Secret Talks between Tokyo and Washington

Secret Talks between Tokyo and Washington

The Memoirs of Miyazawa Kiichi, 1949–1954

Translated and annotated by
Robert D. Eldridge

LEXINGTON BOOKS

A division of
ROWMAN & LITTLEFIELD PUBLISHERS, INC.
Lanham • Boulder • New York • Toronto • Plymouth, UK

LEXINGTON BOOKS

A division of Rowman & Littlefield Publishers, Inc.
A wholly owned subsidiary of The Rowman & Littlefield Publishing Group, Inc.
4501 Forbes Boulevard, Suite 200
Lanham, MD 20706

Estover Road
Plymouth PL6 7PY
United Kingdom

British Library Cataloguing in Publication Information Available

Library of Congress Cataloging-in-Publication Data
Miyazawa, Kiichi, 1919–
   [Tokyo-Washinton no mitsudan. English]
   Secret talks between Tokyo and Washington : the memoirs of Miyazawa Kiichi,
   1949–1954 / translated and annotated by Robert D. Eldridge.
     p. cm.

   Includes index.

   ISBN-13: 978-0-7391-2014-9 (pbk. : alk. paper)

   1. Japan—Foreign relations—United States. 2. United States—Foreign relations—
Japan. 3. Japan—Foreign relations—1945–1989. 4. Japan—History—Allied
occupation, 1945–1952. I. Eldridge, Robert D. II. Title.
DS849.U6M5913 2007
327.5207309'045—dc22   2006029263

Printed in the United States of America

∞™ The paper used in this publication meets the minimum requirements of American
National Standard for Information Sciences—Permanence of Paper for Printed Library
Materials, ANSI/NISO Z39.48-1992.

Contents

Preface   vii

Translator's Preface   ix

1   Joseph Dodge and MacArthur's Headquarters, 1949   1

2   Secret Emissary to Washington, 1950   15

3   Destiny's Peace Conference, 1951   37

4   The Japan-U.S. Talks in Mexico, 1952   67

5   The Ikeda-Robertson Talks in Washington, 1953   79

6   Yoshida's Last Trip to the United States as
Prime Minister, 1954   133

Appendix: Letter from Joseph Dodge to Ikeda Hayato   151

Index   159

About the Author and Translator   165

Preface

This book is a record of the negotiations on the politics and economy of Japan between this country and America between 1949 and 1954, divided into three periods: occupation, peace treaty, and independence.

As someone directly involved, I have written this small work based on the papers and documents of the time not made publicly available until today, as well as the diary I kept during these years.

There still remains a heated debate and great division in public opinion over the path that our country took during these six years. This book was not written to support either view, but instead to record as accurately as possible the facts regarding these bilateral negotiations which have not yet been relegated to pages of history.

However, I am not sure how much I was able to rid these pages of the subjectivity of one personally involved in much of what took place. This naturally will be a likely criticism of the book.

Miyazawa Kiichi
November 1956

Translator's Preface

ABOUT THE TRANSLATION

As introduced below, Miyazawa Kiichi's involvement with national affairs did not end with the publication of these memoirs—a record of the tumultuous times of the latter half of the U.S.-led occupation of Japan and the immediate aftermath during which the young, talented, and international-minded Miyazawa played a central role.[1] Indeed, these memoirs cover just the beginning of his long career.[2] Thirty-five years later, Miyazawa would become Japan's seventy-eighth Prime Minister and serve in key posts throughout the postwar era.

Miyazawa penned this truly insider account on the assumption that the Rightists, following their release from the purge at the end of the Occupation, were back in force and thus those close to Yoshida Shigeru, like Miyazawa and his mentor Ikeda Hayato, had no serious future left in politics or as an official involved in Japan-U.S. relations.[3] The book was published in December 1956, just as the anti-Yoshida administration of Hatoyama Ichiro was ending. It probably surprised Miyazawa greatly that less than four years later, his mentor Ikeda would be named Prime Minister and serve for more than four years and that fellow mainstreamers would occupy that same position for much of the next thirty years, including a two-year tenure by Miyazawa himself from 1991 to 1993. Almost all of those four decades prior to becoming Prime Minister were spent in politics, as was the decade after his premiership (he officially retired in late 2003). He was elected twelve times to the Lower House, and two times to the Upper House, for a total of forty-eight years.

Miyazawa faithfully followed the political philosophy of Yoshida, the mentor of his own mentor, Ikeda. Yoshida allied Japan with the West, the liberal democracies during the Cold War, and emphasized Japan's economic recovery over full-blown rearmament, relying on the United States to provide the bulk of Japan's external security. Although its namesake would argue that such a doctrine never existed, this approach later became known as the "Yoshida Doctrine." Throughout his life, Miyazawa was a firm believer in the "Yoshida Doctrine," arguing that Japan should play a civilian economic role instead of becoming a military power in order to satisfy its ego, in contrast to his contemporary, Nakasone Yasuhiro, and predecessor as Prime Minister by several years, and those politicians that followed, such as Ozawa Ichiro.[4] Miyazawa was the last in the line of followers of the Yoshida School that led Japan through much of the postwar period. His story is Japan's story. If not its author, he at least was one of the central figures in the cast.

This is also the story of the birth, labor pains and all, of the U.S.-Japan alliance for which Miyazawa was sort of a midwife. His was the first account of the Japanese request to have U.S. forces stationed in Japan after the peace treaty, rearmament-related internal and bilateral discussions, and the domestic political dynamics of the conservatives. Of course, he also addressed numerous other issues, such as economic policy, related to the Occupation and early years following the Japan's return to the international community after the end of the Allied Occupation on April 28, 1952. Miyazawa, in short, was "present at the creation," and his memoirs, *Tokyo-Washinton no Mitsudan* (translated here as *Secret Talks between Tokyo and Washington*), reflect this.

Japanese leaders tend not to write memoirs, or at least any that are based on deep reflection or worthy of serious scholarly attention. Miyazawa's is different and is a critical link to understanding the views and perceptions of the Japanese government, both when it was under occupation and then newly independent, struggling to determine its own economic and security policies while aligning itself closely with the liberal, democratic, and economically and militarily powerful United States.

During the years covered in the book, Miyazawa served as Ikeda's secretary, both while the latter was Finance Minister and when he was Minister of International Trade and Industry during respective Yoshida Cabinets. When Ikeda was forced to resign as MITI Minister in late 1952 due to a vote of no confidence after a comment to the effect that it could not be helped that some companies would go bankrupt and company presidents commit suicide in troubled times, Miyazawa, upset with the way Ikeda had been treated both in the Diet and within the Party, and not desiring to go back to the Finance Ministry, decided that same evening to resign from the civil service as well. Ikeda urged him to run in the Upper House elections in the April 1953. Overcoming his own concerns about the socioeconomic viability of a career in politics (see below), he ran successfully with the help of Ikeda and former supporters of his father, a prewar politician from Hiroshima. Only thirty-three when elected, he would serve, as mentioned above, the next fifty years in politics almost non-stop. A long career for someone who initially shunned politics. Miyazawa does not talk about his political career, or even his first election, in the book, but instead concentrates on the interaction between Japan and the United States during this time.

Secret Talks is divided into six chapters covering the six years between 1949 and 1954. Each chapter focuses on a particular year, as well as the major issue of that year for the Japanese government. Chapter 1, for example, is titled "Joseph Dodge and MacArthur's Headquarters, 1949" and discusses the fiscal policies pursued by economic advisor Dodge. Chapter 2, "Secret Emissary to Washington, 1950," looks at Yoshida's dispatch of Ikeda and Miyazawa to Washington to break the impasse in the occupation at the time by requesting that the United States continue to station troops in Japan after the peace treaty. Chapter 3, "Destiny's Peace Conference, 1951," focuses on the thinking of the Japanese government at the time of the peace treaty and the internal dynamics. Chapter 4, "The Japan-U.S. Talks in Mexico, 1952," looks at economic, political, and defense issues between the two countries, as does chapter 5, "The Ikeda-Robertson Talks in Washington, 1953." Chapter 6 covers the year 1954, which was the last year of the Yoshida premiership, hence its title, "Yoshida's Last Trip to the United States as Prime Minister, 1954."

In each of them, Miyazawa describes in detail the many events and personalities he came across during those years, and the respective ideas that were at work at the time as both the United States, generally unaccustomed to its role as occupier and teacher, and Japan, equally unaccustomed to being occupied and a student,[5] were finding ways to work with each other. The bilateral relationship has greatly evolved, but I think Miyazawa would agree that we are still learning how to work with one another.

Some observers, both Japanese and Americans, tend to suggest that the United States, leading the Allied Occupation of Japan (1945–1952), simply had its way with Japan and walked all over it. One of my favorite paragraphs from the book (chapter 1) debunks this myth:

> The biggest issue that Japanese bureaucrats had to think about was how to win over the occupation authorities—the holders of absolute authority—to the bureaucrats' side. There were many examples in which flattery was used to great success, and, while not a lot, some examples in which the bureaucrats opposed a proposed course of action and the occupation authorities came around to accepting the merits of their opposition. The Japanese side also used the classic approach of divide-and-rule, in which it found ways to take advantage of in-fighting within GHQ to press its own views.

The Occupation, and the creation of postwar Japan, therefore can be described as more of a joint endeavor, rather than a simple remolding in the U.S. image. The memoirs of Miyazawa are about this interaction and building of a new Japan.

On the day the war was over, when the Emperor's recorded address was played to the nation, Miyazawa's first reaction was, "There won't be any more air raids now. We can turn the lights on again."[6] Although this was an honest expression of relief that the physical sufferings and other travails of wartime Japan were over, in an other sense, it was an appropriate metaphor—light was returning to the lives of the Japanese people, and Miyazawa, again. Symbolic of this, it is not surprising then that when asked what most, in his opinion, improved in the postwar period, he answered, "freedom."[7] America was the liberator and educator in that regard, although there was a history of limited democracy in Japan already that lost out to the militarists and the problematic structure of the Meiji Constitution.

Miyazawa is often identified as pro-United States, and that he is, but at the same time he is probably the first one to criticize the United States—in his own quiet way—when he thinks its policies, attitudes, or leadership are wrong, or that America is not living up to its own ideals. True friends, in other words, are the ones who tell their partners what they think. In his latter career, he would have plenty of opportunities to do so, but the reader will find many examples herein as well where he and his colleagues attempted to provide the United States with views that it may not have wanted to hear but in fact needed to.

This preface, with a brief overview of Miyazawa's life and times, was written to provide the context behind Miyazawa's involvement in national policy. He is probably one of the most well-known Japanese faces abroad, and, thus, some of the general highlights of his life are known by many Japan observers. And yet, much remains unknown.

My own involvement with Miyazawa began in the fall of 1999 and has continued through today. When I first met him, Miyazawa had already served as Prime Minister and was at the time serving as Finance Minister in the Obuchi Keizo Cabinet. Along with my former classmate, Kusunoki Ayako, then still a doctoral candidate at Kobe University, and our mentor, Professor of Diplomatic History Iokibe Makoto, we visited his large Finance Minister's office to interview him about the Ikeda Mission to the United States in 1950 for an article she and I were co-authoring.[8] Apparently he was impressed with the depth of our archival research and analysis, as he still cites our work in interviews.[9]

Some time after this initial meeting, I went to interview him again, at that point no longer Finance Minister, about Prime Minister Ikeda's visit to the United States in June 1961 for a summit meeting with President John F. Kennedy. Miyazawa served as interpreter then and I was hoping to learn more about Ikeda's views on the question of Okinawa's status, then under U.S. administration, for a future book on the reversion of Okinawa, following up on my earlier *The Origins of the Bilateral Okinawa Problem: Okinawa in Postwar U.S.-Japan Relations, 1945–1952.* It was an insightful interview.

I do not remember exactly when I first thought of translating Miyazawa's *Tokyo-Washinton no Mitsudan* but it was either after the first or second interview with him. As few American scholars of U.S.-Japan diplomatic relations are able to read Japanese, I believed more than ever that this book should be translated. It was not only I that recognized the value of these memoirs—Chuo Koron Shinsha decided to reissue his 1956 book as the first in its new series on the postwar around the same time, and later agreed to this translation.[10]

In the meantime, numerous other projects intervened, including the authoring of a half-dozen books, and it was not until 2005, as I was finishing a one-year sabbatical as a scholar-in-residence at the headquarters of U.S. Marine Corps Forces, Pacific, at Camp Smith, in Oahu, Hawaii, that I could seriously tackle the translation. That same year, Miyazawa's health had taken a turn for the worse and so I devoted the fall of 2005 to finishing the translation. At eighty-six, his health remains frail at the time of this writing.

Having already spoken with the acquisitions editor and staff of Lexington Books, which published my *The Return of the Amami Islands: The Reversion Movement and U.S.-Japan Relations* in 2004, about the project several years before, I followed up with it upon my return from the sabbatical. I would like to express my gratitude for their strong and continued interest in the project.

I would also like to thank the Suntory Foundation for financially supporting the publication and translating costs through its 2006 Overseas Publishing Grant, and of course Chuo Koron Shinsha. I am also grateful to Takashima Junko of Miyazawa Kiichi's Office who always quickly, kindly, and accurately provided information and arranged interviews for me with Miyazawa. Finally, I would like to thank former Prime Minister Miyazawa himself, for agreeing and assisting in the translation and providing his insights both for the following overview of his life and to my own research on U.S.-Japan relations. He did not request the translation, but always generously gave his time to this project, as he has to other projects of historical significance.

OVERVIEW OF MIYAZAWA'S LIFE

Miyazawa Kiichi was born on October 8, 1919, in Tokyo as the first child of Yutaka and Koto. Yutaka, a former junior official of the Home Ministry, was then working at Yamashita Steamship Company. Their marriage was a traditional *omiai*; Koto was the daughter of a famous politician, Ogawa Heikichi, who had served as Secretary General of the *Seiyukai* (Friends of Constitutional Government Party). The marriage was particularly good for Yutaka, as he had political ambitions. He was elected in 1928 and would serve until he was purged after the start of the Occupation.

Miyazawa was raised and educated in Tokyo, and attended top schools, including Tokyo Imperial University (Law Department). It was his time at the seven-year Musashi High School, however, that seems to have had the most influence on him. A private school founded in 1922, just ten years before Miyazawa entered, Musashi was known for its liberal education and the willingness of its school principal to reject the growing militarism that was enveloping Japan in the 1930s. Symbolic of this, Musashi refused to have its students participate in a parade celebrating Japan's aggression in the China conflict in 1937, as requested by the Ministry of Education.

In addition to the school's liberal atmosphere, Miyazawa was influenced in other ways to look at things in a more international and open way. The first influence was that of his father. While still in primary school, Miyazawa's father had told his children that it was not enough to know just the Japanese language and taught them the English alphabet, following up by securing a private foreign tutor to teach Miyazawa and his siblings English. Miyazawa's English ability provided him with opportunities and insights that he would not have had otherwise. The second influence was John Stewart Mill's *On Liberty*, a copy of which an uncle and future politician had given him both to help him with his English as well as to inherit its ideas. "Liberalism was being suppressed at the time and [Mill] gave me the chance to taste liberty."[11]

To Miyazawa, the prewar and later wartime years were "oppressive."[12] He grew up, he would write later, "in a dark time. . . . The difficulty in living in a period during which freedom of speech was gradually strangled, particularly in the prewar and wartime years, can not be accurately described if you have not experienced it. . . . It is like oxygen gradually getting thinner and thinner. It becomes harder to breathe. When you discover there is no more air left, then you are dying. It is the same for a country. Japan was approaching death when the end of the war came."[13]

Miyazawa grew up somewhat lonely and his family lacking money. In winter, he attended school with only a cape on, while the other kids wore fancy coats. "I was so cold it was horrible. I begged my mother for a coat, but we did not have any money. She cried, as I recall . . . I spent my childhood growing up aware of the handicap of being poor."[14] Because his family lived far from the primary school he attended, he was unable to stay around after school to play with his classmates or walk home with them. "It was a lonely existence. I was not able to play the way ordinary kids would. I did not have any friends near where we had moved to either," Miyazawa wrote melancholically later.[15] His father was also busy, and Miyazawa does not have any memories of being with him as a child. "Nevertheless, he was not strict, leaving that up to my mother who handled our education and upbringing," Miyazawa noted.[16]

Because of the above situation, Miyazawa grew up somewhat hardened and independent in his thinking. In any case, Miyazawa's time at Musashi High School allowed him to grow intellectually. In 1937, the same year the war in China began, Miyazawa was one of two students selected to go to Manchukuo, as the Japanese puppet state was known, on a short-term study abroad program. Until that time, the United States had been the destination for these annual trips, but due to the worsening of the currency and other reasons, they traveled within the region. He had heard, however, at the school and elsewhere that Japan's colonial administration was not going well, an administration the school was critical of due to the military's central role. "Perhaps because of these perceptions, I came back thinking that the administration was likely going to fail," Miyazawa recalled.[17]

Miyazawa graduated from Musashi as class valedictorian in March 1939 and entered his father's alma mater, Tokyo University. Later that year, he joined the United States-Japan Student Conference and participated in its 1939 session at the University of Southern California and the 1940 session at Rikkyo University at Tokyo. Miyazawa would later describe his participation as "one of the most formative events of my lifetime."[18] He was even "shocked" by the experience.[19] "Each American student," Miyazawa said later, "has his or her own strong opinion and they have heated discussions. They even criticize their own government. I was impressed and concluded that this was an amazing country. . . . It would be unwise to fight that country."[20] Miyazawa had gone to the United States to argue on behalf of Japan, but came back influenced. He also met his future wife (Yoko) on the trip. Their marriage, in late 1943, was one of love, rather than arranged, something very rare at the time and representative of Miyazawa's independent approach to life.

Miyazawa's graduation from Tokyo University was rushed due to the outbreak of war with the United States some two years later after the trip to the West Coast. As mentioned above, he had long rejected a career in politics and planned to go into the Home Ministry, as several relatives had pursued successful careers there. A family friend, Ikeda Hayato, who worked in the Finance Ministry, encouraged him instead to join his ministry and Ikeda, who was from the same hometown as Miyazawa's father in Hiroshima, became his sponsor.

Ikeda was by no means a star in the ministry and colleagues wondered why Miyazawa had chosen Ikeda to sponsor him. It was not until much later, after the war (the fire raids of which ended up destroying Miyazawa's home and all his belongings), when Miyazawa's skills would be fully utilized and the relationship with Ikeda would blossom into the partnership that it became, as highlighted in the memoirs.

After the war, with his English ability still in tact due to having continued to read the English-language press during the war, Miyazawa was directed to become the secretary to Finance Minister Tsushima Juichi and then Shibusawa Keizo in the Higashikuni Naruhiko and Shidehara Kijuro Cabinets respectively. Already his English-language fluency was being recognized. He was only twenty-six at the time. Subsequently Miyazawa was seconded to the Central Liaison Office, responsible for interfacing with the headquarters of the Occupation forces. In 1949, when Ikeda was named Finance Minister in the second Yoshida Cabinet, he asked Miyazawa to join him as secretary. As the memoirs cover in detail Miyazawa's time as secretary to Ikeda, I will not describe his responsibilities here.

As seen in the memoirs, Miyazawa and Ikeda were inseparable after this point. As noted above, Miyazawa successfully ran in the Upper House elections in 1953 at Ikeda's urging and aligned himself closely with Ikeda and Yoshida afterwards. Miyazawa would subsequently join Ikeda's faction *Kochikai* within the ruling Liberal Democratic Party (established in 1955), at the time of its creation in 1957 and lead it through the 1980s and 1990s. The faction initially served as a "brain trust" for Ikeda who became Prime Minister in 1960, and Miyazawa played a key role in it.

After serving as Party Treasurer and head of the Upper House Steering Committee, Miyazawa was appointed Director of the Economic Planning Agency, his first Cabinet post, in 1962. Some time after Ikeda resigned in favor of Sato Eisaku, due to the detection of cancer, Sato asked Miyazawa to join the Cabinet again as EPA Director, which he did in December 1966. Miyazawa would serve as EPA Director a third time in the late 1970s in the Fukuda Takeo Cabinet.

In January 1970, he was named Minister of International Trade and Industry, serving for a year and a half, and later in December 1974, as Foreign Minister (until September 1976). All eyes turned to him in the summer of 1980 to succeed Prime Minister Ohira Masayoshi, who died during the middle of the elections, but Miyazawa did not run. Instead, in July 1980, he was named Chief Cabinet Secretary in the Suzuki Zenko Cabinet, and continued in that position until November 1982 when the Nakasone Yasuhiro Cabinet came into being. In 1984, he made an unsuccessful bid to replace Nakasone as LDP President, receiving instead the post of Chairman of the Executive Council, his first senior party post, in October. In July 1986, he was named Finance Minister in a Cabinet reshuffle, the last for Nakasone. Miyazawa was retained in the Takeshita Noboru Cabinet, which formed in November 1987, but had to resign in December in order to take responsibility for his nominal involvement in the Recruit stocks-for-votes scandal.[21] This was one of the lowest points in Miyazawa's life, and a time when he thought his career was over. In November 1991, however, Miyazawa was finally named Prime Minister at the age of seventy-two, a political journey that took approximately forty years. He was recalled to public service in the Obuchi Keizo Cabinet, serving as Finance Minister again from July 1998 until April 2000 (when Obuchi collapsed and died from a stroke), but was retained in the subsequent Mori Yoshiro Cabinet, which lasted one year from April 2000 to April 2001. Miyazawa retired from politics in October 2003 at the age of eighty-five, following the announcement of LDP President (and Prime Minister) Koizumi Junichiro to the effect that LDP members over a certain age would no longer be allowed to run on LDP tickets. Nakasone was also targeted, and he initially resisted. Miyazawa, on the other hand, true to form, gracefully retired.

Robert D. Eldridge
Karuizawa, Japan, July 2006

NOTES

1. As the reader likely already knows, Japanese names begin with the surname first, followed by the personal name. I follow Japanese custom for Japanese names throughout the text.

2. Miyazawa has often been interviewed throughout his career, with some of the interviews being turned into oral histories, but has written relatively little himself in book or serial form about his entire life or political career in addition to these translated memoirs. The exceptions are: Miyazawa Kiichi, *Shakaito to no Taiwa: Nyuu Raito no Kangaekata* [Dialogue with the Socialist Party: The Thinking of the New Right] (Tokyo: Kodansha, 1965); Miyazawa Kiichi, *Sengo Seiji no Shogen* [Testimony of Postwar Politics] (Tokyo: Yomiuri Shimbunsha, 1991); and Miyazawa Kiichi, "Watashi no Rirekisho" [My Biography], *Nihon Keizai Shimbun* (April 1–30, 2006) (a twenty-nine-installment series).

3. Interview with Mr. Miyazawa, May 1, 2006.

4. Miyazawa, *Shakaito to no Taiwa*, chapter 5; Miyazawa Kiichi and Kosaka Masataka, *Utsukushii Nihon e no Chosen* [Challenges to a Beautiful Japan] (Tokyo: Bungei Shunju, 1984), chapter 3; Miyazawa Kiichi, *Shin Goken Sengen: 21 Seiki no Nihon to Sekai* [New Declaration for Protecting the Constitution: Japan and the World in the 21st Century] (Tokyo: Asahi Shimbunsha, 1995); Nakasone Yasuhiro and Miyazawa Kiichi, *Tairon: Kaiken, Goken* [Debate on Whether to Revise or Protect the Constitution] (Tokyo: Asahi Shimbunsha, 1997).

5. Of course Japan was a student after the Commodore Matthew C. Perry visits in the middle of the nineteenth century, but by the time of its victory over Russia in the Russo-Japanese war at the turn of the century, it had already graduated.

6. Miyazawa, "Watashi no Rirekisho, No. 7."

7. Miyazawa, "Watashi no Rirekisho, No. 7."

8. The article was later published as Robert D. Eldridge and Ayako Kusunoki, "To Base or Not to Base: Yoshida Shigeru, the 1950 Ikeda Mission, and Post-Treaty Japanese Security Conceptions," *Kobe University Law Review*, no. 33 (1999): 97–126.

9. Mikuriya Takashi and Nakamura Takafusa, *Kikikaki Miyazawa Kiichi Kaisoroku* [Oral History: Miyazawa Kiichi's Recollections] (Tokyo: Iwanami Shoten, 2004), 124.

10. The name of the series was "Shiriizu Sengoshi no Shogen Senryo to Kowa" [Testimonial Series of Postwar History: Occupation and the Peace Treaty].

11. Miyazawa, "Watashi no Rirekisho, No. 4," *Nihon Keizai Shimbun* (April 4, 2006).

12. Miyazawa, "Watashi no Rirekisho, No. 1," *Nihon Keizai Shimbun* (April 1, 2006).

13. Miyazawa, "Watashi no Rirekisho, No. 1," *Nihon Keizai Shimbun* (April 1, 2006).

14. Miyazawa, "Watashi no Rirekisho, No. 3."

15. Miyazawa, "Watashi no Rirekisho, No. 3."

16. Miyazawa, "Watashi no Rirekisho, No. 2."

17. Miyazawa, "Watashi no Rirekisho, No. 4."

18. "Archives: Chapter 1, 1934–1940," The U.S.-Japan Student Conference, www.jasc.org/Archives/archives-book2.htm. Also see Miyazawa, "Watashi no Rirekisho, No. 5," *Nihon Keizai Shimbun* (April 5, 2006).

19. Miyazawa, *Sengo Seiji*, 2.

20. "Archives: Chapter 1, 1934–1940," The U.S.-Japan Student Conference.

21. Although he had done nothing illegal, the scandal was embarrassing for him personally and for the government, the latter because it was trying to pass a 3 percent consumption tax bill at the time. The opposition used the scandal as one of its reasons to oppose the bill. Miyazawa resigned in return for the opposition supporting or at least not preventing passage of the bill.

Chapter One

Joseph Dodge and MacArthur's Headquarters, 1949

THE ARRIVAL OF JOSEPH DODGE

The general elections for the Lower House took place in January 1949, and the Democratic Liberal Party (*Minshu Jiminto*, or *Minjito*), led by Yoshida Shigeru,[1] won. He was about to form his cabinet. On February 1, the U.S. Secretary of the Army [Kenneth C.] Royall came to Japan. I remember first hearing the name of [Joseph M.] Dodge, someone who was traveling in the delegation, in the news around this time.

The Yoshida Cabinet officially formed on February 16, and Oya Shinzo became Finance Minister when, in an embarrassing incident, Izumiyama Sanroku, his predecessor, was caught drinking in the Diet and was forced to give up his position.[2] Oya was then asked to replace him as his temporary successor. At this time, the Finance Minister would meet every Wednesday with Major General William F. Marquat, Director of the Economics and Science Section, General Headquarters for the Supreme Command Allied Powers, in Tokyo. On February 5, Minister of Finance Oya and several of his aides went in to meet with Marquat. Dodge sat in on the meeting. That was the first time I saw Dodge's face and heard him speak.

The Ministry of Finance was facing an immediate problem: with the start of the new Yoshida Cabinet in a few days time, the question of when the ministry would be able to prepare the draft budget for Fiscal Year 1949 arose. Top officials of the Finance Ministry wanted to present the draft to the Diet by March 10 after writing it up, discussing it with GHQ, and getting GHQ's approval. When Oya told Marquat his plan, the latter responded in the way a military officer says things, which sounds like an order: "That is too late. Why can't you get it in sooner? GHQ will need to have time to adequately study it." At that point, Dodge, who was sitting there and still an unknown quantity, spoke up in the following way:

> In coming to Japan for the first time, I talked in great detail with President [Harry S.] Truman and the leadership of the U.S. government. From the U.S. perspective, it seems that Japan is not using the relief goods that we are providing well. In reality, the government of Japan should sell the relief goods to the people and use the money it raises more effectively. However, as it is now, we are unclear where that money is going. Although it is needed assistance, it will not result in the stopping of inflation. I believe that in order to rebuild the Japanese economy, it is necessary to balance the budget in all matters. In order to stabilize the economy, there is no other way to do it other than not spending money. Of course, the government cannot function if it does not spend some money. The people would be in distress. However, the people, who experienced the miserable defeat in war, cannot rise again if they are not in some degree of distress. What is most necessary for the people of Japan is, in one word, austerity, and what is most necessary for the government of Japan and the occupation forces to do is the courage to force this austerity on the Japanese people. Simply put, everyone should forget about their dreams for the time being. Furthermore, there is no other way but to start again from a "hard-headed" realistic stance.

This was an overview of what he said and when we heard this we collectively thought that a tough old guy had come upon us. But, over the next year or two, everything that he called for in his talk went exactly as he said, something that no one predicted at the time.

DODGE AND MACARTHUR'S HEADQUARTERS

It was not only we who were surprised. Dodge was also trying to reason with the Americans in GHQ.

The Economic and Science Section, in charge of the economic and finances of the headquarters, was comprised of several civilians under a major general (Marquat) in sort of a council system. Many of these civilians were extreme New Dealers, those who strongly believed that humans had the ability to manage the economy. For several years until this time, they believed they could do so in Japan, a defeated country with no food or clothing. In fact, they tried to implement it several times, but the prices they set lost out to those of the black market. Strikes were held in order to force wages to catch up. At that time, the phrase, "negative cycle of prices and wages" was used to describe the situation that was occurring. The government, sometimes as many as ten times a year, would prepare supplementary budgets to deal with this crisis.

When Dodge stated "austerity" was the basis of rebuilding the economy and that it was necessary to throw away one's dreams and return to a position of realism, it was the people in this section who were the most surprised. They seemed to strongly question in their gut "who this greedy banker was coming here, saying big things. Doesn't he know that the handling of an economy and society of a country is different from running a bank?"

Dodge also surprised everyone when he said that he wanted to take his time in looking over the draft budget being prepared by the government of Japan, almost as if he had not heard the Finance Minister's explanation that he hoped to submit it by March 10 and Marquat's comment that that would be too late.

On February 16, the second Yoshida Cabinet was formed and Ikeda Hayato became the Finance Minister. I became his Secretary, and he came to me to talk about how we should proceed.

The biggest issue that Japanese bureaucrats had to think about was how to win over the occupation authorities—the holders of absolute authority—to the bureaucrats' side. There were many examples in which flattery was used to great success, and, while not a lot, some examples in which the bureaucrats opposed a proposed course of action and the occupation authorities came around to accepting the merits of their opposition. The Japanese side also used the classic approach of divide-and-rule, in which it found ways to take advantage of in-fighting within GHQ to press its own views.

In fact, I thought it would be interesting to have the new Finance Minister try to clearly separate or distinguish the differences between Dodge's thinking and the approach taken to date by the New Dealers. Marquat was a figurehead, and the New Dealers under him had continued to bully the Japanese authorities responsible for the economy. The latter individuals had been raised to try to limit spending to the greatest degree possible, so their view was that the most important thing to emphasize was limiting financial expenditures rather than stabilizing prices or raising wages. The New Dealers had blocked this approach for several years and a great deal of frustration had built up. While not sure who Dodge was, Japanese authorities wanted to borrow the power of this seemingly stubborn, older man. At the least, rather than getting into the boat of the New Dealers, the feeling was that Dodge's boat would be a smoother sail. When we did get in Dodge's boat, it turned out to be a much more difficult and rough voyage, but that was later.

In addition to these behind-the-scenes dealings, because the newly created Yoshida Cabinet had to submit the 1949 budget draft to GHQ shortly after its formation, it went ahead and submitted the draft already considered by the bureaucrats in the Finance Ministry during the elections to GHQ at the time of the Cabinet's formation.

During the election, Yoshida's Democratic Liberal Party had made several electoral promises to improve the economy. They included: a decrease in the income tax, an ending to the unpopular turnover tax, an increase of 100 billion yen in public works spending, and a simplification—to the greatest extent possible—of the complicated and troublesome planned economy. The draft prepared by the Finance Ministry only included those items that fiscally worked well.

Even the fiscal authorities, who were having difficulties collecting taxes, were in favor of a reduction of the income tax and turnover tax, as well as a simplification of economic planning, but they were opposed to spending a lot on public works. As a result, it became possible to greatly reduce this unnecessary fiscal support and an axe was taken to this spending.

JAPAN'S ECONOMY AT THE TIME

While I do not plan to go into great detail, I should at least explain the situation at the time of Japanese industry for the benefit of younger readers. For most products, there was a fixed price. Although there were differences between companies, the production costs for steel, fertilizer, coal, and other items forming the basis of industry were for the most part above these fixed prices. As a result, the government had to pay producers for the additional costs incurred in order to maintain fixed prices for consumers.

Moreover, similarly, for imported goods, in order to maintain those fixed low prices domestically, the government had to pay the difference in the costs between the fixed price and the real price for the imported items. Similarly, for exported items, the government paid producers for the difference between the actual price and the selling price in order to maintain the competitiveness of Japanese companies.

As is explained later, the reason why it was said the Japanese economy was on "stilts"was that the Japanese government was paying the additional costs for both imported and exported products. As a result, the entire Japanese economic structure was not standing on a firm business basis, but on an unstable "false bottom."

It is impossible to accurately determine how much money was spent in fiscal support at its most egregious. The reason for this was, as mentioned before, that the government pooled the money acquired from sales of U.S. relief goods (at the time, these items were called *hoshutsu busshi*, released or surplus goods) and as a result there were no exact financial records kept during this time. Because Dodge separated the funds acquired by selling these aid items into a new category "collateral money," maintaining fiscal records afterwards became easier. In addition, Dodge set about bringing order to these government expenditures, which until this point had been badly handled. As is described later, despite this effort at better fiscal management, the additional expenditures of the government for Fiscal Year 1949 still amounted to 200 billion yen, nearly one-third of the budget.

In the first draft budget prepared by the bureaucrats in the Finance Ministry, these expenditures had been reduced to 70 billion yen, but in truth, looking back at the time, it was not based on any rational accounting or particular confidence. Instead, it seems to have been both a feeling by the bureaucrats to cut spending as much as possible because the New Dealers were going to raise it in any case, as well as an act of desperation against inappropriate electoral promises by a political party, namely the promises of the Democratic Liberal Party to cut taxes and increase spending for public works by cutting this other spending.

In any case, Dodge began to study this draft budget, as did the new Yoshida Cabinet. Within the Cabinet discussions, many critical comments were heard to the effect that the funds set aside for public works were too low and that they did not meet electoral promises.

CUTTING THE "STILTS"

As reported in the newspapers, the Dodge-Ikeda talks first began some two weeks afterward on March 1, 1949. And beginning that day, the substance of the Dodge Line, said to be the symbol of the coming recession, started to appear.

After studying the Japanese fiscal and economic system for approximately half a month, Dodge gave the following analysis:

The Japanese economy is standing on the two stilts of financial support for fixed prices and American surplus goods. In order to become a truly health economy, these stilts have to be eliminated. To do this, we need to determine how long in fact each of these stilts is. Japanese fiscal practices to date have led to the money being used for financial support and other relief measures for just about everything not being reflected properly in the budget. It is necessary first to show — he used the word "expose" — these expenditures. Second, the Reconstruction Finance Corporation (*Fukko Kinyu Kinko*) has invested a great deal of money after the war. In the draft budget prepared for this year by the Finance Ministry, the GOJ planned to take out another 40 billion yen from this fund. However, this was unacceptable. It was a near-crime to put money into the economy in the name of investing when the economy was on the brink of collapse due to inflation. Now more than ever was the time to turn off the pipe. Third, the electoral promises to cut income taxes and turnover taxes are essentially mistaken. It is necessary to close the pipe on the one hand, and continue to pump water from a tub on the other hand. These two actions form the basis of my approach. Taxes play the role of pumping water up. Turnover taxes are considered "bad taxes" by the general public, but I have never heard of a country or an era in which there was such a thing as a "good tax."

Dodge essentially stated the above overview, and this became the basic thinking of the Dodge Line, which guided the Japanese economy for the next one or two years. With this, all of the electoral promises of the LDP, such as cutting taxes and increasing spending on public works, were cancelled.

Yet, there was one thing on which Dodge very much saw eye-to-eye with Minister of Finance Ikeda. Dodge was very happy about the fact that in the budget prepared by the Finance Ministry introduced earlier, money for financial support was greatly cut. However, within GHQ, where there were many New Dealers, they believed that such financial support represented the quick road to increasing production without raising prices. True to fashion, they produced a lot of documents to try to pessimistically explain that if financial support for the steel industry were cut, prices for steel products would soar, affecting all industries and leading to the prices of everything increasing. Even Dodge was unable to show any courage to challenge this.

Then, on March 1, Dodge asked Finance Minister Ikeda, "You keep on saying to cut the financial support, but what do you think would happen in the end to prices? For example, what about steel?" To this question, Ikeda immediately responded, "I think that if financial support for steel is cut, the effect would only be so much, but in reality, I don't think the figures are accurate in the first place. There is no choice but to make dramatic cuts in the support."

I do not think Finance Minister Ikeda had any strong opinion on this question, but it was an electoral promise of the Democratic Liberal Party to end controls over the economy, and he was probably forced in his position to call for the ending of financial support because it would become a source of revenue in their attempts to cut taxes and increase spending for public works.

DR. FINE'S PROTEST

In any case, at this point, Dodge and Ikeda really saw eye-to-eye on this issue. When Finance Minister Ikeda jokingly said, "the fastest way to teach a child to swim is to throw him into the sea. If it looks like he will drown then you can save him at that point," Dodge listened with a smile on his face.

Two days later on March 3, Dodge asked Ikeda to discreetly come to see him. Ikeda brought me along. Dodge told us, "It appears the ruling party generated a great deal of support when it promised in the election to eliminate the turnover tax. As I said the day before yesterday, I am opposed to that because I think it is necessary to collect as much revenue as possible under the name of taxes. No matter how hard you or the Prime Minister try, it will be impossible to implement the cut. I have given a lot of thought to the matter, and would like to suggest that I announce my opposition to the tax cut. If I do this, then the position of the government and the party should be safe." Ikeda said he was opposed to Dodge's doing so, and asked that he not make such a statement.

March 9 was a Wednesday, the day that the Finance Minister and Major General Marquat had their weekly meetings. Dodge did not attend the meeting, but the leader of the New Dealers, Dr. [Sherwood] Fine, said, "I do not think I can agree with his thinking about the need to balance the budget. What would happen if both production and exports go down? The most important thing is to stabilize prices and increase production." We heard this and thought, "There they go again." Fine seems to have wanted to say both that it has been objectionable that a direction, different from the one they pursued to date, was being followed after Dodge arrived in Japan, and that he was offended in some way by Ikeda becoming close with Dodge.

In response, Ikeda, with a serious face, said, "As Finance Minister, I believe the balancing of the budget is the most important thing. While you speak of stabilizing prices and whatnot, an economy that is built on top of relief support will never be able to compete with foreign countries. No matter how pretty the flowers in a greenhouse may be, if cold winds of outside blow in the flower would die. I want to help break the glass of the greenhouse." Fine made an unpleasant face, and Marquat said sarcastically, "That was a fine speech." Despite appearances, Marquat and Ikeda did not get along after this point and their fractured relationship would continue until the end of the Occupation.

That afternoon, Dodge and Ikeda met again. Dodge told Ikeda about the press conference he had with a group of Japanese reporters. Dodge proudly stated he was "giving the Japanese public a mental massage through the newspapers" and when asked what that meant, he replied, "I am giving the Japanese people a head massage to get them to come closer to my thinking." We knew he was an old guy who was quite organized, but we also thought maybe his head needed a massage too. We of course did not say this.

At the press conference he gave, when asked, "if production and lower prices [were to] be sacrificed in order to stabilize the economy," Dodge responded that he wanted "stability without fiction." The interpreter, Dodge told us, apparently mistook "fiction" for "friction" and when the interpreter said that he wanted "stability without friction," everyone got confused. At the time, no one really knew Dodge, the person.

The same day, Finance Minister Ikeda told him, "Hearing your explanation, I think the budget to be prepared is going to be a stringent one and if so, we need to prepare measures to deal with unemployment." Dodge responded, "in my mind, unemployment countermeasures end up creating unemployment. Instead of establishing public works projects for those unemployed, the effect of inflation that is created by public works is the more dangerous thing."

VETOING THE GOVERNMENT'S BUDGET

We began to learn the contents of the GHQ draft budget that Dodge was working on, using the Japanese government's draft as the basis around March 20. When we first looked at it, we realized it was completely different from what we expected. Although its name, "Draft Budget for Fiscal Year 1949," was the same, its contents were entirely changed from the Japanese version. It was completely modified. We recognized that we were in for some tough times ahead.

Finance Minister Ikeda met with Dodge and asked him directly about it. Yes, it was true, he was told. I won't go into details here, but the funds for public works, part of the electoral promise, were halved from 100 billion yen to 50 billion yen, income taxes and turnover taxes would not be eliminated and continue to be collected as before, and train fares and postal rates would be raised 50–60 percent. Everything that could be taken would be taken, and nothing should be disbursed out. This was truly a budget crunch for the people of Japan. We were aware that Dodge was calling for "austerity" but this was really severe.

The amount of financial support to be cut was more than 200 billion yen. When asked about it, Dodge said he wanted to cut more but he could not do so alone on his own authority. However, even then, it was necessary to bring to light the issues that were previously hidden, and if the support could be limited to a certain amount, then that in and of itself would be a big accomplishment. While this was true, it would be difficult to explain this to the general public made up of nonspecialists. Dodge, in any case, was quite satisfied, saying in a self-congratulatory manner, "This is the best budget draft, I think. This is neither deflationary nor inflationary in nature. This is a disinflation budget."

From Ikeda's perspective, however, this budget did away with the DLP's electoral promises, and looked nothing like the budget originally discussed by the Cabinet. It was as if it wasn't even necessary for Ikeda to have been Finance Minister.

Ikeda was the type that if there was nothing that could be done then he believed it was good to try to relieve oneself quickly of any stress. When Prime Minister Yoshida told him to delay announcing the Dodge draft, Ikeda prepared to resign as Finance Minister and traveled to Hakone to get away for a while.[3]

A big clash was seen at the Cabinet meeting. Namely, criticism existed among those in the DLP Diet Members Association over the inability of the government to submit a budget, despite the Party having an absolute majority in the Diet. When the criticism of Ikeda got intense with everyone standing up at the same time and shouting at him, Yoshida appeared and calmed things down. It was probably because it was during the Occupation, but Yoshida was also faced with this pressure.

I am not sure, but I think Yoshida had been carefully watching Dodge and behind him, Washington, for a long time. He likely decided that it was best to work with Dodge because he did not know what the U.S. would do in the case he misplayed his hand.

The Finance Minister afterwards decided not to complain about expenditures. Regarding revenue, he asked if it might be possible to do something face-saving on the issue of reducing income taxes. Ikeda met with Dodge three times on March 24, 25, and 28 about this, reminding him of the campaign promises.

Regarding the reduction of income taxes, Dodge said that Japanese tax rates might be as much as 20 percent too high. However, the structure for collecting taxes was random. The Communist Party had been conducting an anti-tax movement and tax officials belonging to labor unions participated in the movement and did not cooperate in the collection of taxes. In addition, the method for assessing taxes was not done using any sort of documentation and new, appropriate taxes were unreasonably high. In light of the above, it appeared that taxes were approximately 20 percent high. However, Dodge thought lowering taxes before the problems were improved was dangerous. Moreover, Dodge repeatedly said that Japan could wait to make any changes until the arrival of an expert by the name of [Carl S.] Shoup, scheduled to come in April.

At this last stage, the tax experts in the headquarters persuaded Dodge that the tax rate was high and that because it was too high, it was necessary to talk about an additional tax. In the end, Dodge gave in. However, right around almost the same time—I think it was March 28—two elder statesmen-like gentlemen from the DLP, Mr. "U" and Mr. "H" (because both men acted voluntarily, there is no need not to provide their names but because they are still both alive, I wish to protect their privacy[4]), requested to meet Dodge and explained to him the need for reducing taxes. We heard about this later. How the atmosphere of these talks went can be best described first by Dodge's comment that he "did not like giving in to political pressure in Japan" and second by the fact that the meeting ended early.

With the budget problem being cleaned up, Dodge began to think about proper accounting methods for separating and estimating the income from surplus goods from America, as described before. This became known as the Counterpart Fund (*Migaeri Shikin Tokubetsu Kaikei*). Around the same time, fiscal matters began to take shape with the introduction of this special account. However, nothing had been done with regard to finances so Dodge began to think about financial regulations. At the time, Dodge said, "the problem was of course with the Bank of Japan. While there is a Board of Directors with the Bank of Japan, in fact it is under 'one man control' by its president. It is not a Board of Directors, but rather no more than a 'Board of Managers.' It is necessary to build an organization that establishes policy more." Dodge began to talk about this more, and eventually this led to the establishment of the Policy Committee of the Bank of Japan. However, regarding this Policy Committee, Dodge himself later said it was a mistake.

DECIDING THE RATIO OF 1 DOLLAR = 360 YEN

One more thing that Dodge did that year was setting the yen-dollar exchange rate. Setting the rate over the next year or two was expected to be quite problematic, because Japan was suffering from inflation and it was difficult to establish a date to set the exchange rate. Around this time, I was thinking that even if the Dodge budget were realized, it would take at least half a year to see how things were going. So, when setting the rate was discussed, I thought at the minimum it would be the latter half of 1949. Yet, at the time of the Dodge-Ikeda meeting on April 2, I think it was, when Dodge exposed the support funds and tried to reduce them, he also explained that regarding support funds for imported goods, it was necessary to have a set exchange rate in mind when calculating the funds. He told Ikeda that he had a rate of 330 yen to the dollar in mind.

It is true that if there was no exact exchange rate in mind, it would be impossible to calculate the amount of support funds, and thus we agreed with Dodge's logic. Likewise, the rate he suggested was simply for discussion purposes, and thus did not really have any particular implication. However, when an actual figure of 330 was mentioned, Finance Minister Ikeda thought that setting a rate of 330 yen to the dollar would make it quite tough for Japan. Moreover, if we did not wait a half a year or so after the start of the 1949 budget, it would be difficult to estimate how things were going. What Ikeda was trying to say was that the rate should probably be set sometime in July, and at about 350 yen to the dollar. Dodge told us that he had to go back to the United States in the beginning of May, and I had a premonition that the rate might get set by that time. However, in truth, we did not talk at all about specific numbers to one another afterward. The problem of setting the rate was that much of a taboo within GHQ, and despite Dodge and Ikeda having become personally close, both avoided mentioning it.

However, in the morning edition of the newspapers on April 23, a United Press story with a Washington dateline suddenly appeared, reporting that the exchange rate would be set at 360 yen to the dollar and that the new rate would be effective April 25. This came to us as a bolt out of the blue. In fact, on the afternoon of April 23, GHQ made an official announcement, the contents of which were identical to the UP story. And on April 25, the exchange rate of 360 yen to the dollar was put into effect, and has been in effect through today.

I am guessing, but I think Dodge spoke with only a few people when deciding on the rate of 360 yen, and was in the process of checking with Washington to be on the safe side when the story was scooped by UP. Because of the story breaking, the date of the rate going into effect was probably moved up considerably.

It was in this way that the yen-dollar exchange rate was decided upon, and has not changed at all during the past seven years.[5] In the beginning, there were several times where rumors appeared to the effect that the rate would change, but today the argument for changing the exchange rate has seemed to have died down. While it appears that Dodge had a very good view of the future, another important factor is that the Japanese economy forced itself to adjust to the rate or that the intervention of a powerful force during the Occupation made it easier to do so. At least in regard to GHQ and the Japanese government, there was only one time when either side looked seriously at revising the rate. As far as I know, this was only time to date that such a consideration took place.

The date was September 19, 1949, when all of a sudden, an announcement was made that the British pound was being reduced. The rate went from $4.03 to the pound to $2.80, but despite this, the situation in Japan was surprisingly stable. In the four to five months after the budget began, the effects were more positive than expected and the economy was already showing signs of stabilizing. Indeed, those with uptight personalities were already predicting the coming of a "mini-depression." In any case, a sense of confidence began to emerge that the economy would do well at the rate of 360 yen. On that morning, Shuto Hideo, Director of the Economic Stabilization Office, Inagaki Heitaro, Minister of International Trade and Industry, Ichimada Hisato, President of the Bank of Japan, Kiuchi Nobutane, Chairman of the Foreign Exchange Committee, and some others, met with Finance Minister Ikeda in his office. When asked what Japan should do about the exchange rate, the conclusion was quickly reached that the "current rate should be continued," and this was announced to the press.

That morning, I contacted GHQ, as it was necessary to check its intentions. Because Dodge had already gone back to the United States, GHQ itself could not decide. A great deal of time had elapsed while it was trying to contact Dodge in Washington. One person responded by saying that GHQ "had no objection to the Japanese government announcing on its own that it did not have any intention to change" the exchange rate. Another person said, "let's watch the situation for a while." These two people spoke to others in their headquarters and eventually came back and told me something to the effect of "no comment." Because this was going nowhere, and the Japanese decision was reached with no problem so quickly, we decided to go ahead and announce our decision without waiting for an official response from GHQ.

We told GHQ, "the Japanese side announced that it has no intention of changing [the exchange rate]. As a result, we would like you to cooperate with this announcement." At this point, someone from GHQ said, "While I can not make any promises on behalf of GHQ, we not only have no problem with Japan's announcement of its desires, we also were very happy with it." This was quite confusing to say the least.

In the end, GHQ publicly announced the following day on September 20 that "for the time being there would be no change in the exchange rate." No matter how one looked at it, the expression "for the time being" was a ridiculous one, something that we were unhappy with. Officials from GHQ said that MacArthur himself specifically introduced this phrase, and there was nothing they could do to change it. This was probably true. Fortunately, no reverberations happened domestically, but in retrospect, thinking about it today, it was a silly announcement.

This was the only time that I know of in which the rate of 360 yen was ever seriously reconsidered. There were of course many rumors over the years, but they ended up being just that, rumors.

THROWING AWAY DODGE'S LETTER

There was one strange thing that happened after Dodge returned to the United States on May 2. In September, when a correspondent for Kyodo News Agency visited Dodge in America, Dodge asked him, "In early August, I sent Finance Minister Ikeda a long letter through GHQ. I assumed it would be released to the general public and wrote it for public consumption, but I have not yet seen it in any of the newspapers. What happened?" This was the first time the reporter had heard about it, and asked his contacts in Tokyo. No such letter had come to us. Thinking it was curious, we asked GHQ about it. Considering the likely contents of the letter, we thought it would have been the Economic and Science Section that would have received the letter. No matter how many times we asked them, we did not get a satisfactory response.

After many days had passed, we learned that the staff of the Economic and Science Section had in fact received the letter, but they pretended not to know anything about it. Unfortunately, we never learned what was written in that letter.[6] My guess is that the jealousy exhibited by the staff of the Economic and Science Section toward Dodge only got worse as Dodge got more and more well known, resulting in this episode.

I think the major break with the headquarters (superficially, it was between the headquarters and Ikeda) that occurred immediately after Ikeda's trip to Washington as Finance Minister the following year had a distant connection with this incident.

NOTES

1. Throughout the book, Miyazawa often used the full name and titles of individuals, although they had been mentioned previously. I have taken the liberty of sometimes simply using family names after they appear in the story and not overly repeating their titles. Moreover, Miyazawa often wrote short, sometimes one-line paragraphs. Where the flow was consistent, I have merged paragraphs to make the sentences read better.

2. Izumiyama was also accused of molesting a female Diet Member as well. Miyazawa, *Sengo Seiji no Shogen*, 13.

3. Hakone is a mountainous resort area southwest of Tokyo, near Mt. Fuji.

4. As fifty years had passed since the writing of the memoirs, Miyazawa told the translator their names: "U" was Utsumi Yasukichi and "H" was Hashimoto Kingoro.

5. The exchange rate would not change until 1971, when U.S. President Richard Nixon took the United States off the gold standard and forced the reevaluation of the yen.

6. The translator was able to locate a copy of the letter in the Papers of Joseph M. Dodge in the Burton Historical Division, Special Manuscript Collection, Detroit Public Library. The copy appears as Appendix A at the end of this book. He would like to thank the library staff for its assistance in locating the letter.

Chapter Two

Secret Emissary to Washington, 1950

THE FIRST TRIP TO THE UNITED STATES AFTER
THE START OF THE OCCUPATION

By February of the following year, 1950, a strong desire had emerged in Japan
to conclude a peace treaty in the next couple of years and become independent
again. Nevertheless, this was not being realized, and a sense of frustration began to be felt among the people of Japan. At the same time, the Dodge Line
had begun in Japan the year before and inflation, which had plagued Japan for
much of the postwar, came to an end. However, on the other hand, the stop-
page in money flow and salary rises became severe. Economists warned of
businesses about to go under, exclaiming a "mini-depression." Moreover, the
impression was widely held among the people of Japan that this recession was
the result of an occupation by an uncaring foreigner, Dodge. The economic
struggle in their daily lives began to turn the people of Japan against the Occupation.

The feelings of the people of Japan at the time were beginning to manifest
themselves as anti-Americanism through the unseen opposition to the occupation itself and in the dissatisfaction with the severe lifestyle being forced
upon them by the Occupation authorities. In addition, an Upper House election was scheduled in June this year, with half the seats up for re-election.
Prime Minister Yoshida wanted to reduce the frustration of the people and, after succeeding to do so, use that success to win the election. A concrete way
to do this, Yoshida believed, was to send Finance Minister Ikeda to the United
States as the latter had already gotten to know Washington's thinking during
his two rounds of negotiations with Dodge the previous year. As far as I know,
Yoshida began to formulate this plan sometime in the beginning of 1950 or in

15

February. The biggest problem, however, consisted of the views of Gen. Douglas A. MacArthur the Occupier. MacArthur believed that he was responsible for everything going on in Japan, and as long as he was in that position the government in Washington should stay out of the way. At the same time, he liked to show to the people of Japan that he was their new Emperor.

By this point I had gotten to know the inner workings of GHQ. I often sensed from the bootlickers among the military that they looked at him as someone above the clouds, and when I had the chance to meet MacArthur and heard him lecture us for close to an hour, I too felt that he was a great man. But at the same time, I could not help but feel that he believed himself a god, incapable of making mistakes and therefore above criticism. This made me think what it must have been like to meet an insufferable Prussian Emperor in the past.

As a result, if Yoshida did not skillfully handle the sending of his most skilled bureaucrat to the country of the occupier, and thus escaping from his control, it would not only lead to MacArthur's vetoing the entire trip, but could easily come back to haunt the Japanese government through a change in MacArthur's attitude toward it. The following confidential letter from Prime Minister Yoshida to Ikeda, who was Finance Minister at the time, reveals this situation:

The Honorable Ikeda, Finance Minister[1]

Greetings. Regarding your trip to the United States, I will be meeting Gen. MacArthur next week and will ask his permission at that time. Until then, it is necessary to keep this matter confidential or else we will be unsuccessful. Definitely do not tell anyone else. I am confident that it won't get out but I just want to make sure.

　　Sincerely yours,

Yoshida Shigeru

(1950) February 24

While I included the entire letter here, the essence of it was that if things weren't handled carefully, it wouldn't work, and if word leaked out, for example, to a newspaper before MacArthur had the opportunity to officially give his permission, the opportunity would be lost. Yoshida apparently told MacArthur very carefully that the "reason he was sending the Finance Minister to the United States was to have him study about the U.S. finance and the economy, as a developed country, in an effort to see how this can be applied to Japan. [Ikeda would] also give a report on the results of the Dodge Line implemented over the past year."

Dodge had reportedly asked MacArthur on the occasion of his departure at the end of his second visit to Japan at the end of last year about sending the Finance Minister to the United States. MacArthur and Dodge were both Republicans, and sharing many classical style ideas, seemed to get along quite well with one another. As a result, one can imagine that Dodge's suggestion had a strong influence on MacArthur when he assented to Prime Minister Yoshida's request.

As Ikeda began getting ready for his trip to the United States, Director of the Economics and Science Section Marquat said to him one day, "I think you are a great financier but it might be good for Japan's future as well as your own if you visited the United States. How about it? If you are interested, I can speak to Gen. MacArthur about it."

The reason Dodge came to Japan the year before and the Dodge Line was implemented in the first place was basically because Washington had identified the fact that Marquat and his staff who were technically responsible for the Japanese economy were unqualified. As a result, the jealousy they felt toward Dodge turned into passive resistance and sometimes outright opposition to Dodge and Finance Minister Ikeda, who was seen as Dodge's alter ego in this matter. As was mentioned earlier, this was seen fairly often and thus when Marquat made that seemingly friendly suggestion we all, as a matter of fact, felt very uncomfortable.

However, with the trip to the United States a near reality, we decided to begin our preparations. Initially, Finance Minister Ikeda truly thought his mission was only to discuss finance and economic problems with Dodge and try to find a solution to the issues at hand. I do not intend to go into a detailed explanation of those problems here and now, but briefly, during the past one year, the economic base of the country was made firmer, so much so that signs of a "stability depression" were appearing. The objectives laid out by Dodge—turning off the "water spigot and letting the water accumulate"—had largely been accomplished. In fact, the foundation began to crack. In 1950, it became necessary to move along the way to rebuild the economy and relieve the severe lifestyles imposed upon the people of Japan. This is generally how the government thought at the time.

As a result, Finance Minister Ikeda wanted to raise this in Washington, and discuss concrete problems, such as the further reduction of income taxes, as was originally proposed by Dr. Shoup the year before but was seen as not going far enough, the release of funds that been superficially assigned by Dodge the year before but never properly used, the raising of the salary base of 6307 yen (the so-called 63 base), the release of savings by the people in postal accounts, the relaxation of debt repayment (the policy of using taxes to repay loans through balanced overly balanced finances), and the establishment of an Import-Export Bank to finance exports and imports in light of the fact that the Japanese economy was increasingly becoming connected with the international one.[2]

TRYING FOR A PEACE TREATY

In order to have the people in Washington listen to our requests, we had to have them understand the domestic situation at the time in Japan. In other words, as I explained at the beginning of this chapter, we had to emphasize to them that the frustration with the Dodge Line and the unhappiness with the long occupation were gradually evolving into anti-Americanism and to get them to understand this. If they did not, then they would not understand the results of these measures. This view began to dominate our thinking.

In going to Washington, we could not avoid asking the obvious question, "Just when is America going to allow Japan its independence again?" However, in doing so, we would likely be asked, "To what extent has Japan made preparations to become independent?" Things that happened in the past are easy to forget, but the debate at the time in Japan was over whether it should pursue an "early peace" or a "full peace." The former was the argument that it was better for Japan to go ahead and conclude a peace treaty with the democratic countries of the world led by the United States. Those who called for this were mostly conservatives. In contrast, the Socialist and Communist Parties led the call for a "full peace" with both the Western and Eastern camps, because a "one-sided peace" would not bring about an end to the state of war with the Soviet Union.

There was one problem with the conservative's call for an early peace. That was of course the issue of the defense of Japan following the peace treaty. Even if Japan would be protected by the United States, it would not be easy to find a way to convince a large majority of the people for the need for an independent country to have a foreign military stationed in it.

It was widely assumed that because Finance Minister Ikeda was deeply trusted by Prime Minister Yoshida, he knew the Prime Minister's thinking on this issue. However, that assumption is incorrect. As far as I know, Yoshida did not make known to anyone his concepts regarding the biggest problem of the time, the Peace Treaty. Moreover, even though he told Ikeda just about everything on other issues, Yoshida seems to have felt that the area of foreign affairs was exclusively reserved for the Prime Minister. As a result, when the Prime Minister answered at the Diet, in response to questions like, "Do you plan to recognize the stationing of U.S. forces in Japan in the event of a one-sided peace?" that "It was a hypothetical question and would be answered if such a thing were to happen," I don't think anyone in the Cabinet really knew what he was truly thinking.

In any case, it was not until the eve of Ikeda's trip to the United States that he learned what Yoshida's thinking was on these matters. At this time the Prime Minister told Ikeda, "It is all right for us to request the [continued] presence of the U.S. military." Looking back on it, this revelation was the concept behind what became the U.S.-Japan Security Treaty. While the original purpose of the trip began with the coincidental suggestion to have Ikeda visit the United States, the greatest reason for the trip now became to request the continued presence of U.S. forces in Japan, as is explained later.

As mentioned earlier, because of the situation with GHQ, the Finance Minister departed Japan on April 25 under the pretext of looking into the financial and economic situation of the United States Shirasu Jiro[3] and I accompanied him.

THE FINANCE MINISTER OF A DEFEATED COUNTRY

Our treatment in Washington was somewhat unexpected. For a Cabinet Minister and his entourage of an occupied country receiving aid from America to be put up in a second-rate hotel was not unreasonable, but our two-week schedule was very tight meeting with the various departments in the U.S. government and visiting banks, and we had to follow this schedule.

One day, we met Dodge and complained to him about this very tight schedule and told him we did not come here just to sightsee. Dodge responded, "We were well aware of that. However, it we did not set it up like this, the headquarters in Tokyo would have been unhappy. If a decision is made about Japan here going over MacArthur's head, then there will be many problems later. We can talk about what you wish to talk about in the evenings and on Sunday." In fact, this is the way it happened. We limited our talks to the evenings and on Sunday.

Ikeda was very much aware of the importance of the mission he was given, namely to relay the Japanese readiness to accept the presence of U.S. forces after the peace treaty. He began to look for the right time to relay this. Before I go into this, I wish to briefly explain the details of one more financial and economic problem.

The requests of the Japanese side were first relayed to Dodge. After he studied them, he sent them on to the leadership of the respective departments. We spoke about the requests two or three times at these gatherings. Dodge acted as chair of the meetings. He carefully avoided making anything like a conclusion, but sent detailed reports of the meetings to the headquarters in Tokyo and allowed them to make a decision, at least in form only.

At these meetings, the representatives of the State Department asked rather penetrating questions. As explained later, at the time, the State Department was in favor of an early peace with Japan, while the Army Department was cautious, and thus the two were diametrically on opposite sides of the debate. The State Department felt that the severity of the Dodge Line on the people of Japan was actually causing much of the unhappiness of the people there, and that this was triggering the need for an early peace. This was perhaps the correct view. In their questions, therefore, they asked somewhat leading questions like, "Aren't there people who are having difficulties because money is tight now?" They did so right in front of Dodge, and so Ikeda responded frankly, "Yes, that is right. This is why we have come here to ask Mr. Dodge's assistance." We were happy to be able to come to America and speak freely like this because in occupied Japan, it was hard to even breathe.

In the end, the participants accepted most of the problems we raised at the meetings. Our biggest problem was the lack of documentation, and the fact that we had no way to prepare materials to provide at the meetings. Over the course of the meetings, it became necessary for Ikeda to prepare his ideas for a supplementary budget for 1950, as well as an overview of the establishment of an Import-Export Bank. However, at the time, the Embassy in Washington did not exist nor did any Japanese government agencies, and the only Japanese in Washington were basically two newspaper reporters (Nakamura [Shogo], who is now the American General Bureau Chief of the *Asahi Shimbun*, and Sakai [Yoneo] of the *Tokyo Shimbun*), and so for any facts and figures we had to find the right time to call in the middle of the night back to Tokyo. For the most part, our calls to the Finance Ministry in Yotsuya never got through without some sort of problem. And when they did go through, the person we were looking for at the Ministry was not there. We ended up using a lot of money on these international calls without much to show for it. When we finally got the documents ready, we had to have the Departments of the Army and State print them off as we did not have a typewriter or paper at the hotel we were staying at.

We arrived in Washington on April 27, and went directly to meet with the Undersecretary of the Army, Tracy S. Vorhees. At that time Vorhees told us, "It is being said that the Army is opposed to a peace treaty with Japan, but please make no mistake about it; what the Army is really concerned about is that if a peace treaty were signed, Japan would be completely exposed, and what would happen if the U.S. military were to leave."

Several days later, we met Lt. Gen. [Robert L.] Eichelberger, who had been the Commander of the Eighth Army in Japan before then. The views of these two became clearer with this meeting:

First, when MacArthur called for an early peace, I personally was quite troubled by it because the Soviets had blockaded Berlin and the United States had its

hands full with defending Europe and was not able to pay much military attention to Japan. Second, from the Army's perspective, it is not so much the formality of a peace treaty, but the issue of the defense of Japan that we are most
concerned about. Third, the State Department desires an early peace with Japan,
but they will have to find some way in which to continue to station U.S. troops
in Japan. To say that they would be in Japan to observe the enforcement of the
peace treaty is not enough. Fourth, the idea that it would be alright if Japan were
to become neutral is completely unrealistic. (He said he it was not "worth a
dime," to be exact.) Looking back, America was probably a bit too firm with
Japan. I think this was a fundamentally wrong policy. If we had known that the
Soviet Union was going to be as expansionist as it is, we should have left Europe to Germany and Asia to Japan. That might have been much better. If we
could go only go back to the fighting in the Philippines and Bataan and undo
what happened.

Just right around that time one morning, James Reston of the *New York
Times* had written the following:

The Four Ministers Conference will be held soon, and Secretary of State [Dean
G.] Acheson is likely to touch upon the Japanese Peace Treaty, but nobody here
expects them to do more than touch the surface of it and other problems. The
State Department has one view of the Peace Treaty; the Pentagon has another.
Acheson and MacArthur believe it is necessary to go ahead with a peace treaty
even without the Soviet Union. The Joint Chiefs of Staff opposes this, arguing
that if a treaty were signed with Japan, it would invite attack by the Soviet
Union. The reason the Soviet Union has not attacked Europe is because it has to
plan for a two-front war if it were to attack Europe as the United States is in control in the Far East. If America were to leave the Far East following a peace
treaty with Japan then Soviet Union would be free to attack Europe at will. This
is the Joint Chiefs' view. The British, French and other countries in Europe view
the situation similarly, and for this reason, they will not join Acheson in his call
for a peace treaty with Japan. One more concern the Joint Chiefs of Staff holds
is that if the Soviet Union does not join in a peace treaty with Japan, the state of
war between the Soviet Union and Japan would continue and the Soviet Union
would possess the legal right to strike Japan any time.

We felt that Reston faithfully captured the difference in thinking that existed
between the State Department and the military at the time.

YOSHIDA'S SECRET MESSAGE

Finance Minister Ikeda thought long and hard about to whom he should deliver the message entrusted to him, and eventually decided that Dodge, who

was both a Minister in the State Department as well as an advisor to the Army Department, was ideal because he would offend neither side. One afternoon on a day we had off, May 3 to be precise, Ikeda and I visited Dodge's office and sat down across from Dodge and Dr. [Ralph] Reid, who was an administrative assistant and soon to be Deputy Budget Director.

Explaining that he had a message from the Prime Minister, Ikeda spoke about the peace treaty for a little more than two hours, sharing his ideas and desires. Dodge spoke as well, making sure to preface everything with the fact that they were his "personal opinions." Reid prepared summaries of the comments of both sides. A few days later, Reid brought this memorandum of conversation by and asked me to add or delete to it as I thought appropriate. Based on instructions from Ikeda, I made two or three minor changes.

This memo is an important document, and I retain a copy of it today.[4] One copy each was probably sent to [John Foster] Dulles (later Secretary of State), the Department of State, the War Department, and to Gen. MacArthur in Tokyo. I have avoided speaking about this document until now, and with the exception of some parts that could be problematic, I will go ahead and introduce a summary of its contents below. The first part was all Ikeda speaking.

For many reasons, there are strong voices in Japan desiring an early peace. Within the Diet, the political opposition has centered its attack on the point, originated with the Communists but reportedly joined by the Socialists who have grouped themselves into a united front calling for a full peace. They oppose anything other than a full peace and are against providing America with bases. The Yoshida Cabinet also desires a peace treaty with as many countries as possible, but the continuing of the occupation until those countries that now view Japan as an enemy change their view would be hard to accept. It therefore thinks there is no other choice but to try to get the best peace treaty at the earliest time possible. The political question for the party now in power is whether or not to carry the treaty question and their position on it as part of the party platform in the approaching elections for the House of Councilors, and what this position should be. The opposition often claims in the Diet that GHQ interferes in all levels of Japanese politics and economy and as a result, their democratic privileges are not actual in relatively minor matters of policy affecting the day-to-day life of the Japanese and in the actions of the Diet with respect to these. They have been looking for more latitude in these matters which they claim in some cases have been denied them. The opposition does not believe that this in with the approval of SCAP, but that nevertheless it exists. It criticizes the government as only saying yes and blindly following the Occupation Army. Because of this as well, we feel it necessary to sign a peace treaty as early as possible.

I would like to relay the following message from Prime Minister Yoshida: "The Japanese government desires the earliest possible treaty. Even after such a peace treaty is signed, U.S. forces will probably be necessary for the security of Japan and the Asian region. If the U.S. government is unable to make such a request, the Japanese government can study the way in which to make such an offer. A study of the constitutional angle by constitutional scholars has led to the conclusion that if the maintenance of U.S. bases were made a requirement of the treaty it would make it easier from a constitutional perspective. Nevertheless, according to these scholars, offering such bases would not be in violation of the constitution."

The paragraph above in quotation marks represents Prime Minister Yoshida's message.
Ikeda continued,

In reviewing the attitudes of the Japanese people, they had not forgotten the statement of Secretary of the Department of the Army Royall in February 1949 to the effect that Japan was not necessary to the United States. In particular, looking at what happened later, it appears that America's attitude with regard to Taiwan is not clear. It was further colored by the Communist gains in Indochina, the fact that South Korea is not strong and could, perhaps, easily be abandoned. The Japanese people are skeptical that the U.S. will defend these areas in Asia.

Regarding the last part, it is very interesting that less than two months after this the Korean War started.

The Japanese people are desperately looking for firm ground. There is also the possibility that the Soviets may offer a peace treaty in advance of the United States and might include in that offer the return of Sakhalin and the Kuriles. If this should prove to be no time for a Japanese peace treaty then perhaps America could grant Japan more freedom in the conduct of its own domestic political and economic affairs to give as much as possible the effect of a treaty with the U.S. and create a de facto treaty situation. The Japanese people expect this from the Yoshida Cabinet and if this did not happen then the political situation could become unstable again.

The above is how Ikeda's comments would appear if they were summarized.

THE COMPLICATED ATMOSPHERE IN WASHINGTON

In response, Dodge, ever careful to note that what he was about to say was not official, that it was completely his own opinion, spoke:

As the general international situation between the Soviet Union and the United States deteriorated, and particularly as this appeared to exist in the Far East, it

was certain to raise serious questions as to the advisability of an effort to establish a peace treaty with Japan under these conditions at this time. This in no way
denied the general desire and objective of a peace treaty, but as the general situation deteriorated, the military and strategic position of the United States rose
in importance as a consideration. This, if true, would lead to a natural conclusion that the U.S. position in Japan should probably be maintained at its
strongest. In any case, the peace treaty issue would likely be taken up at the Foreign Ministers Meeting in London, but it is uncertain if the positions of each
country would be made clear at that time or not. What can be said now is that
the U.S. government desires a peace treaty at the earliest time with Japan and
that the conditions will be set to make this happen early.

The above was the gist of Dodge's comment. After this exchange, and the
drafting of the memo, the following was included for the record: "Mr. Ikeda
was informed that his views and the views of his government would be summarized, as they have been above, that this summary would be subject to his
review and approval, and would then be placed in the hands of the proper officials of the Department of State and the Department of the Army." He proceeded to sign it with his name, Joseph Dodge.

Dr. Reid brought the summary of the May 3 memo, now typed, to me on
May 6. After reviewing it, Ikeda signed his name and it became the official
record of the meeting. At this time, I asked Reid where he intended to dis-
tribute copies of the memo. He replied that he would have to consult with
Dodge about it but that he thought one should go to [W. Walton] Butterworth,
one to the Secretary of State's advisor, Dulles, one to the Deputy Undersecretary of the Army [Carter B.] Magruder, and one or two more to other places.

When one copy made it to MacArthur's headquarters, a huge problem
emerged. We were not told at the time that a copy was going to be sent. However, Dodge was sending daily detailed reports (written to keep GHQ informed so as not to place Ikeda in a difficult position upon his return to Japan)
to MacArthur, which we were aware of, and there was no special reason to
oppose one copy going to MacArthur's at this time. Indeed, our feeling then
was that because MacArthur himself was an advocate of an early peace, we
did not think at the time that he had any reason to oppose our views. We tried
to be very careful in our phraseology when we talked about the excessive intervention by the Occupation Army. We were only telling the truth and thus
did not think it would cause any problems.

Despite this, a big problem emerged in the end probably because we went
from a suffocating Occupation environment to America, which was very free,
and as soon as we breathed that free air, we became intoxicated and completely lost our senses. As a result, we could not recalibrate ourselves to the
thinking back in Japan under Occupation. In any case, the May 3 memo was

the first expression of Japan's desire to move the peace treaty along by telling the United States that Japan would recognize the stationing of U.S. forces in Japan after the peace treaty.

The basis of the U.S.-Japan Security Treaty was born here. The peace treaty could be signed in September the following year because of this. I still believe now that the framework for peace with Japan, called the Yoshida-Dulles formula at the time, was not mistaken in itself. Of course, the base problems that exist now are the result of this, but as I explain in detail later, it was not the formula itself that was at fault but the fact that there were many mistakes made in its implementation.

Nevertheless, if the Korean War had not broken out, the signing of the peace treaty might have been delayed longer. That is because the U.S. military, as the occupying force, would have been able to stay as a garrison force after the treaty. In principle, people may have accepted this, but the feeling of the people of Japan would have felt that the occupation was continuing.

When we were struggling with this question, the Korean War by chance broke out and the name "United Nations Forces" came into being for the first time in history. With this, the idea was in fact more easily acceptable among the people of Japan that it was the UN Forces, and not just one country, the United States, that was responsible for protecting Japan's security.

THE INCIDENT OVER THE PRESENT FROM THE U.S. TRIP

Confident in his having relayed the Prime Minister's message about the peace treaty and in having resolved the different economic and financial issues facing Japan, Ikeda departed Washington for Japan, via New York. While in New York, Ikeda received an order from Prime Minister Yoshida to depart in time to meet him in Kyoto on May 21, as he was going around the country to campaign in the Upper House elections.

Upon returning to Japan, Ikeda realized that he would have to make some sort of statement at Haneda Airport. However, Ikeda was well aware that the relationship was quite delicate between Washington, MacArthur's headquarters, and the Japanese government—the occupied—regarding economic and financial matters. In fact, when in Washington gaining the agreement of Dodge on a host of economic issues, Dodge said, "This will likely be a huge present [for your government]. However, it is MacArthur's headquarters that holds the key to this present and thus it would not be good to open the present as soon as you arrive at Haneda." We were quite aware of the warning this implied.

More than this, the feeling of the people desiring a peace treaty was as I explained before and thus it was necessary to say something about it. While it was not likely that the State Department, which was in favor of an early peace treaty, and the more cautious Army, would quickly resolve their differences, we could not just come out and say that directly. We decided to hint to the people that the peace treaty was still some time from now. We thought about how best to say it for some time.

Since Japan did not have a diplomatic representation to speak of at the time within America, we were unable to print off a prepared statement to be used upon arrival at Haneda. So, on the way, when we stopped off in Honolulu, we found a Japanese language newspaper publisher who printed our statement in Japanese for us. The printer also prepared an English version that was a direct translation.

As a side note, when Foreign Minister Shigemitsu [Mamoru] visited the United States [in 1955], there were some problems over the interpretation of the joint statement released at the end of the trip concerning whether Japan had promised to dispatch troops overseas. Readers may remember that it eventually escalated into accusations that the English and Japanese versions were different.

While a somewhat personal experience, I myself was involved in the drafting of three different joint statements, one in 1950, described now, one in 1953 when Ikeda met with Assistant Secretary of State [Walter J.] Robertson as Yoshida's personal emissary, in what was known as the Ikeda-Robertson Talks, and finally for the summit between Yoshida and [Dwight D.] Eisenhower in 1954. From these experiences, in retrospect, I would say that the least amount of problems emerges later if the draft were originally written in English. When preparing the English draft, I was also thinking about how it would sound in Japanese. If the final English version came out well, but the Japanese strange, or the Japanese version good but the English one difficult to read, we would work on them both, with each becoming only slightly awkward, but which made the intention clear and removed any differences between the two. One would think that it would be possible to turn both of them into fine pieces of writing, but I often found that I did not have that level of language ability.

The problem in the 1950 statement was that the peace treaty was not necessarily far off, but at the same time was not immediately around the corner. To tell the truth, while somewhat devious, we had to both be able to give some glimmer of hope to the people of Japan in the Japanese version while at the same time be able to have an English version that would satisfy the concerns of the United States or its headquarters. The Japanese version read, "For the time being, if the domestic political situation remains stable and the economic recovery proceeds, the day in which our country, as a de facto peaceful country, will resume a high place in international society is not far off." In the English version, it says that Japan will resume a high place *de facto. De facto*, as everyone knows usually means "not by law but in fact," but there are many instances when people use the phrase without intending it to have such a restricted meaning. If GHQ made a claim about the phraseology, we intended to use that practice as the reason for any competing interpretations. In writing this, it may appear as boasting, but we really did use our heads in these situations, but in retrospect now, it is somewhat annoying that we even had to do that.

The time immediately after arriving at Haneda in the early morning of May 21 was so confusing that I have no real memory of it. The Prime Minister's Secretary told us to immediately go to Kyoto. When we asked if we should first go to MacArthur's to pay our respects, the Secretary responded that it was all taken care of and we did not have to do so. Since it was the age before domestic flights, we went to Kyoto by train, but have no recollection of what time or even from where we boarded. My diary this day only says, "May 21. Arrived at Haneda at 4:45 a.m. Lots of people met us at the airport."

On the ride to Kyoto, we asked about things during our absence. From a report filed by the two Japanese correspondents, there was a vague impression that some discord was emerging with the headquarters, but that was about it. Even today, I am not sure of the real reason. In the short few hours since returning from the most free country in the world, I had not yet adjusted back to the oppressive atmosphere of the Occupation.

GENERAL HEADQUARTERS DELIVERS A SEVERE REBUKE

As we were approaching Kyoto, the conductor brought me a telegram. It not only broke the spell of freedom, but was also written in English to boot along the following lines:

To Mr. Miyazawa Kiichi, Secretary to Finance Minister, from Finance Director Watanabe [Takeshi] in care of Kyoto Station Master

I was ordered by Major Generals Marquat and [Courtney] Whitney to report to you by telegram the following before the Finance Minister begins electoral campaigning.

1. The purpose of the Finance Minister's trip to the United States was to examine the situation in the United States, and to explain Japan's situation, something of which the Finance Minister was very much aware. It was inappropriate for him to negotiate in a political manner while in the United States this time regarding economic problems.

2. According to Dodge's letter, among other sources, Dodge made it
   clear that you were to speak to the Supreme Commander of the occupation regarding Japan's future policies. It is unlikely that in talking directly with the U.S. authorities a decision could be reached.
3. It is a serious breach of etiquette on the part of the Prime Minister and
   the Finance Minister to try to use a lessening of the Dodge Line in a
   political campaign. If this in fact happens, problems will likely
   emerge with GHQ when trying to implement future economic stabilization programs.

My first reaction when I read this was, "what jerks!" While my language
may be somewhat vulgar, there was no other way to express this. Especially
the last part, which said, if this order was not followed then "problems
w[ould] likely emerge," was the ultimate in bad form. It was an unpleasant
message, no other way to say it, particularly the tone of GHQ saying, "you
people are being occupied." I was really angered by this.

However, the fact that this telegram was sent in the name of both Major
Generals Marquat and Whitney suggested that situation was serious. To be
honest, I think these two generals weren't even worth criticizing, but in any
case MacArthur brought them from Bataan in the Philippines with him. Not
only did they not get along personally, but they also clashed in their work. For
example, when Whitney antagonized the National Personnel Authority (*Jin-
jiin*) and recommended a salary increase for public workers, Marquat had to
oppose it for economic reasons. The two got along like a cat and dog. The fact
that they both took action meant only one thing: MacArthur was in the background.

That evening, Finance Minister Ikeda boarded the train to go back to Tokyo
after giving the Prime Minister a detailed report in Kyoto. The next morning,
we went to Major General Marquat's office to pay our respects after returning. Although we had an appointment, Marquat's deputy came out and said
that Major General Marquat had urgent business and could not meet with us
and that he would receive us instead.

As this strange situation continued over the next couple of days, the newspapers began to report that the "relationship between GHQ and the government has increasingly been getting chilly." While not factually incorrect, we
could not talk about what really happened. Perhaps I was still suffering from
jetlag or something, but I did not feel that the chilliness was directed at us personally. While this might seem like a strange confession, I had thought until
then that Major General Marquat was a really high-ranking man, but after going to the Army Department in Washington, I realized that there many people
of such rank just hanging around in the hallways there and that such a rank

was nothing special. A strange wave of confidence came over me, but in the end Marquat did not get over his feeling of self-importance.

But what was problematic was not whether or not we were scorned but the fact that we wanted to announce the results of our meetings in Washington in time for the Upper House elections and thus had to speak with GHQ on the timing. If Marquat, saying he was out of the office, could not meet us, then we could not publicize our results.

A few days later, a letter from Dr. Reid came on another matter, and in it he wrote that Dodge had sent the final memorandum relating to the meetings in Washington to GHQ, and thus the headquarters should have a full picture now of what took place. It was clear that GHQ was not awaiting any new instructions from Washington.

DISCORD BETWEEN GHQ AND THE JAPANESE GOVERNMENT

We really did not know what to do at this point. Looking back, that situation seemed to last about half a month or so, but when I checked my diary I realized that recollection was incorrect. The situation was resolved by May 30, which meant that it only lasted less than ten days. It was tough, so that is probably why it seemed to have lasted longer. During those ten days, a lot of people were made busy trying to resolve this issue. The reporters in Washington even sent Marquat telegrams trying to explain what Ikeda said to them to help our case. It was really an unpleasant period.

While ridiculous, the plan was to have the Finance Minister submit to the Prime Minister a report of his trip with a description of the policies he wished to pursue from now on (in other words, the requests he made in Washington and the results of the consultations). The Prime Minister in turn would forward this on to Supreme Commander MacArthur with a note asking for his "pledging our loyalty." In response, MacArthur would write back and the issue was resolved at the time. By doing this, our status as the occupied would be restored and MacArthur's headquarters would be able to regain its prestige and authority.

MacArthur's response to Prime Minister Yoshida arrived on May 25. I still remember it now, but the gist of it had to do with Ikeda's view that his plans had to be implemented next year. The letter said that with the election just around the corner, he would be laughed at for promising things for next year, but they could say that a supplementary budget for this year would be released at the time they were forming next year's budget. Seizing on this point, Yoshida, as President of the Liberal Party, said rather boldly on May 30 that the party would lower taxes and raise salaries through a supplemental budget in the second half of the year. There was no particular scolding after that.

However, we had lost the opportunity to pay our respects to MacArthur upon our return home to Japan. On the eve of our departure, MacArthur lectured us for close to an hour, but after our return he did not even respond when we said we could visit him at a time of his convenience. The next time I saw MacArthur in person was the following year when he was departing Haneda after being relieved of command by President [Harry S.] Truman.

MR. DULLES BEGINS WORKING TOWARD
THE PEACE TREATY

After we returned from Washington, the State Department and Defense Department had been able to compromise and the desire to move ahead with an early peace treaty increased. In addition, we sensed that something large was afoot given that Dulles, who seemed to welcome overwork to work, was assigned the task of arranging the peace treaty. In fact, in early June, in the announcement regarding Dulles's pending trip to Japan, it said that the purpose of the trip was to explore "the timing and approach to be used for the Peace Treaty with Japan." Moreover, the press reports from Washington stated that "the U.S. is looking to create a security structure for the Asia-Pacific region" and that "the peace conference would likely be convened in January next year."

After visiting Korea, Dulles arrived in Tokyo on June 22, if my memory is correct, and just three days later North Korea declared war on the South. It was quite surprising that Seoul fell so quickly, within a few days.

In this way, the long conflict began on the Korean peninsula, and in Japan a heated argument began in Japan on the issue of Japan's defense. Politicians and scholars debated the question of whether the clause in the Japanese Constitution denies the right of self-defense. For the general public, this had not been a serious problem in the past. Indeed, the question probably consumed MacArthur more for he was the one who was responsible for establishing the postwar Constitution and in the position to handle military operations against the Soviet Union.

Therefore, on January 1, 1950, as the occupier of Japan, MacArthur openly stated in his New Year's address that "Japan has the right to self-defense," in contrast to what had been said in the past. Moreover, in the Prime Minister's policy speech before the Diet in the middle of January, Yoshida basically stated the same thing. Nevertheless, it did not become a tangible issue to the general public until the end of July when MacArthur issued a directive to the

Japanese government "authorizing it to take the necessary measures to establish a National Police Reserve" following the start of the Korean War on June 25 and the introduction of U.S. forces on the 27th.

In the years following the end of World War II and this point, U.S. occupation forces and Japanese police provided security within Japan. However, when third country nationals caused violent disturbances, it was the U.S. military that imposed order, with the Japanese police not lifting a finger. Many Japanese hoped for a police force that was fully equipped to deal with these domestic problems.

Despite the fact that MacArthur's directive was a direct result of the Korean War, the use of the term, "National Police Reserves," was probably in response to this desire of the Japanese people.

Around this time, Finance Minister Ikeda visited Yoshida, who was resting in Hakone. On the way back to Tokyo, I remember Ikeda saying to me, "The Prime Minister is very happy that the National Police Reserves are to be created. He repeated over and over, 'Yokatta ne, yokatta ne!' [it's great, it's great]." As explained before, with the domestic security situation the way it was and a major conflict in a country nearby, most Japanese seemed to welcome the news of the directive in a similar manner.

On August 10, a Potsdam Directive was issued to allow the Occupation Army's directive to go into effect and officially permit the establishment of the National Police Reserves. Over the next several years, the NPR would later become the National Safety Force and then the Self Defense Force, spawning a debate over the relationship between the Constitution and the military.

Around this time, the effects of the Dodge Line, which had been in effect for more than a year, were quite visible. Indeed, money had actually begun to become tight, and the war in neighboring Korea did not really impact this at all. While the economy was not yet growing, it was no longer as weak as it once was.

On August 15, the fifth anniversary of the end of the war approached and the newspapers began to print headlines that suggested things were looking up for the average person in being able to purchase foods and other daily necessities. Indeed for the ten years from before the time of the start of the Greater East Asia War to now, "clothing tickets" were issued, and that policy was ended at the end of September that year (1950). For those raised after that time, you might think that it is normal to be able to purchase clothes or shoes if you pay for them, but during the war until 1950, all clothing had point values, and even if you had the money, without the accumulated points you were not allowed to buy the clothing.

Symbolic of this time was an incident concerning the publication of a translation of [D. H.] Lawrence's *Lady Chatterley's Lover* by Ito Takeshi, someone who was until then practically unknown outside of his circle. The book was considered pornographic and the translator was indicted. As a result, it gained the attention of the general public, touching off a big discussion.

At the beginning of September 1950, President Truman publicly announced that he had told the Far Eastern Committee, comprising the countries involved in the Allied Occupation of Japan, discussions on the peace treaty would formally begin with Dulles to be in charge of the negotiations with each country.

DODGE VISITS JAPAN AGAIN

Regarding economic issues, in late October, Dodge visited Japan because the time to prepare the 1951 Fiscal Year budget was approaching. By this point, the financial situation had been stabilized for the most part, and the Japanese government was beginning to think about ending the "rice" controls as part of the process of cutting the stilts on which the economy was standing, namely aid.

Dodge had said in the past that it was necessary to strip the Japanese economy bare, and so he did not oppose ending rice controls in principle. I thought the timing was right because of expectations that a large amount of rice, some 63,000,000 *koku*, would be harvested.[5] Indeed, I sensed it was more the officials in the Ministry of Agriculture and GHQ who thought American-style farm support, which protected farmers by maintaining a certain level of prices for agricultural items, should be started.

Finance Minister Ikeda was in the forefront of the debate to end price controls and the Cabinet had basically come around to this view. In fact, in early November, the government and the ruling party had agreed in effect to end price controls for rice and other main staples around April the following year. In my interactions with Dodge, I didn't think it would be difficult to overcome any doubts he may have had. Yet, one morning in the middle of November, we were asked to see Dodge. Prefacing his remarks by saying, "In regards to the issue of price controls for rice," he then began to write out a lot of questions for us:

1. In light of the situation today, what is most important for the safety of the people of Japan today?
2. Who can guarantee that ships importing food to Japan won't be blown up somewhere, sometime?

There were twelve of these kinds of questions.

When we tried to answer these questions, it appeared that Dodge was not even listening to us. We did not know what to make of the situation. Indeed, there were some people within GHQ who strongly called for ending price controls and they watched Dodge's sudden change of colors closely and with indignation. It was not until somewhat later when we found out what had happened. That morning, a meeting of the senior leadership in GHQ was held. It appeared that forces of Communist China had launched a counterattack that morning just as South Korean forces had reached the border between North Korea and China, and GHQ was at that moment studying the intelligence reports of this serious situation. Indeed at the end of the month, MacArthur made a special announcement stating, "Communist forces had advanced southward and the situation on the Korean peninsula had entered a new stage. The situation was beyond his authority." This was an attempt to pressure President Truman to allow him to bomb Manchuria and send forces across the border. This statement became the direct cause of MacArthur's dismissal by Truman, but in any case, GHQ judged the situation serious enough as to believe that Japan might be directly attacked. We learned later that this was the reason for Dodge's sudden change in his point of view and for the twelve questions he gave us. Therefore, if this situation had not occurred, it is likely that the problem of price controls on rice would have been resolved by the end of 1950.

DODGE'S FAILURE

I have one more gloomy memory of our interaction with Dodge that year. The issue was quite a trivial thing, but that summer, the workers of the National Railways demanded a one-time pay bonus, and the Central Labor Committee (*Chuo Rodo Iinkai*) ruled in their favor. The ruling was binding on the government "as long as it had the funds to do so."

There was other work to do as well—repairing Kyoto Station after a fire that year, building new freight cars for the National Railways, etc.—but as long as the ruling was legally binding on the government, it had to direct the funds from its budget to pay for the one-time bonuses. Dodge was of the belief that the establishment of rigid pay scales and labor laws was to allow defeated Japan to live within its means. One time, Dodge even said to me, "If I knew Japan had a Labor Standard Law, I wouldn't have even bothered to come to Japan." This is how much he thought that improvements on the railways or bonuses were unnecessary.

Nevertheless, the time remaining in the Diet was getting shorter, and when we raised this issue with him he became upset as expected. However, this was the law and while it was something we were not particularly happy about it had to be done. This explanation alone took half a day.

By evening, Dodge resigned himself to the submission of the bill to the Diet. But he said, "However, only a certain amount of budget (it was about 5 billion yen) should be used, as there is nothing more and therefore impossible to use." In addition, he said to add the phrases, "this will not be a precedent for other public workers," and "it will be necessary to cancel the building of new freight cars." While this was logical, there was only one style in which bills could be presented, and thus these conditions could not be included. It took almost an hour for him to accept this. With this, Dodge, showing his reluctance, signed "OK" to the English translation of the bill to be presented to the Diet. He then informed the Government Section, which had been waiting for his decision (the GS examined all pending legislation and budgets that the Japanese government prepared for submission to the Diet), by telephone of his approval. The GS in turn informed the Japanese government, which went ahead and submitted the bill for the one-time bonus.

We took the document that Dodge had signed and as we were leaving, mentioned that "it would be necessary to amend the budget. The amendment shall be presented to the Diet tomorrow morning." Dodge's expression changed all of sudden. "Budget? What budget?" he said to himself, in a strange way. When his staff explained that an amendment permitting the shifting of funds to pay for bonuses away from building new freight cars was necessary as a formality, it did not appear to register with Dodge. When Finance Minister Ikeda tried to explain that an automatic amendment to the budget became necessary since he gave the approval, Dodge let out a short outburst and grabbed the signed document that was on the desk.

Because Dodge enjoyed the deep trust of MacArthur as his highest advisor on financial matters, he was able to carry himself at GHQ in such a way. However, the directors of the heads of the sections responsible for politics and the economy were all military officers, and Dodge had to save their faces, a task apparently not easy for him. In this case, to amend the budget, formally, the permission of Major General Marquat, who headed the economic section, was necessary. This meant that Dodge inadvertently made the decision unilaterally.

To complicate matters, it was the Government Section that was responsible for things related to salaries, and it was Major General Whitney, MacArthur's closest aide, who was in charge of that. Like Marquat, Whitney came with MacArthur from Bataan but he outdid Marquat for MacArthur's affection and was at a slight advantage and thus the two almost never got along on any matter. Whitney supported the bonus, hoping it would lead to the democratization of Japan's workers. Marquat opposed it due to his concerns about a sound economy. On top of their difference of opinions, the fact that Dodge went ahead and approved indirectly the budget revision, which was really Marquat's jurisdiction, was likely to add fuel to the fire. (Following MacArthur's dismissal, they both returned to America together, and Whitney regularly visits MacArthur's "personal headquarters" in a New York hotel.)

Having stolen the document he had just signed, Dodge took it to Marquat's office, but Marquat had already gone home for the evening. There was some discussion on the phone, but nothing appeared to have been settled. After that, Dodge returned to the room we were in. Without saying anything to us, he grabbed his hat and tore off into the hall uttering, "good night" or something to that effect and plodded off down the hallway. Those of us left in the room—Ikeda, myself, and Dodge's aides—sat around vacantly for several moments. Because Dodge had taken the one piece of proof—the paper with his "OK" on it—to show that it was possible to pay for the bonuses as per the bill about to be introduced in the Diet, which was the biggest issue at the moment.

Finally, Finance Minister Ikeda said to the aides, "What in the world was that all about?" They all answered in unison, "Dodge is wrong. There was nothing wrong in what the Japanese government was doing. We will be your witnesses anytime." At that point, Ikeda said in Japanese, "If that is the case, please write it down." I did not understand what he was asking, and did not interpret it. This is unfortunate because Ikeda was trying to get them to put down their testimony on paper right then and there.

When we returned to the Diet it was already half-past nine, and the bill to pay for bonuses was proposed, but without the GHQ's approval for the revised budget, the situation was in flux, something that the newspaper reporters were picking up on. Various rumors were afloat that night, including that the relationship between the government and GHQ was cooling quickly and even that the government was in danger of collapsing.

In the long years that I interacted with Dodge, this event was the one happening that was most unlike him. He would always come to Japan during the cold time, from around November to winter. At that time, heaters were not common and having to work all day may have led him to react in this way. As far as I know, this was the only time when he acted less than a gentleman.

NOTES

1. This letter is also reprinted in Yoshida Shigeru Kinen Jigyo Zaidan, ed., *Yoshida Shigeru Shokan* [The Letters of Yoshida Shigeru] (Tokyo: Chuo Koronsha, 1994), 37.

2. For more on the Shoup Taxation Mission, see U.S. Department of State, *Foreign Relations of the United States, 1949, Vol. 7, The Far East and Australasia, Part 2* (Washington, D.C.: Government Printing Office, 1976), 846.

3. Shirasu, a businessman, had become a close friend of Yoshida when the latter was Ambassador to England in the 1930s and participated with Yoshida in the Yoshida "anti-war" group that tried to bring about an early end to the war. After Yoshida joined the first postwar cabinet (of Higashikuni Naruhiko) as Foreign Minister, Shirasu joined the Central Liaison Office as Counselor to assist in interfacing with the Occupation authorities. He was appointed as the first Director of the Trade Agency (Boeki Cho) in 1948. He participated on the trip to the United States in his capacity as a private advisor to Yoshida.

4. A copy is also available as "Discussion of Japanese Peace Treaty with Mr. Ikeda, Finance Minister (May 2, 1950)," *Foreign Relations of the United States, 1950, Vol. 6, East Asia and the Pacific* (Washington, D.C.: GPO, 1976), 1194–98.

5. *Koku* is a unit of measuring in Japan, equal to 180.3 liters.

Chapter Three

Destiny's Peace Conference, 1951

MACARTHUR GETS DISMISSED

When General MacArthur was dismissed in the beginning of April 1951 at the end of a long period wrought with friction with President Truman and the Allies over the handling of the Korean War, the Japanese people experienced something strange. Those who were called "Intellectuals" described it as the manifestation of the principle of civilian control over the military in American democracy and thus Japan should learn from this, but for most of the people, there was the sense that the absolute authority of the Occupation was crumbling if the person that they revered almost like a new Emperor, who until then was above rebuke, suddenly lost all his power and was subject to a great deal of criticism.

Even then, it was quite interesting to observe the various expressions on the faces of the staff at GHQ. The younger officers, up to say the lieutenant level, or those who openly supported Truman, or even those who felt for MacArthur, constantly talked about the dismissal, but the very senior level of the command, those that were believed to be close to MacArthur, such as Whitney and Marquat, held even more complicated feelings. It became a competition between those that considered themselves close to MacArthur and had vied for his affection in the past to see whom MacArthur would bring back with him at the time of his departure. As a result, the dismissal released a new round of rivalry among the senior staff. It was a strange atmosphere to witness—I heard one person say to Marquat, "Of course, you're going with MacArthur as well, aren't you?"

In any case, within GHQ and around Japan, there was a general feeling that MacArthur was being crucified. The send-off for him was huge. People lined the streets from Tokyo's Hibiya district to Haneda airport on both sides, something not seen before or after. I think it was April 16 when the Cabinet, including Prime Minister Yoshida, and other members of the Japanese government went to bid MacArthur farewell. With no choice but to go, I stood behind Finance Minister Ikeda near the airplane. At the designated time, MacArthur, his wife, son, and Whitney came and shook the hands of each of the Cabinet officials gathered. Whitney said to the Cabinet Minister "M" standing to the right of me, "Yes, we shall return soon." I wondered what in the world he was talking about.[1] Some years later, I heard from Prime Minister Yoshida that Whitney said to him, "God bless you," but Whitney had caused Yoshida so many problems over the years that Yoshida wanted to say back to him "God blame you." (Examples of the trouble Whitney caused Yoshida were seen when Ashida [Hitoshi] and Nishio [Suehiro] tried to create a coalition of the Progressive and Socialist Parties as well as Yamazaki [Takeshi]'s short-lived rebellion. Whitney was behind both moves pulling the strings.)

In any case, the people who came to bid farewell, unlike the ordinary people, were those who had suffered in some way directly at the hands of the Occupation. Even if we were personally grateful to MacArthur, there were likely few people who were truly sorry to see him go. Although there was an eerie silence throughout the farewells, as soon as MacArthur got on the top landing of the stairs to go inside the plane, one of the Cabinet Ministers screamed out, "General MacArthur, Banzai!" and everyone raised their arms. If someone who looked the other way and did not do this, he would have been labeled a serious "resistor," I imagine. This label was something that was feared at the time in Occupied Japan.

Early on in the Occupation, MacArthur quickly saw that conflict was coming with the Soviet Union and prevented its occupying Hokkaido, and he also opposed the Emperor's going to trial for war crimes. Knowing him as well as he did, Prime Minister Yoshida retained a deep affection for MacArthur until the end. Even after MacArthur's dismissal, Yoshida would speak very highly of MacArthur's accomplishments when Americans gathered. In 1954, when Yoshida visited the United States, he went out of his way to go up to New York to see MacArthur. In addition to his personal affection for him, Yoshida had a tendency to do what he wanted to when the mood hit him and his desire to visit with MacArthur would increase the more MacArthur became embattled.

THE PEACE TREATY DRAFT

The peace treaty preparations begun by Dulles the year before were proceeding, and a draft treaty prepared by Dulles was ready in March 1951. The draft was prepared in order to allow the Allied countries to study it. In drafting it, Dulles and his aide, Minister [John M.] Allison, who had been sent to the Political Advisor's Office within GHQ for this purpose, sought out the opinions of Japan as well. This draft is called the "March 1951 Draft." At the Peace Conference, the U.S. State Department handed out copies of it to the delegates of each country as part of the reference materials to compare it with the final version (the August 13, 1951 draft).[2]

I think it was on July 20, when the United States sent out invitations to the Allied countries inviting them to San Francisco for the peace conference, that it announced it would "not release the contents of the August 13 draft until then in order to overcome a misunderstanding that exists in Manila on the treaty." This was a reference to the issue of compensation. Namely, Dulles had initially planned not to require of Japan in principle the payment of reparations, as per Japan's strong request.

The legal basis for this was found in the decision of the Far Eastern Committee to place the direct expenses for supporting Japan during the Occupation as the first in the list of claims against Japan. This meant that if other countries were going to claim reparations against Japan, first America, which sent Japan many relief supplies such as clothing and other things during the Occupation worth several billion dollars (today, these are called the GARIOA [Government Appropriation for Relief in Occupied Areas] claims), would have the right to be repaid first its billions of dollars by Japan. Therefore, the reasoning was that if this were done, there would be nothing left to pay for reparations and thus these countries should give up on its demands for reparations. However, this was unacceptable to the Philippines and Indonesia and they showed signs of not even wanting to participate in the Peace Conference. Dulles finally decided to include the minimum amount for reparations in the August 13 version. As a result, the March version did not have the current clause in it regarding compensation and instead left it up to each country in principle to use the assets left by Japan or its private citizens for compensation (Article 14 of the March draft).

This was the biggest difference between the two versions, but there is also another issue, the territorial clause relating to the status of Southern Sakhalin and the Kurile Islands, that has become a problem now. Namely, in Article 5 of the March draft, the clause read, "Japan will return to the Union of Soviet Socialist Republics the southern part of Sakhalin as well as all the islands adjacent to it and will hand over to the Soviet Union the Kurile Islands." This was the phraseology used by influential people in Japan at the time. The proposal to not specifically name the Soviet Union was what lead to the rewriting of the article in its current form.

If the March draft were left unchanged, the territorial problem between Japan and the Soviet Union likely would not have occurred. Similarly if

Dulles had been willing to take on the Soviet Union more strongly, we would not have had to relinquish rights over the islands to an unnamed party in the current vague form that the article has proscribed. In any case, the March draft has the southern part of Sakhalin to be returned and the Kurile Islands "to be handed over" to the Soviet Union in the same language it seems as the Yalta Agreement.[3] This must have bothered the conscience of the American side, and thus the change.

THE MANEUVERING OF THE DEMOCRATIC PARTY ON THE EVE OF THE PEACE CONFERENCE

In early July, we learned that the peace conference would be held in San Francisco in early September. Within Japan, high expectations were seen toward the coming independence, and abroad, such as in New York, Japanese government bonds (valued at approximately $100) were apparently being purchased for as much as $102. On the other hand, regarding the question of Japanese security following the peace treaty, the general understanding among Japanese people was that because some sort of arrangement was likely to be worked out between Japan and the United States, America would likely be in charge of Japan's defense for some time.

Since the time of my trip to Washington in May the year before, we could determine that a security agreement to be signed at the time of a peace treaty was being worked out based on the improved atmosphere between the State Department and Defense Department and statements to that effect by Yoshida. However, in truth, the Cabinet was left in the dark on the details and the talks proceeded quite secretly.

Japan was unable to stand the occupation any longer; yet, it was unable to handle its own defense if it became independent. At the time there was little criticism out of the ordinary of the decision, known as the Yoshida-Dulles formula, that Japan had no choice but to enter into a security treaty with the United States. However, it can not be denied that within just a few years, many base problems, which lead to the rise in anti-Americanism seen in the slogans, "Yankee Go Home," had its origins in this formula. As I discuss later, I do not believe that the formula itself is to blame for the situation that emerged, but instead is related to the numerous mistakes made afterward in realizing the formula. In any case, Japan, about to be granted independence, was unable to see that far into the future.

Many politicians at the time had their heads occupied thinking about the domestic problems related to the peace conference. As the peace conference approached, a movement started to try to welcome the treaty in a bipartisan manner, at least among the conservative parties, a desire particularly strong within the ruling Liberal Party. At the time, this movement was called the "Democratic Party Machinations." These efforts had a long history. In fact, beginning a year before in January 1950, Prime Minister Yoshida attempted to bring into the fold Inukai [Takeru] of a faction of the Democratic Party that was in favor of a coalition government with the Liberals, but a group led by Shidehara and others within the Liberal Party (then known as the Democratic Liberal Party or *Minjito*) strongly opposed this. After some complicated dynamics, this effort finally bore fruit. On the eve of the peace conference, the other conservative party was the "Democratic Party" led by Tomabechi [Yoshizo] as Supreme Committee Chairman, following Inukai's departure, with Miki Takeo as Secretary General.

Around July 20, as our country accepted the official invitation to attend the peace conference, the Liberal Party requested the Democratic Party to participate in a plenipotentiary delegation so that the conservatives could participate as one group at the peace conference. However, Tomabechi, Supreme Committee Chairman of the Democratic Party, who had called for bipartisanship in the past to which the Liberal Party did not respond, released a statement saying he was unhappy with this sudden request and said their participation was not possible. The opposition to the peace treaty of the Democratic Party, which was like that of the right wing of the Socialist Party, did not appear to be one that opposed the peace conference in principle. However, they called for the government to hold a special session of the Diet prior to the peace conference to explain the contents of the draft peace treaty and the post-treaty U.S.-Japan security relationship.

In response, the government's view was consistently opposed to doing so because the final version, which was ready on August 13, had to be announced by America and it would be a breach of international trust if the Japanese government publicly discussed the contents prior to that. The leadership of the Liberal Party suspected Democratic Party Supreme Committee Chairman Tomabechi of actually wanting to attend the Peace Conference but because of the complicated history between the two parties and the situation within his party, publicly he had to be critical. As a result, when Liberal Party Secretary General Masuda [Kaneshichi] met with Tomabechi and Miki of the Democratic Party on July 28, I think it was, they were able to narrow their differences. Namely, the positions of the two parties could be written up on the same paper. The Liberal Party stated that if the Democratic Party would confirm its intention to participate in the Peace Conference then it would hold a special session of the Diet. The Democratic Party's position on the other hand was that if the Liberal Party held a special session of the Diet and if it were satisfied with it, then it would participate in the Conference. In other words, the problem was how to save face for the Democratic Party. However, when it came to these delicate, or shall we say childish, situations within the

Liberal Party, the Prime Minister would often throw a fit and say that it was necessary to break off talks with the other party who knew absolutely nothing and order something to that effect. At times like this, Yoshida would get really angry or at least show that he was angry to get the other side to give in a little. In those cases, I do not think Yoshida even knew which one it was. In any case this was quite common.

Nevertheless, at times like this the go-betweens would be trembling at Yoshida's every change of mood if they were not familiar with his temperament. The person tasked with negotiations this time was Secretary General Masuda. At the time, Masuda's relations with Hirokawa [Kozen], chairman of Executive Council (*Somukai*), were really bad, fighting over the Prime Minister's favor on just about everything. Hirokawa was much closer to the inner workings of the party and he blocked Masuda's efforts.

On the one hand, because the Executive Council, based on the thinking of Hirokawa and the bullishness of the Prime Minister, passed a resolution calling for the ending of negotiations with the Democratic Party on July 30, Secretary General Masuda was no longer able to proceed. Yet, on the other hand, the time to choose the plenipotentiary delegation was rapidly approaching and on the evening of July 31, Secretary General Masuda, Executive Council Chairman Hirokawa, Policy Affairs and Research Council Chairman Yoshitake [Eichi], House Steering Committee Chairman Ozawa [Saeki] went to Hakone to sound out the Prime Minister again and there they got another scolding.

Prime Minister Yoshida's feelings at the time, based on what I heard indirectly later was essentially complete frustration at the site of these grown men, who not only arrived without a single concrete proposal but also included individuals who were doing their best to undermine each others efforts, line up before him with their heads bent forward. Yoshida reportedly said afterward that he "was really angered" and that is probably what in fact happened.

And the Prime Minister at this time—in his anger—said in a threatening tone that he no longer wanted to deal with the Democratic Party, that he would not call a Diet session, and that if Tomabechi wanted to join the Cabinet in order to become a member of the plenipotentiary delegation he would meet him the day after. We were not the only ones who were dumbfounded. When Masuda told Miki, Secretary General of the Democratic Party, about this, Tomabechi was driven into a corner. "Have you ever heard of such a foolish thing? Even if Yoshida were to come here officially I would not meet with him." As a result, both sides stopped talking to each other.

According to what I heard from Finance Minister Ikeda a few days later, that same evening, Yoshida's beloved daughter, Aso Kazuko, was also there in Hakone and after the members of the Liberal Party snuck away she pointed out to the Prime Minister that if he angered the Democratic Party—the largest opposition party—it would only make the passage of the peace treaty that much more troublesome. Yoshida well understood this logic; this is probably why he was patient for so long and had the party undertake the operation to get the Democratic Party on board. However, at the important juncture he lost his temper. He likely regretted it afterwards.

The following morning, August 1, the Prime Minister came down from Hakone to Tokyo although there was no Cabinet meeting scheduled. He called Chief Cabinet Secretary Okazaki [Katsuo] and Masuda, Hirokawa, and Yoshitake from the day before and said, "Let's continue with the operation vis-à-vis the Democratic Party. However, because this involves the selection of plenipotentiaries, it is not a party matter but one of state. For this reason, from now on Okazaki will be primarily in charge." To me, it also appeared as a defeat for both Masuda and Hirokawa. However, the Democratic Party was another matter. Because Secretary General Masuda had told Miki, the Secretary General of Democratic Party, what was said the night before, who in turn told a gathering of the party members, the party membership passed a resolution to not engage in any negotiations at all on this issue.

TOMABECHI AGREES TO BECOME PLENIPOTENTIARY

I will introduce my diary in full for August 3, two days after the above events.

August 3 Friday. Clear sky, hot.

Finance Minister Ikeda telephoned early this morning. He told me he received a phone call from Prime Minister Yoshida in Hakone, who wants to meet immediately. I left with Ikeda at 8:30 and arrived at the old Mitsui mansion in Kowakudani a little after 11:00. Finance Minister Ikeda spoke with the Prime Minister for over thirty minutes. On the way back, Ikeda told me that the Prime Minister is thinking of visiting Washington, if possible, following the Peace Conference. For this reason, he wants to have Finance Minister Ikeda and Ichimada of the Bank of Japan accompany him. He would also like both men to attend the Peace Conference as Ministers Plenipotentiary.

After saying that he was in agreement with this, Ikeda stated one condition, that the Prime Minister confer immediately with Chairman Tomabechi of the Democratic Party and request him to participate as well as a Minister Plenipotentiary. In addition, Ikeda added that he was aware that the Prime Minister had rejected the idea of visiting Tomabechi the night before last [August 1], this was probably due to the Prime Minister's not fully understanding what had happened in the talks between the two parties' Secretaries-General up to that point. He then explained the situation. As a result, the Prime Minister agreed to meet with Tomabechi. Ikeda said that he would try to arrange the meeting so that Tomabechi would visit the Prime Minister's residence in Meguro, but if for some reason he was unsuccessful and was forced to select a third location, he wanted all such arrangements left up to him. The Prime Minister reluctantly agreed to this. In addition, Ikeda asked the Prime Minister for permission to have me accompany him to the Peace Conference, and this was granted.

In the car on our trip back to Tokyo, we then studied how the above might be best relayed to Tomabechi. In our conversation, former Admiral Toyoda Teijiro's name came up. He is an old friend of Miki Takeo and Ikeda thought it might be worthwhile to ask him to do so, but as Toyoda is currently a purgee, we would have to make sure that he would not be inconvenienced by it. When we were discussing the above, we met two cars from Tokyo carrying Mr. and Mrs. Aso and Chief Cabinet Secretary Okazaki [Katsuo]. We spoke beside the road under the hot sun and were told that the two gentlemen were on their way to Hakone just then to encourage the Prime Minister to meet with Tomabechi. When Finance Minister Ikeda told them that the Premier had already assented, everyone was pleased. However, Aso felt that, given the party resolution of the previous evening [August 2], it would be nearly impossible for Tomabechi to visit the Prime Minister's residence in Meguro and that there was no choice but for the Prime Minister to visit Tomabechi. Finance Minister Ikeda, pointing out that there would be no problem if the Prime Minister agreed to that, asked what we should do if he did not. As everyone thought about this, I suggested that in that even we might make reservations at the Korinkaku restaurant in Shiba Takanawa. Everyone agreed to this.

Upon arriving in Tokyo, I went directly to Korinkaku in Takanawa, handed the manager my calling card, and left after telling him that we might borrow a banquet room that night and requesting him that he keep it a secret as it would not involve anyone suspicious.

At 7:00 p.m., an emergency cabinet meeting was held. The Cabinet decided to open a three-day extraordinary Diet session and that interpellation on the peace treaty draft would be conducted along with selection of the Ministers Plenipotentiary. Since only two nights earlier, the Prime Minister had stated he would not hold an extraordinary session and would not seek a Minister Plenipotentiary from the Democratic Party, it appeared that no one knew what was going on. It seemed that no more than three or four members of the Cabinet were aware of the plan for Prime Minister Yoshida to visit Tomabechi that evening.

In the middle of the meeting, Agriculture Minister Hori Shigeru telephoned Tomabechi at his residence (around 8:20 p.m.). After learning that Tomabechi was at home, he apologetically requested that he stay at his home for the time being. About thirty minutes later, while the Cabinet meeting was still in session, Agriculture Minister Hori received a phone call from Hakone. It appeared that Aso had succeeded in convincing the Prime Minister to meet with Tomabechi and that he would be coming down from Hakone.

The Cabinet meeting finished at 9:00. A press conference was held at the Finance Ministry. The press corps persistently asked about the Finance Minister's trip to Hakone earlier that day, but the Finance Minister did not give them any answer of substance. The press did not yet realize that the Prime Minister was at that very moment on his way from Hakone to visit the Tomabechi residence. The Finance Minister left saying that there might be something to announce later this evening.

Around 11 p.m., I was told that Aso had telephoned the Finance Minister's residence to the effect that the Prime Minister's call on Tomabechi had ended in success. I then returned with the Finance Minister to reopen the press conference. However, because there was word from the news desks of each of the reporters to the press corps that Chief Cabinet Secretary Okazaki was announcing the Prime Minister's call on Tomabechi, the press conference ended immediately. From there, I accompanied the Finance Minister to a restaurant in Shinbashi to meet with the Prime Minister, returning home at 1:00 a.m.

Within the Democratic Party, there were still some like Ashida Hitoshi and those considered to the Left such as Kitamura Tokutaro and others who were still not satisfied, and said they were waiting for the Diet session to open and hear the government's explanation before deciding. However, most people in the party said that this meant in fact that Tomabechi would participate in the plenipotentiary delegation. In fact, the official decision did come only after the opening of the special Diet session, but because the government's explanation of the Japan-U.S. Security Treaty was insufficient, Tomabechi's participation was conditioned on limiting it to only the peace conference.

In addition, there were many predictions that the Soviet Union would not participate in the peace conference but on August 13 it told Washington that it would in fact participate. Because of this, we became concerned that the conference might become more problematic than was expected.

THE PRIME MINISTER'S DELEGATION
GOES TO SAN FRANCISCO

The Prime Minister's delegation decided to leave on August 31, and I was to be a member of the group. The security was extremely tight. A truce existed in the Korean War, but the United States continued to view the Soviet Union as the enemy and was concerned that it might try something against the Japanese delegation on the eve of the peace conference. On the day before the departure, our luggage, unlocked, was collected at Haneda Airport, inspected and scanned to see if there were any hidden time bombs, and then brought into the hanger with the plane and guarded during the night under the lights.

Our plane departed in the evening of August 31, and was given a courtesy escort by U.S. Air Force fighter planes for part of the way. After several hours on the plane, when things began to settle down, I noticed there was someone on the plane I had never seen before. That person looked as if he was trying not to be noticed, and acted like one of the flight crew. After a while, we learned he was an FBI agent sent from Washington a few days before to Tokyo to escort the Prime Minister to San Francisco.

We arrived in Honolulu the next day and stayed the night. At that time, the security was tight. For those of us who had been away from a military atmosphere, it was kind of silly we thought. Prime Minister Yoshida had requested we take the Northern route, which would pass Alaska, in going to San Francisco. One of the reasons for this was that if we took the Southern route through Honolulu, we would have to participate in all sorts of receptions. Yoshida was not one who enjoyed receptions to start out with, and on top of this, he would also be tired from the flight. This appears to have been the main reason for his requesting the Northern route. However, from the perspective of the U.S. military, which was charged with providing security, the Northern route was too close to Soviet territory, and considering the flying time of their long-range aircraft, it would be hard to guarantee our safety. We thought this was a little extreme, but in any case this showed how seriously America took our security.

BEHIND THE SCENES AT THE PEACE CONFERENCE

On the morning of September 3, the day after we arrived in San Francisco, Dodge visited us at our hotel. He was a member of the U.S. delegation, but this morning, he and [Noel] Hemmendinger, the current Director of the Office for Northeast Asian Affairs, and Finance Minister Ikeda and I spoke for about two-and-a-half hours on a number of things. The budget after the peace conference was one of the things that came up, but the main topic was the money owed to the United States during the Occupation, the so-called GARIOA. How did Japan plan to pay for GARIOA, and questions of this nature.

Prior to our departure, Finance Minister Ikeda had done some calculations on the payments with interest, and he proceeded to present this to Dodge as one way of paying for it. We discussed this for some time. Perhaps by coincidence, or perhaps Dodge was thinking along similar lines, this approach was adopted almost in full for the U.S. proposal to West Germany the following April. West Germany in fact signed an agreement with the United States along these lines.

In Japan's case, however, primarily for domestic reasons, the two sides were unable to reach an agreement along these lines. The U.S. side continued to push repayments the following year (1952) in Mexico City, the year after that (1953) during the Ikeda-Robertson talks, and finally when Yoshida visited Washington the following year (1954), and I was put in a difficult spot each time. As is well known, the problem remains unresolved today.

I thought Dodge was some person to not forget at this celebratory time of the peace conference the liabilities Japan incurred during the Occupation. Moreover, until this time, Prime Minister Yoshida planned to visit Washington after the peace conference, and that is why he desired Ikeda and Ichimada to be a part of the delegation, as mentioned before. However, both Dodge and Hemmendinger said that the people involved in Japan issues had been so busy over the past year as the peace treaty approached that once it was over they would be breathing a big sigh of relief and therefore no one in Washington would want to talk business all of a sudden again. Moreover, in their opinion, most countries viewed the peace treaty as too soft on Japan and if the Prime Minister of Japan went to Washington immediately after the peace conference, it could be seen as "favoritism towards this adorable Japan" and some jealousy might emerge. Or so this was the explanation. While looking at this time from today it might seem ridiculously too much, Japan-U.S. relations were in fact in sort of a honeymoon period and therefore such an explanation was not seen as strange, as my diary at the time shows. In this way, Prime Minister Yoshida's delegation's trip to Washington was naturally called off.

The atmosphere of the Peace Conference has been described in great detail by Japanese reporters and today several works about it have appeared, so here I will describe the relatively unknown episodes from behind the scenes. What I mean by this is that the unexpected participation of the Soviet Union necessitated coordination between us and the host of the conference, the United States. Furthermore, an even more important issue was the issue of reparations in the draft treaty, about which the countries of Southeast Asia were particularly unhappy. While these countries agreed to attend the peace conference, several of them still had not made clear their intention to sign the peace treaty.

Because the Soviet Union was expected to try to disrupt the conference to some extent, the United States was very concerned that the dissatisfaction of the countries of Southeast Asia would be used by the Soviet Union. Thus, the United States desired for the leader of the Japanese delegation, Prime Minister Yoshida, to sincerely try to improve the atmosphere with the countries that harbored concerns about the treaty.

In light of this, Prime Minister Yoshida visited the U.S. delegation at the Palace Hotel on the evening of the day after his arrival in San Francisco. He met with Secretary of State [Dean G.] Acheson, who was scheduled to serve as chairman of the conference, and Dulles for about one hour. The following is what I was told took place during the meeting.

Acheson stated that despite the participation at the conference of the Soviet Union, he intended to do his best to proceed with it as a ceremonial opportunity for the Allies to welcome Japan as a peaceful member of the international community. As a result, he intended to permit no changes to the treaty text because over the past year the United States had engaged in lengthy negotiations with the Allies already. He said he would make this point clear in the conference's Rules of Procedure[4] and that he would limit the speeches by the delegates to one hour.

Next, Secretary of State Acheson stated that he was uncertain whether several of the participating countries would actually sign the peace treaty. Of course the Soviet Union and its satellite countries could not be counted on, but also the actions of Pakistan, Ceylon, and Indonesia were not clear. Indeed, Indonesia from all estimates probably was at this point not going to sign the treaty. While the Philippines was likely the most dissatisfied with the treaty, because of its long relationship with the United States, the Americans would probably be able to convince the Philippines to support the treaty.

Those countries in any case were unhappy with Article 14 of the treaty, which dealt with reparations, and because Japan is also expressing reservations to Article 14, the successful conclusion of the peace treaty is in doubt. While Japan might be dissatisfied with different aspects, it was important for it to actively show that it intended to enter into negotiations on reparations in a spirit of good faith with these countries. Of course it is not necessary at this time to make comments on the timing and actual manner in which reparations would be made. The above comments represented Secretary of State Acheson's views.

At this point, Dulles explained the thinking behind Article 14 regarding reparations in the following way: "Japan has an excess of industrial labor, and facilities that aren't being fully used. On the other hand, the countries demanding reparations have the necessary natural resources. These resources could be brought to Japan and Japan could manufacture and produce items for consumption in those countries for no profit. Japan would benefit by giving employment to its people and this formula could lead to the re-establishing of trade channels between Japan and those countries." As was mentioned earlier, the clause relating to reparations was not in the March draft treaty and was inserted relatively late in the drafting of the treaty. Because of this, Japan was not fully consulted on this matter so, while we could understand the logic behind the reparations paid for by manufactured goods or in services, many complex problems have emerged in practice in the years since when trying to implement it. These problems were not adequately forecasted at the time. Even if they were, the situation was at the time that the treaty in any case would not pass if Japan opposed Article 14.

Regarding this, Dulles raised the issue of the Ryukyus-Okinawa problem.[5] Just around this time, a hunger strike took place on Amami Oshima demanding reversion to Japan because Amami Oshima was part of the islands to be separated from Japan.[6] Dulles said these actions in the Nansei Islands were regrettable:

America is to administer the Ryukyu and other Nansei Islands because of their strategic necessity. It has no territorial desires. It is clear that sovereignty would be left with Japan. This is exactly as I have often told you (Prime Minister Yoshida). The countries of the world, including Japan, think the United States' attitude toward the peace treaty is generous. The United States is not going to take your wealth nor did it stop opposing the demands by other countries to place restrictions on Japan's maritime transportation or other economic relations. The demonstrative movements such as the hunger strike are unacceptable. We hope for some self-restraint by the Japanese now.

This was followed by a delicate exchange between Acheson, Dulles, and Prime Minister Yoshida over the question of the two Chinas, in other words the government of Taipei and that of Peking, and how Japan was going to handle its future relations with either of these countries. I will not write about that discussion here, but will just say in general that while Dulles appeared to be strongly leaning in favor of Taipei, Acheson gave the appearance of being much more logical and calm about the issue.

At the end of the meeting, Dulles explained that the security treaty was essentially finalized and agreed to, as Yoshida knew, but if it appeared to be completed, the Soviet Union and other countries might take it up during the peace conference and try to make it an embarrassing situation. If it comes up at all, Dulles said, the two countries should just say that for the time being discussions were still continuing and that the signing of any treaty would take place only be after the signing of the peace treaty. Of course, Yoshida agreed to this.

In the afternoon of the following day, Senator [H. Alexander] Smith, an alternate delegate to the U.S. delegation, visited Prime Minister Yoshida at the Mark Hopkins Hotel and for a little while had a pleasant talk about generalities, but on the issue of the two Chinas—his tone was, if it could be summarized briefly—"You wouldn't think of sacrificing the government of Taipei for that of Peking, now would you?" While it was true that a de facto truce was in effect in the Korean War, the United States had lost many men and considered Communist China an enemy in Korea. From the U.S. point of view, this was to be expected. Prime Minister Yoshida responded with his regular speech on this issue—even if one is concerned about trade with Communist China, they will push their own conditions and thus it will not go smoothly in any case.

In addition, Yoshida, as was his style, asked about Gen. MacArthur, and Smith said that when he saw him a month earlier in New York he was in good health. Smith also reportedly told Yoshida that MacArthur might come to San Francisco (in fact he did not come). Prime Minister Yoshida also attempted to meet with the leadership of the countries that were unhappy with the reparation issue in the treaty. On September 4, when he met with the Philippine representative [Carlos P.] Romulo, Prime Minister Yoshida genuinely apologized for the psychological and physical damage caused by Japan to the Philippines during the war and that Japan hoped to make up for this in the form of reparations and would faithfully fulfill the obligations of Article 14 although its economic ability, as Romulo knew, was not fully capable of it at the time.

I had heard that Romulo was an eloquent speaker. In addition he dramatically told us of the strong voices of opposition to the peace treaty within the Philippines (explaining that there were demonstrations in Manila calling for the Philippines "not to be a puppet of the United States and Britain" and "the return of the honor and self-respect of the people of the Philippines"), and of how his house was set afire and he had to flee to the United States after traveling with MacArthur in Bataan and Corredigor after Japan had invaded the Philippines.[7] Prime Minister Yoshida listened sympathetically the entire time. Using this as his preface, Romulo then went on to talk about the reparation issue in the following way: "I want you to make concrete promises while you are in San Francisco, Mr. Yoshida, on how and when Japan intends to pay the reparations. Words are not enough. I have heard that you intend to go on to Washington after the conference. Before then I wish for the two of us to speak." In response, Prime Minister Yoshida said, "I had intended to visit Washington but because of the ratification issue, I plan to return immediately to Japan. However, regarding the problem of reparations, I would very much like to speak with you too at any point and anywhere. Your country or Tokyo would be fine."

Romulo expressed his desire that at any rate experts from both countries meet while in San Francisco to discuss the issue more and Yoshida agreed to this (in fact, on September 5, between the afternoon and evening sessions of the conference, Director of the Treaties Bureau Nishimura [Kumao] met with [Diosdado] Macapagal, a Philippine representative, and his staff at the Saint Francis Hotel for a long time and were able to go into some detail on the issue). Considering Romulo's style, the meeting between him and Yoshida must have been difficult. He spoke on the premise that he would sign the peace treaty, and later told the U.S. that there was no chance that he would not sign the treaty.

The same day, Prime Minister Yoshida met with Indonesian Foreign Minister [Ahmad] Subardjo, the senior representative of that country, and explained Japan's intentions. Compared to Romulo, Subardjo's reception of Yoshida was more positive. He stated that in his speech before the conference he hoped to cite Yoshida's message that Japan "was prepared to enter into negotiations at any point and any place on the reparations issue" and that he wished Japan would designate the appropriate person in order to begin discussions on the matter. In response, Yoshida immediately designated Treaties Bureau Director Nishimura and that afternoon Nishimura met with Indonesian Ambassador to the United States Ali [Sastroamidjojo].

Because of Secretary of State Acheson's pessimism about Indonesia's willingness to sign the treaty voiced two days before, we took the meeting between Yoshida and Subardjo quite seriously. From what I heard after the meeting, Subardjo's attitude was quite amiable and the impression gained was that Indonesia's signature would not be a problem.

Yoshida spent all this day, September 4, meeting with the above individuals as well as the representatives of Ceylon, Minister Plenipotentiary [J. R.] Jayewardene for a tea party, and Pakistan, [Chandri Mohammad Zafrulla] Khan. Both of these meetings were more friendly than expected.

Prime Minister Yoshida met with British Foreign Minister [Herbert] Morrison, who headed up that country's delegation, after the signing of the peace treaty on September 8. The meeting lasted for about thirty minutes. Morrison's attitude during the meeting was typical of the British, sober. "There are many people in England who are still unhappy with Japan. The way to overcome this over the long run is for Japan to continue with the social reforms undertaken during the Occupation." He continued by explaining the positions of his party, the Labor Party, and that policy could not be decided while ignoring the views of labor. Moreover, he said that while the instances of nationalization of major industries won't all prove successful, there are success stories and nationalization of them cannot be blamed for all the problems. It is a question of both time and objective observation. Moreover, Morrison called Yoshida's attention to the issue of damages to the property of British citizens in prewar Japan. Yoshida informed him that just two months before, a Cabinet decision was made to provide compensation to these people.

In addition to the above, several people from our delegation met with members of the delegations of other countries on several occasions to follow through on the promises made by Prime Minister Yoshida on the question of reparations (the major example being the talks with the Filipino delegation).

WAS THE PEACE TREATY A SUCCESS?

Even if the Yoshida plenipotentiary delegation did not conduct these behind-the-scenes efforts, the countries participating in the peace conference
would still likely have signed the peace treaty, but objectively speaking, we
felt it was necessary that our delegation bow for the time being and apologize to the countries which directly suffered at Japan's hands. While such
actions might be seen as problematic today after all the changes that have
taken place in the world in the past five years, the situation at the time as
seen from the countries that were victorious in the war was that compared
to the Versailles Peace Treaty and the earlier treaty with Italy, the San Francisco Peace Treaty was extremely generous (for example, the treaty with
Italy went into effect when the four powers—the United States, Britain,
France, and the Soviet Union—ratified it, while the Japanese treaty only
went into effect when Japan did so). While it is true that the country was
still under occupation, free speech was possible as there were no longer any
special restrictions on our newspapers and in them there was no disagree-
ment with how the delegation conducted itself. (One example was an analysis in the *Asahi Shimbun* of July 12, 1951, entitled "An Unprecedented
Treaty of Reconciliation.")

The First Problem—the Kurile Islands

Since then, over the past few years, several difficult issues have emerged
from the peace treaty, which was seen initially as a satisfactory one. They
continue to greatly trouble Japan today. One is the territorial problem over
the Kurile Islands, Kunashiri, Etorofu, and other islands; the other problem
is that of the friction between the U.S. military and their bases and the Japanese people.

   I am unable to say how the problems of today could have been prevented
or nipped in the bud at the time of the peace treaty as to do so both goes beyond my abilities and probably those of others without the passage of many
decades. Here, however, I would like to show to what extent the officials
dealing with the peace treaty were aware of the potential problems in it by de-
scribing what took place at the time.

Dulles's Views

On the afternoon of September 5, the second day of the conference, Dulles,
representing America as the drafting country, spoke on the spirit of the treaty
and its terms before the assembled delegates. I will introduce what Dulles

said regarding the territorial problem of the Kurile Islands based on the official transcripts at the time:

What is the territory of Japanese sovereignty? Chapter II deals with that. . . . The Potsdam Surrender Terms constitute the only definition of peace terms to which, and by which, Japan and the Allied Powers as a whole are bound. There have been some private understandings between some Allied Governments; but by these Japan was not bound, nor were other Allies bound. Therefore, the treaty embodies article 8 of the Surrender Terms which provided that Japanese sovereignty should be limited to Honshu, Hokkaido, Kyushu, Shikoku, and some minor islands. The renunciations contained in article 2 of chapter II, strictly and scrupulously conform to that surrender term. Some question has been raised as to whether the geographical name "Kurile Islands" mentioned in article 2 (c) includes the Habomai Islands. It is the view of the United States that it does not. If, however, there were a dispute about this, it could be referred to the International Court of Justice under Article 22. Some Allied Powers suggested that article 2 should not merely delimit Japanese sovereignty according to Potsdam, but specify precisely the ultimate disposition of each of the ex-Japanese territories. This, admittedly, would have been neater. But it would have raised questions as to which there are now no agreed answers. We had either to give Japan peace on the Potsdam Terms or deny peace to Japan while the Allies quarrel about what shall be done with what Japan is prepared, and required, to give up. Clearly, the wise course was to proceed now, so far as Japan is concerned, leaving the future to resolve doubts by invoking international solvents other than this treaty.

The above was what Dulles stated regarding the problem islands. Even if one were to re-read it now, there is little suggestive here, but two or three things are clearly spelled out in his statement.

Namely, first, the United States was making clear its view that Japan and the Allies not a party to the understandings between some of the Allies, for example, the Yalta Agreement, were not bound by them. Therefore, if during discussions between Japan and the Soviet Union the latter were to try to use the Yalta Agreement as a proof of Soviet claims over the islands, America's interpretation of the issue would be that trying to use the Yalta Agreement to bind Japan was impossible. (It is a separate question whether America itself was bound by the Yalta Agreement.)

Second, America interpreted the Habomai Islands as not being a part of the "Kurile Islands." While Dulles used the name "Habomai Islands," it is not clear if he intended for Shikotan, for example, to be included or not, and just what exactly he meant by the Habomai Islands because no one asked him.

Third, the United States recognized that its thinking is not absolute with regard to the question of whether the "Habomai Islands" should be included in the Kurile Islands renounced by Japan, and suggested that further discussion might be needed, including taking it to the International Court of Justice.

Fourth, the article's having Japan simply renounce sovereignty over the islands in question without their final disposition being decided would likely become a problem in the future. If discussions continued on this point, the peace treaty itself would be delayed indefinitely. Dulles also stated that if a problem emerged in the future, it could be resolved by "invoking international solvents," but by doing so the problem was put off for the future and what's more, there was no guarantee that the United States itself would take the initiative in trying to help.

From what I can tell, the above points were the expressed opinions of the U.S. government at the time regarding the problematic Northern Territories.

The Soviet Union's Views

The Soviet Union was clearly frustrated with the clause in which Japan unilaterally renounced sovereignty over the islands (without the final disposition being decided). In the afternoon of September 5 during the conference, the senior Soviet representative [Andrei] Gromyko attempted to make several amendments.

In one comment, he demanded, "the Soviet Union's sovereignty over the Southern Sakhalin and Kurile Islands should be made clear" within the treaty. The Soviet Union had until then on more than a dozen occasions sent the United States its requests for amendments in the form of memorandum, including on this question. More problematic was the fact that the March 1951 draft prepared by Dulles had actually recognized Soviet sovereignty over the islands, but as was mentioned earlier, the final version was rewritten to have Japan relinquish sovereignty only. Gromyko's call for amending the article was an issue up until the last night of the conference, in other words, until after Yoshida had made the speech accepting the treaty, but because the suggestion for an amendment was made at the wrong time, it was ruled out of order and not considered for discussion.

In large conferences like this, there are many instances when a country suffered an embarrassing loss because its representatives were not read up on the rules of procedure. Below follows the exchange as to how the Soviet Union lost its bid to have the amendment accepted, based on the transcripts of the conference and my own notes:

(The time is around 8:40 p.m., September 7, after Japan's delegate, Yoshida, had made his speech accepting the treaty on behalf of Japan.)

Soviet Representative Gromyko: Mr. Chairman, first of all, I would like to ask you in what order will the Soviet amendments [on September 5] to the treaty be taken up. And also if you intend to have a vote and in what manner, on those Soviet amendments.

President (Acheson): The Chair was, at the time of the speech of the Soviet Delegate, sitting among the delegations. The Soviet Delegate was asked by the presiding officer, the Vice President of this Conference, whether he was proposing amendments to the treaty; and in the hearing of the present presiding officer, the Delegate of the Soviet Union said that he was making a statement. Therefore, the presiding officer does not have before him any motion or any proposal to make amendments to the treaty in any respect whatever; and, therefore, he is unable to answer the question put by the Delegate of the Soviet Union.

President: Order, please.

Gromyko: The President has described the situation incorrectly. Our amendments, in addition, have been presented to the present Conference as a part of the Declaration of the Soviet Delegation. On this basis, the proposal of the Soviet Delegation should be followed by a decision and it is for this reason that I am asking the question.

President: I can only repeat what was said a moment before. If the Soviet Delegation wishes to propose his statement, which he declared at the time he made it, was merely a statement, as an amendment to the treaty, the way is open for the Soviet Delegation to appeal from this ruling of the Chair. If the Chair is overruled, we will then proceed to suspend discussion upon the motion before us, and we will consider that further amendments to the treaty are open. . . . The Soviet Delegate has challenged the ruling of the Chair. Under my prerogatives I am entitled to allow five minutes on either side of this.

Polish Representative: Are we an international conference or not? It is what Mr. Dulles called it on July the 12th a ceremony? A great Englishman once said, "To preach freedom of discussion is not enough, you have to practice it. If you don't practice it and preach it, it is sheer hypocrisy."

U.S. Delegate Dulles: I arise to support the ruling of the Chair. We made clear, beyond the possibility of doubt, at the time of the invitation, that the conference was to be a conference, which, following eleven months of negotiation, and the negotiation of a text of a treaty which we described as the "final text," was called to sign that text. This was understood by both the Soviet and Polish delegations. They did not need come here unless they wanted to.

President: Discussion having been concluded concerning he question of supporting or not supporting the ruling of the Chair, I now ask for a show of hands. All those in favor of supporting the ruling of the Chair will indicate by raising your hand. (Show of hands.) All those opposed to the ruling of the Chair, will you please raise your hand? (Show of hands.)

President: Order please. Quiet in the gallery. The gallery will please maintain order. The ruling of the Chair is supported by a vote of 46 to 3.

Because of the above exchange, the Soviet Union's amendment proposal was not adopted for formal discussion and subsequently died. There were many opinions among the delegates as to why the Soviet representative did not try harder to disrupt the proceedings. Likely, it had to do with the fact that the odds were against the Soviet Union at this conference, as well as the treaty draft being quite thorough and well drafted. The Soviet Union has consistently pushed its amendment proposal (in which the question of the right to navigate the straits was included) both in San Francisco as well as recently when Prime Minister Hatoyama [Ichiro, Dec. 1954–Dec. 1956] went to Moscow and the Soviets stubbornly raised it again.

In addition, another thing that is apparent from the above exchange seen in the transcripts is that the conference was in many ways a ceremony—in exchange for the Allies not raising any issues, Japan, which would accept the treaty, would not either. The United States, Britain, and Japan all shared the common recognition that if the above were not the case, a final peace treaty would not be possible. In the private meeting between Acheson, Dulles, and Prime Minister Yoshida described earlier, this thinking was clearly reflected in Acheson's comments.

Delegate Yoshida's Statement

Even if the above thinking was the case, this did not mean that Yoshida did not take up the issue of the Northern Territories in his acceptance speech. However, as was written above, because we were aware that the conference was ceremonial in nature, it has to be admitted that the statement he made was less than aggressive in nature:

With respect to the Kuriles and South Sakhalin, I cannot yield to the claim of the Soviet Delegate that Japan had grabbed them by aggression. At the time of the opening of Japan, her ownership of two islands of Etoroff and Kunashiri of the South Kuriles was not questioned at all by the Czarist government. But the North Kuriles north of Urruppu and the southern half of Sakhalin were areas open to both Japanese and Russian settlers. On May 7, 1875, the Japanese and Russian governments effected through peaceful negotiations an arrangement under which South Sakhalin was made Russian territory, and the North Kuriles were in exchange made Japanese territory. But really, under the name of "exchange" Japan simply ceded South Sakhalin to Russia in order to settle the territorial dispute. It was under the Treaty of Portsmouth of 1905 concluded through the intermediary of President

Theodore Roosevelt of the United States that South Sakhalin became also Japanese territory. Both Sakhalin and the North and South Kuriles were taken unilaterally by Russia as of September 20, 1945, shortly after Japan's surrender. Even the islands of Habomai and Shikotan, constituting part of Hokkaido, one of Japan's four main islands, are still being occupied by Soviet forces simply because they happened to be garrisoned by Japanese troops at the time when the war ended.

Rereading Yoshida's speech today, it is true that it was not more than him speaking freely and saying what he wanted. However, as was explained so far, it is arguable whether Japan had the ability to say, "unless this point or that point is not amended, we will not accept the Peace Treaty. We would rather the occupation continue." It is interesting to consider the actions of the U.S. and British governments, which were drafting the peace treaty, were still limited in what they could by the Soviet Union due to the Yalta Agreement, which they were a party to, in that they did not force Japan to give the Northern Territories to the Soviet Union.

However, while Yoshida spoke somewhat freely, there is room for debate as to whether it was possible for any clearer expression of Japan's desires given the fact that the conference was a "ceremony" and the concern over not irritating more the countries already dissatisfied with the reparations clause. An *Asahi Shimbun* editorial from this time (September 9, 1951, morning edition) stated, "Delegate Yoshida's statement makes clear that the Kurile Islands and Southern Sakhalin were not stolen or the result of aggression by Japan and we think it was done to show that Japan is not entirely satisfied with the way in which the disposition of the islands was handled in the Peace treaty as was being intended to show that Japan may call for its territorial rights in the future over the Shikotan and Habomai Islands. Unfortunately, this intention was not made clear in his speech."

Looking back on the sometimes-forgotten atmosphere at the time, the opinions in the editorial represents the thinking of Yoshida and to some extent the general public at the time. In other words, there was no reason to handover the Habomai and Shikotan Islands to the Soviet Union as they are a part of Hokkaido. Even the disposition of the outer islands, such as Etorofu and Kunashiri, are not fully to our satisfaction, but the immediate problem, the leadership at the time for the most part felt, was Habomai and Shikotan.

Because I introduced Yoshida's speech on the Northern Territories, I will now introduce the section of his speech relating to the Ryukyu Islands, which have become an issue of late:

As regards the Ryukyu archipelago and the Bonins which may be placed under United Nations trusteeship, I welcome in the name of the Japanese nation the

statements by the American and British Delegates on the residual sovereignty of
Japan over the islands south of the 29th degree, north latitude. I cannot but hope
that the administration of these islands will be put back into Japanese hands in
the not distant future with the reestablishment of world security—especially the
security of Asia.

Yoshida's acceptance speech was quite anti-Communist in content, and because of this, his taking up the Ryukyu and Ogasawara Islands in the first part
of his comments about the territorial problems was, without a doubt, bold on
his part. The domestic situation, such as the hunger strikes in the Amami Islands that so irritated Dulles as described earlier, was reflected in his speech.
Moreover, because the situation with the Ryukyu Islands is often compared
of late to that of Etorofu and Kunashiri, I recall the speech by British Foreign
Minister [Kenneth G.] Younger, who was the British delegate to the conference, in support of the American position:

> As regards the Ryukyu and Bonin Islands, the treaty does not remove these from
> Japanese sovereignty; it provides for a continuance of United States administra-
> tion over the Ryukyu Islands south of 29 degrees north latitude; that is to say that
> those islands nearest to Japan itself are to remain not only under Japanese sover-
> eignty, but under Japanese administration as well. This is in marked contrast with
> the provision for the complete renunciation of Japanese sovereignty over the
> Kurile Islands, the other principal group which approaches close to the main is-
> lands of Japan, and which is now occupied by the Soviet Union. We have agreed
> to the renunciation of Japanese sovereignty over the Kurile Islands, we think that
> this comparison should be borne in mind by those who criticize the provisions re-
> lating to the more southerly of the Ryukyus, and to the Bonin Islands.

He was of course saying this to the Soviet Union.

THE SECOND PROBLEM—
JAPAN-U.S. FRICTION OVER THE "BASES"

One more big problem with the Peace Treaty that was affecting the relationship today was the base problem, namely the anti-Americanism seen in
the slogan, "Yankee Go Home," which was due to the friction caused between the people of Japan and the bases in Japan based on the Japan-U.S.
Security Treaty and the Administrative Agreement that finalized the basing
arrangements.

On the surface, the Japan-U.S. Security Treaty was separate from the Peace
Treaty. Prime Minister Yoshida judged that this was the only way an early
peace could be arranged. As was explained in detail earlier, he had Finance

Minister Ikeda go to Washington in 1950 to relay this view. From that time, the two treaties came together to form one concept. For convenience sake, this can be called the Yoshida-Dulles Formula, and I personally do not think that this approach was mistaken (I am of course aware that there are other influential opinions out there to the contrary).

Speaking more to the point, the Japan-U.S. Security Treaty itself was not flawed, but it seems with the drafting of the Administrative Agreement, several issues that were not anticipated emerged. Some thought was put into the Administrative Agreement the same year as the Peace Treaty, but the actual negotiations began in late January 1952 and continued for about one month. Dean Rusk, the U.S. Assistant Secretary of State, went to Korea as Ambassador and conducted negotiations with our Foreign Ministry officials.

The talks were undertaken in detail at the working level between the Japanese and U.S. governments and when agreement could not be reached, the matter would be referred to discussions between Foreign Minister Okazaki and Ambassador Rusk. It is necessary to point out that outsiders, like myself, have no idea about the difficulties encountered during the negotiations. However, while being an outsider, I would like to express here frankly some things I felt at the time. Namely, I think our negotiators sometimes lost sight of the principle that with the peace treaty coming into effect, the positions of the two countries had changed—the U.S. military was now a guest in Japan, not in charge of Japan as it had been, and thus it could not do anything that went against the wishes of the host government.

Traditionally, an occupation army is required to depart within ninety days following the end of the occupation, and thus ninety days after the coming into effect of the peace treaty, the U.S. military had to go home. If both countries agreed that it was necessary to have the U.S. military continue to be located in a certain area or use a certain facility, then it was necessary for the U.S. and Japan to work out a new agreement to that effect. In other words, even if the U.S. wished to continue to be located at a certain place, if Japan did not approve then the U.S. military would have to leave. This was a principle that had to be respected. The situation in which Japanese officials had to run out every time the U.S. Air Force tried to construct an airfield on someone's farmland and ask them to leave was not only audacious, but should never have happened in the first place.

In a draft I saw at the time the Administrative Agreement was being discussed, I recall there being a clause to the effect that "Regarding the places (they were called 'Facilities and Areas') the United States desires to station forces, it will discuss with Japan within ninety days of the peace treaty coming into effect in order to gain Japan's consent. However, if discussions are not completed within ninety days, the U.S. will be permitted to continue to use the places temporarily until the discussions are finalized." It is the sentence beginning with "however" that is completely wrong—consult with us within ninety days or else the United States will be there until the talks finish. What is the point, then, of setting a ninety-day limit? If there is no meaning in setting such a limit, it is almost saying as if there is no meaning to having the peace treaty coming into effect and gaining independence.

I was surprised and asked the Foreign Ministry to delete this clause from the draft text. After that what surprised me even more was the fact that even though the clause was removed from the Administrative Agreement itself, it reappeared in its exact form in the "Okazaki-Rusk Exchange of Notes" that took place at the time of the signing of the agreement. What's more is that by the time I became aware of this, the Administrative Agreement had already been signed between the two countries.

Of course, I realize that such a written-out interim measure was necessary because there were so many complicated issues surrounding the areas and facilities the United States desired and thus it was nearly impossible to go from a situation in which they were using them for seven years and then suddenly switch over to Japanese control with the peace treaty coming into effect. On top of this was the fact that the securing of budget and land to build replacement facilities by the Japanese government for the buildings the U.S. military was requested to vacate in order to move outside of the central parts of cities.

Still, even if there were several reasons, it is difficult to understand why no time limit was placed on the interim measures. I would go so far as to say that the reason for the ill feeling that exists toward the U.S. military is the frustration at the Occupation mentality that seems to pervade their forces. I believe that the fundamental cause of this is related to the problems found in the Administrative Agreement. Even Fukushima Shintaro, who served for a long time as Director General of the Procurement Agency, recently wrote (in the September [1956] issue[8] of *Bungei Shunju*) to my great surprise that "Even now there may be some bases which we have not officially provided [to the U.S. military]." In other words, without the knowledge of the country, which is a sovereign state, a foreign military may now still be occupying parts of it. In light of this situation, is it any wonder that cries of "Yankee Go Home" can be heard?

Because I believe the Yoshida-Dulles approach to the peace treaty itself was not mistaken, I am disappointed with the mistakes made at the time of the signing of the Administrative Agreement. (I repeat that as I am not fully aware of what took place at the time of the Administrative Agreement, I may be mistaken in my understanding of it and do not hesitate to apologize for this.)

MY THOUGHTS TODAY

To give an overview of the few years between the peace treaty and today, there were probably some sacrifices that have allowed Japan, which was so thoroughly defeated in the war that we thought it would take thirty or even fifty years to recover and thus decided to bear the unbearable, is able to now enjoy the peace which we have. In the case of Etorofu and Kunashiri, as well as with the administrative agreement, these problems simply showed their faces relatively early. As the months and years go by, even bigger problems may arise.

The role of a politician probably is to discover at an earlier stage where these problems lay waiting and develop countermeasures all without the general public becoming aware and anxious about it. I still believe Yoshida Shigeru was a distinguished politician. However, even someone as distinguished as he was unable to see that clearly into the future.

Indeed, while few, there were some people at the time who vaguely were able to imagine the situation today. Within a few years of independence, these people became much larger in number as nationalism increased. There was little hope that nationalism wouldn't rear its head among the people of Japan. As nationalism increased, it was certain to be directed at the former occupier and the country that continues today to station its forces within Japan—the United States and its military. This can be called a natural reaction of humanity to seek a position of equality against a stronger counterpart; it is not related at all to the rational judgment that having U.S. forces here is in Japan's national interests.

In order to relieve these pressures ahead of time, it is necessary for statesmen to take preemptive action. It will be important to take a strong stand vis-à-vis the United States and consciously choose to the place and time, which the public can witness, in which to do so in order to impress the public. It is only in this way that the feelings of the people of Japan won't reach the exploding point and can be diffused. West Germany's [Konrad] Adenaur is someone who has done this and has been preaching this for several years.

At the time when Prime Minister Yoshida was naming the first [postwar] Ambassador to the United States, I once asked Finance Minister Ikeda, "Which type of person do you think Prime Minister Yoshida will name as the first Ambassador to the United States? Will it be someone who will purposely pick fights in Washington on occasion or will he choose someone who is a nice guy and whom the leadership in Washington will adore?" Ikeda directly asked Yoshida this it seems and after some time I was told, "The Prime Minister said he will of course choose someone who is trusted and liked is best as Japan's first ambassador."

PRIME MINISTER YOSHIDA'S FEELINGS
IMMEDIATELY AFTER THE PEACE CONFERENCE

The popularity of the Yoshida Cabinet was at an all-time high after the San Francisco Peace Conference. According to the results of a survey conducted by a large newspaper and announced on September 25, 1951, 58 percent of the respondents said they did when asked, "Do you support Yoshida?" Compared to earlier surveys when the same question was asked in October 1949 (43 percent) and April 1950 (32 percent), Yoshida's popularity had grown dramatically. I do not think any cabinet in either the prewar or postwar has likely received this level of support.

I still wonder today why Yoshida did not resign at that time. His not resigning was not just for self-preservation or to preserve his honor. With the peace treaty, a new Japan was being born, not a continuation of the old one. At the time this new Japan was being born, the previously purged officials were returning to politics and the business world. For example, Hatoyama Ichiro, who is a problem today, was released from the purge in the middle of July just before the peace treaty.

While there were some exceptions, of those that were being released, many were leaders of Japan up until its defeat. Many of them do not think or wish to believe that Japan completely changed with its defeat. I am not defending purges, a modern form of barbarism, but defeat in the war was a sort of revolution that formed a division between the old and new. It was not a question of the people of the previous era being bad and those after being good, but rather one of sensibilities. A gap so large that compromise was impossible had emerged. If Yoshida saw this and using the high public support of his cabinet at the time as a backdrop to pick any one he wanted and chose someone from the younger generation, Japanese politics after that for a few years until today probably would have been quite different. While it is difficult to outright state that politics would have been better in that case, it is quite possible to imagine a political structure in which the feelings of the postwar public would have been better reflected more quickly.

However, what I want to say right now is not this point, but the impression I had that Yoshida and those around him did not see the peace treaty as a time for him to resign his office. Rather, Yoshida seems to have felt that now with the peace treaty and independence, he was free to attempt things that he had been unable to do during the Occupation. Moreover, he and his associates felt the strong sense of responsibility to fulfill the promises Japan made to numerous countries at the time of the peace treaty. I do not know if Yoshida himself today thinks whether it would have been better to resign at the time. I have a sense that it would be "no." However, I sometimes hear today from people who are strong supporters of Yoshida and like him from the bottom of their hearts that he should have resigned at that point.

All I wanted to do here was to record that at the time, I did not see at all any serious discussion of his resigning.

DODGE'S LAST VISIT TO JAPAN

After returning from San Francisco, the Cabinet, led by Finance Minister Ikeda, began to put together the supplementary budget and the budget for 1952. Although Japan's independence was agreed upon at the peace conference, it would be another half-year before the Occupation army left and thus Japan could not go ahead and develop the budget completely on its own.

At this time, the problems emerging domestically at the time were whether to raise the salaries of public servants and whether to eliminate restrictions on rice, but in San Francisco the focus of the discussions with Dodge were on completely different matters. Dodge explained that with independence, Japan would have to be ready for the tasks associated with being a sovereign state. It could not, he argued, talk carelessly about tax cuts when faced with large expenditures such as reparations, repayment of foreign debts, the increase in the strength of the National Police Reserves, etc. In any case, this was the last chance for him to be able to involve himself in Japan's budget.

Dodge likely thought he was being altruistic. On the evening of October 28, his ship arrived in Yokohama. Upon arriving, there was no doubt that.he would release a statement to the press and that message was likely to be an attempt to preach why the "Reduce Taxes, Reduce Taxes" calls by the Japanese government were not a good idea. However, if he outright stated his "opposition to tax reductions," it would appear that, although independence was within sight, the Japanese government was still unable to take decisive and autonomous actions due to being under occupation.

After a request by Finance Minister Ikeda, I, with a few others, boarded a Customs boat and approached the *President Wilson*, which was moored out in the bay, in the early morning of the day it arrived. Fortunately, Dr. Ralph Reid (who would become Deputy Director of the Budget Office), whom Dodge trusted the most, had come to Japan ahead of him. Perhaps he thought that it was not good to overly provoke Japan on the eve of its independence, but he seems to have felt the same way and boarded the launch with us.

Dodge had just woken up and was not in a particularly good mood, but we all began to negotiate. Regarding this key issue, he had prepared fifty copies of a long statement to the effect that "Reducing taxes was not good for Japan about to become independent." Eventually, he reluctantly decided not to use it and instead hastily prepared a handwritten statement in time for his press conference. Upon going ashore, Dodge was surrounded by members of the press at the Customs Office. Because they were specialists in economics, the journalists understood what the main issue was and easily got right to the point in their questioning of Dodge:

> **Question:** What is your opinion about the intentions of the Japanese government to reduce taxes for the next fiscal year?
>
> **Answer:** I had planned not to talk about this but since I have been asked, let me respond by asking you a question. Could you tell me where there is another country in the entire world that has lowered taxes two years in a row and is planning to do so a third time? All of the other countries in the world are doing the exact opposite. (It is as if Dodge was saying, don't you realize America is at war now?)

Yet, after about a month of talks on the budget, Dodge eventually turned a blind eye to the plan to reduce taxes due to the fact that Japan was soon to be independent. However, he pointed out that putting things, such as financial support for the bereaved families of Japanese soldiers, in the budget was difficult. With his typical gravity, Dodge said, "If you do that then you will be taken to task by the Philippines in your discussions on reparations. Don't you understand the feelings of the families of Filipino soldiers killed by Japanese forces?"

Finance Minister Ikeda also lost in the discussions on ending controls on rice. The main reason was that at the time there was little success over the black market in rice, and consumers, who no longer felt any pain from the controls, actually feared the ending of them would lead to a rise in prices. Producers, particularly those in the prefectures known for their rice production, on the other hand, feared the dropping of the price of rice if controls were ended. During his stay, Dodge received about 100 letters everyday on this problem, with the number of those in favor of keeping controls outnumbering those in favor of ending them by a ratio of 10 to 1. This appeared to truly affect Dodge's thinking on the issue. Nevertheless, this issue had been around for some time, and he knew Ikeda was quite serious about it. Moreover, he probably felt that Japan was to become independent in any case, so he compromised by saying that he would not really oppose it if the Japanese government were to end the controls by first setting very high delivery goals (he used the figure 27,000,000 *koku*) and then storing as much as possible. However, in fact, it was the Governors Association (*Chiji Kaigi*) that decided how much to produce, and they could not even agree to 25,000,000 *koku*, let alone 27,000,000. As a result, no agreement was reached in time and Finance Minister Ikeda ended up losing.

The government and the Liberal Party had in fact agreed on several occasions to end the controls, but the last decision they made had the following sentence in it when announced to the public: "The government plans to undertake the ending of controls when all the various conditions are ready." The rather timid explanation then was that, "Now, the situation was not quite ready." As a result, nothing was done that year. From around this time, the controls on rice were protecting the producers more than they were the consumers. In thinking about the situation today, when farmers make up less than half the population and the fact that agricultural economy cannot support our country as an industry, it probably would have been better to have gotten rid of the controls at this point.

NOTES

1. Mr. "M" was Masuda Kaneshichi.
2. Both drafts are available in *Foreign Relations of the United States, 1951, Vol. 6, Asia and the Pacific, Part 1* (Washington, D.C.: Government Printing Office, 1977).
3. With regard to the islands in question, the Yalta Agreement stated: "The southern part of Sakhalin as well as the islands adjacent to it shall be returned to the Soviet Union. . . . The Kurile Islands shall be handed over to the Soviet Union."
4. The text of the Rules of Procedure can be found in the U.S. Department of State *Bulletin* 25, no. 638 (September 17, 1951): 450–52.
5. For a detailed history on the peace treaty and Okinawa, see Robert D. Eldridge, *The Origins of the Bilateral Okinawa Problem: Okinawa in Postwar U.S.-Japan Relations, 1945–1952* (New York: Garland, 2001).
6. For more on the Amami reversion issue, see Robert D. Eldridge, *The Return of the Amami Islands: The Reversion Movement and U.S.-Japan Relations* (Lanham, Md.: Lexington Books, 2004).
7. This story is told in General Carlos P. Romulo, *I Walked with Heroes* (New York: Avon Book Division, 1961).
8. Fukushima Shintaro, "Chotatsucho no Hikigeki: Gyosei Kyotei ni Tsumi Ariya" [The Tragedy of the Procurement Agency: The Administrative Agreement is Full of Sins], *Bungei Shunju* 34, no. 9 (September 1956): 80–86.

Chapter Four

The Japan-U.S. Talks in Mexico, 1952

THE SURPRISE DISSOLUTION OF THE DIET

The peace treaty went into effect on April 28, 1952. Our country became independent again on this day. In December the year before, much debate was seen in the ordinary session of the Diet on the issues relating to independence—in addition to approving the peace treaty and the security treaty, the respective peace treaties with India and Taiwan needed to be ratified, and new laws to improve upon those introduced during the Occupation or to be modified to fit a sovereign Japan had to be decided.

Furthermore, there were many other things to be debated in this, an unusually long Diet session of 235 days that ended on July 31. For example, the National Police Reserves, a name that we had gotten accustomed to using for some time, merged with the Maritime Police (*Kaijo Keibitai*) and from the middle of October came into being as the National Safety Force (*Hoantai*) with the National Safety Agency (*Hoancho*) coming into being before that on August 1. But what became more apparent from a political perspective after this long Diet session is that within the Liberal Party, which had supported the Yoshida government, a great internal conflict was emerging and it looked as if the Yoshida cabinet was starting to show the signs of terminal illness.

At the time, the biggest reason for this unhappiness was interpreted as Prime Minister Yoshida's decision to override opposition from within the Liberal Party and name someone close to him as Secretary General of the party. In a sense, the naming of Fukunaga [Kenji] as a Secretary General was no doubt a direct cause (at the time, it was called the "Secretary General Fukunaga Problem"), but looking back on it today, one could probably see the roots of the discontent in the flow of the history at the time.[1]

As explained earlier, around the time of the peace treaty, purged politicians began to be released from the restrictions and with the return of independence all of these people were freed from this detestable yoke. It was only natural therefore that they came to desire returning to politics once this leash was removed. However, during their long hibernation, the world had changed dramatically. While the time between defeat and independence was only seven years, the changes the country experienced were dramatic. If history had gone its course naturally, it may have taken at least one hundred years for these changes to be realized. Moreover, it was not simply a superficial passage of time but the fact that many near impossible things occurred during this period making us view these seven years as a "revolution."

Following the peace treaty, the public began to tire of Prime Minister Yoshida and members of his party who, as leaders after this revolution, were trying to block the efforts of those from the pre-revolution period who were trying to take the helm again. In addition to the fact that his penchant for secrecy and cronyism became a problem, Yoshida was often criticized for his policies of gradual rearmament and balanced budget (often called deflation finance policy) after close coordination with foreign countries, especially the United States. Thus it was quite easy for the old forces, led by Hatoyama Ichiro, to find slogans by which to call for the replacement of the new forces headed by Yoshida.

Hatoyama's group first appealed to the spirit of friendship and love. Second, they called for the adjustment of relations with the Soviet Union and Communist China, going beyond Yoshida's slavish devotion to the United States. Third, Yoshida's "piecemeal" style of defense had the effect not only weakening the feeling of independence, but because it had to do with the constitution, there should be a call for rearmament. Fourth, fiscal policy should be positive and constructive.

Of course, these people did not openly criticize Yoshida's policies as long as they held out the hope that the government would pass from Yoshida to Hatoyama in the future peacefully. When Yoshida suddenly called for the dissolution of the Diet when the new ordinary session of it began in late August following the 235-day-long session mentioned above, these forces began to openly oppose Yoshida, and from this time on, criticism of Yoshida was heard more and more.

From Yoshida's point of view, the San Francisco Peace Treaty enjoyed the strong support of the people and Yoshida hoped for Japan to follow along these tracks in the post-treaty period, and as such he still believed that there was much to do. At the same time, Yoshida was obliged to listen to public opinion and could not prevent the formerly purged politicians from seeking the support of the voters in a general election. As a result he came to decide on calling an early election.

In the "Secretary General Fukunaga Problem" mentioned before, when rebellious forces within the party began to show some strength, Yoshida, who was never one to back down from a fight, apparently had wanted to delay dissolving the Diet for as long as possible. However, when the rebel forces fell under the control of rival Hatoyama Ichiro, they became even more powerful. Yoshida was aware of this but continued to think that everything was still all right and that he could ride out the Diet session. The general public thought that dissolution of the Diet would be put off until much later, and most people spoke instead of a Cabinet reshuffle. Around this time, on August 22, Ikeda and a few other Cabinet members met with Prime Minister Yoshida and suggested that an early dissolution of the Diet should be considered as the situation was no longer manageable. In this way, the "nukiuchi kaisan," or surprise dissolution, was decided. I heard that when Prime Minister Yoshida visited Nasu Imperial Villa on August 25 to brief the Emperor on the political situation, he told him that he was thinking along these lines.[2]

At the 14th Ordinary Session of the Diet, called on August 26, the election of the Speaker of the Lower House was held. During these proceedings, members of the Cabinet were called one-by-one outside the chamber to sign a document approving the dissolution of the Diet. Because it was done in this way, some Cabinet members did not know about it at all and several were not able to sign it. That evening, the Director of the Cabinet General Affairs Office brought the signed document to Nasu Imperial Villa. The Emperor, on the "advice" of the Cabinet, as per Article 7 of the Constitution, performed his duty to dissolve the Diet.[3]

On the morning of August 28, an emergency Cabinet meeting was held and the Lower House was dissolved that day. Initially, the plan was to dissolve the Diet on August 27, but by chance, Ono [Banboku], who was elected Speaker of the Lower House on the 26th, was in Nasu paying his respects to the Emperor, and the opinion was that the Prime Minister should inform the Speaker prior to dissolving the House. As a result, it was put off until the 28th. Interestingly, Ono, who was probably in Nasu to request the Emperor's presence at the opening of the ordinary session scheduled for August 31, was not aware that the Emperor had already been told the Diet was to be dissolved.

To the surprise of the general public, Prime Minister Yoshida dissolved the Lower House in this way. Even within the Cabinet, there were those who did not know about it until that morning and those who were even still talking about legislative issues for the Diet. Looking back on these events, Prime Minister Yoshida's methods at the time were quite forceful. This was one of the reasons for the criticism of his secrecy and cronyism. It also explains why several Ministers under Yoshida viewed this is as lacking virtue and why they eventually would call for his resignation. These strong feelings against Yoshida's abrupt ways led many to join in the anti-Yoshida movements.

ARRIVING IN MEXICO

With the Diet suddenly dissolved at the end of the month, we were in for a little bruising. That was because Finance Minister Ikeda and I were scheduled to depart Haneda Airport for Mexico at the end of the month on the 31st. From the middle of the Occupation period, our country had repeatedly asked the Occupation forces to permit us to join the various international organizations at the earliest opportunity. This was true in particular for the World Bank and International Monetary Fund, which we had already asked about during our visit to Washington, D.C. We attempted to make this request known through former Deputy Secretary of the Army [William H.] Draper of the New York financial community.

However, in the end, admission to these two financial organizations would not be possible until after Japan regained its independence. Because the signing of the agreement joining them was held on the 13th that month (August) in Washington, it became necessary for the Finance Minister, in his capacity as the Governor of the Bank of Japan, to attend the Board of Governors meeting on September 3.

Our country was interested in borrowing funds from the World Bank to develop an electric power station on the Tadamigawa.[4] Regarding this, we tried to raise this with [Eugene R.] Black, President of the World Bank. In addition, we also began preparing for questions about Japan's biggest problem following independence, namely "defense," from Secretary of the Treasury [John W.] Snyder and Dodge, who recently became advisor to the Secretary of State, who we knew would be in Mexico City for the meeting.

The public became interested in the so-called "defense problem" of the public around this time. The National Safety Agency was established on August 1. While telling the members of the National Police Reserve (they did not yet call them the Safety Agency forces), "Now is not the time for Japan to rearm," its first director, Prime Minister Yoshida, also reportedly said to the assembled forces that "they represented the basis of the construction of a new national military." Moreover, the Safety Force advertised the hiring of an additional 35,000 personnel (this was related to the fact that the 28,000 who were hired two years ago were leaving at the end of August with 60,000 yen in severance pay), the hiring of former military officers of the rank of colonel to become officers in the National Police Reserves, and the establishment of an air school in Hamamatsu with the United States loaning about ten planes (based on discussions with Major General [Thomas E.] Watson [USMC], the advisor to the Police Reserves). All of these things relating to the establishment of a defense structure were being discussed in the Diet around this time.

The government was being criticized by the Socialist Party for pursuing "slow but sure rearmament" while the Progressive Party and the Hatoyama Ichiro faction decrying the lack of an independent spirit by doing rearmament secretly and not moving ahead publicly. We departed Japan for Mexico City on August 31, leaving behind this uncertainty that the dissolving of the Diet brought. The annual meetings of the International Monetary Fund and the World Bank were, to be honest, like a party, which did not particularly lead to any results. However, because it was the one opportunity for all of the Finance Ministers and Governors from the National Banks to meet in one place, there were significant discussions at working levels and at social functions outside of the main meetings.

Changing planes during the course of the trip, we did not make it to Mexico City in time for the start of the meeting, but we were able to meet with President Black of the World Bank for our one-hour meeting scheduled the afternoon of September 3.

THE JAPAN-U.S. TALKS IN MEXICO

President Black was quite interested in helping the newly developing areas of Southeast Asia as one of the activities of the World Bank, and asked about Japan's thinking about Asia as a whole. However, we did not have any specific knowledge that would convince a banker.

At the time, the West, especially the United States, was very interested in India's future direction. There was a strong desire in Washington to win India's heart, and this view was reflected within the World Bank. Black asked us about the plan that Takasaki Tatsunosuke of Japan was promoting. If I remember correctly, the plan was to create a joint venture between Japan and India using World Bank funds and build a blast furnace in India from which Japan would import inexpensive steel. Black showed strong interest in this at one point.

When Minister of Finance Ikeda raised the issue of electric power, particularly the issue of Tadamigawa, Black appeared interest and said that he would like to send a team to look into the matter as quickly as possible. When we told him that "Prime Minister Yoshida would like to invite him as soon as his schedule permits," Black limited his response to something to the effect of his wanting to go. All in all, he seemed less than enthusiastic.

The next day, we met with American Treasury Secretary Snyder for about fifty minutes. Dodge sat in on the meeting. The following day, we spoke with Dodge for a couple of hours. This was the first time in bilateral negotiations that we addressed defense issues from head-on. Secretary Snyder, expressing the views of the leadership of the U.S. government, stated that he wished Japan would increase its defense capabilities as quickly as possible, as called for in the Japan-U.S. Security Treaty. He also mentioned several times that to help the Japanese economy, the United States would undertake its procurement in Japan with dollars. My impression was that the first part of what he said was something he could say as a member of the Cabinet, but he did not know too much after that.

In our conversation with Dodge the next day, however, we really got into a lot of detail. Dodge's assistant made a rather vague comment—"In the U.S., research findings from the Defense Department suggest that the National Police Reserves could reach 180,000 (at the time there were 110,000 personnel) and that within a few years it could reach 325,000"—but our opinion was not specifically asked on it. Dodge told us that Washington was currently studying giving Japan about 300 million dollars in military assistance as part of the Army budget for the next fiscal year (which was to begin in July 1953 until June 1954). We wanted to know what form this money would take. If it were money that could be touched, then it would no doubt make news when we returned to Japan. However, we were not prepared for this and were in a hurry, so we let it go by thinking it not particularly important. At this point with a truce on the Korean Peninsula, there appeared to be much left over in the Army budget. Now might be a good time to draw out this money.

In Mexico, we also visited with [Fritz] Schaffer, the West German Minister of Finance, and [Ludwig W.] Erhard, the Economic Minister, where we heard Erhard's "social market system" economic views, but it is not necessary to introduce them.

ONE LADY AND FIFTY FINANCE MINISTERS

Finally, there is one small personal experience I would like to share based on my diary at the time. I need to let the reader know at the outset that it has nothing to do with politics or the economy.

At 9:00 p.m. on the day we arrived from Japan, September 3, the Finance Ministers and Governors of the Central Banks attending the meeting were invited to a dinner party by the Mexican Finance Minister at the National Bank of Mexico (*Banco de Mexico*). However, the Japanese representative, Minister Ikeda, hated functions like this, and what's more, he could not speak English, so he told me to go with him. However, even if he ordered me to attend, I was still not a Minister or a Bank Governor. I tried to demur as it was a formal party and those not invited could not obviously go, but in the rush of the day paying our respects on the Mexican President [Miguel Alemán Valdés] and meeting with World Bank President Black, it got late in the day. That evening, officials from our Embassy encouraged me to attend the dinner, saying they had arranged for me to go. I was very uneasy about this, not sure whether the hosts were in fact aware of it or not.

I went to the second or third floor of the Bank of Mexico building where the guests were assembled having cocktails. No matter where I looked, there were Finance Ministers and National Bank Presidents all looking elegant. I began to get more and more nervous. I looked for someone I might know, but more than half were dark-skinned people conversing in languages I was not familiar with. I found U.S. Federal Reserve Bank Chairman [William McChesney] Martin, whom I had met a couple of times before. He was only about forty years old, a person that someone young like me could probably talk to. However, as the U.S. Federal Reserve Chairman, he was a very important figure and many people were gathering around him and it was quite hard to approach him. I looked for Dodge, but of course he would not be there—he was neither the Secretary of the Treasury nor the Chairman of the Federal Reserve. With this, I became quite despondent.

More than this, I was most concerned about what would happen when the doors to the dining room were opened and as I went to the table discovered that there was no seat for me. The pathetic sight of me just loitering around the table in front of everyone was something that I thought first and foremost would not be good for Japan, which recently regained its independence.

I started to look for a chief attendant to ask quietly if I indeed had a seat. Most attendants are black, strong, and sturdy, and so finding them is usually not a problem. However most of the guests were black, strong, and sturdy, too, and I could not tell the difference between the attendants and guests. I was afraid that my calling a Minister a waiter by mistake might lead to a break-off in diplomatic relations.

Eventually I found a man in a white tuxedo jacket, and thought I had found the chief attendant. The invitations had clearly stated that it was to be a black jacket affair, and so I thought the man in the white had to be a waiter. This too was a mistake. That person turned out to be a Finance Minister from some country. When I tried to speak to him, he did not understand English and a cold sweat came over me. However, I became relieved when I thought what would have happened if he had understood me.

I then saw someone way off in the corner who did not move at all. I thought that he must be from the Mexican FBI or something, and I was right. He called a Vice Minister or Protocol Officer from the Mexican government. When I explained the situation, the person said, "Of course you are invited. Please enjoy yourself." Yet, his response was all too easy and I began to worry thinking that there is no way that a Mexican can remember a Japanese name that well.

Well, the doors to the dining room opened and everyone made their way to the table. Following from behind, I saw that my name card was indeed there by a table setting. It even had "His Excellency" in front of it and I got excited, except for when I sat down. Having flown for three days and nights, and sweating during the evening, my tuxedo felt uncomfortable on me. When I saw the menu, it was all written in French. Items that look good normally appeared less so when I realized that we would be here until after midnight trying to get through the eight-course dinner. However, what I was most surprised about at the dinner was not the food. It was about a woman who appeared at the dinner.

A band appeared as dinner started. There were about five or six members who had guitars and violins, all wearing cowboy-like costumes. All had beards, so it was hard to tell their ages. The music appeared to be a form of Spanish madrigal (but, then, what do I know?). After performing several songs, a woman entered like a flower blossoming. Her skirt was wide and she had a shawl on her exposed back (this became fashionable a year or two later in Japan, something that fashion models would wear). Of Spanish descent, she was clearly a beauty. She began singing. She was no doubt good. I thought she would finish after four or five songs, but she gave no appearances of wanting to end. The guests by this point had begun to feel the effect of the drinks and some Finance Ministers and Central Bank Chairmen began calling out lustfully. We learned that her name was "Veronica."

Miss Veronica (or Ms., I am not sure. In either case there was not a big difference) continued to sing for about an hour later. The atmosphere became more and more rowdy. She began to visit each of the Finance Ministers and Central Bank Chairmen and while singing, shared a drink with them. They seemed to already know her and would hold her hand and kiss her. Miss Veronica gradually made her way to the seats of honor and she came to Treasury Secretary Snyder and Chairman of the Federal Reserve Martin. Everyone appeared to be watching with interest as to what would happen.

Age-wise, Snyder was an old grandfather figure and Miss Veronica, acting coquettishly, touched him on his back. Martin was quite nervous and everyone laughed but she did not do anything to him. Miss Veronica sang four or five more songs after this, and when the dessert time approached, she grabbed someone's menu and began going around asking for autographs.

When the Finance Minister of one country sitting next to me took out his fountain pen to sign, the ink did not come out. When it did not work after shaking it a few times, he turned to Miss Veronica and said, "Lately my thing has not been working, too. It must be old age." They both laughed loudly together.

When it came to my turn, I started to tell her that I was neither a Finance Minister nor a Central Bank Chairman, but Miss Veronica asked in a big voice, "What's the matter? Don't you have name?" With this, I hurriedly, but solemnly, signed the menu.

On the way home, I wondered to what profession she belonged. The next morning I asked one of the locals, but was not given a clear answer. The closest comparison would be like the *geisha*, whom Japanese are so proud of. However, I do not think even we have anyone like this who can entertain single-handedly seventy guests at one time for three hours.

In any case, I am glad that at this particular time there were no female Finance Ministers or Central Bank Presidents.

THE WAR BETWEEN YOSHIDA AND HATOYAMA BEGINS

We returned quickly to Japan because elections were about to be held. We got a call from Ambassador Tsushima [Juichi][5] in New York when we stopped off in Honolulu for one night on the way back. Since July 20, he had been meeting with the representatives of Britain, the United States, and France regarding the disposition of Japan's foreign exchange. There were many problems from the prewar that had to be dealt with, and the role of negotiating with these representatives was a job that only Tsushima could do. On the telephone, Tsushima told us that the negotiations were going to take a little bit longer, with his counterparts being who they were, but that he should finish during August. Unlike West Germany and Italy, Japan does not alter agreements part way through and instead follows through with them, he said. After returning to Japan on the 27th of that month, the agreement was reached between Japan and those countries.

When we returned to Japan, it was election time and the Hatoyama group had clearly stepped up its attacks on Prime Minister Yoshida. These smart politicians knew exactly what policies of the Yoshida Cabinet were not popular, and stepped forward to call for a new approach to politics. These policies were the ones I referred to before, such as the spirit of friendship and love, improving relations with China and the Soviet Union, unabashed rearmament, and more spending.

Within the party, there were those that viewed these attacks as an opportunity for the Prime Minister himself to make his views clear on these issues. For example, on the issue of rearmament, Yoshida responded to this criticism in the following way during a speech in Nagoya:

> If we were to carelessly undertake rearmament today it would be necessary to increase taxes. And were taxes to be raised, we would still have to use upwards of 80 percent of revenue for national defense. If this became the case, then Japan's economy recovery would be done for. Our party is not going to pursue rearmament. We will maintain our policy of gradually increasing Japan's self-defense capabilities in proportion to the increase in national power.

In the days when the Liberal Party had an absolute majority in the Diet and could simply rest on its laurels, Yoshida would only answer, "We will not rearm" to questions of this nature from the Socialist Party. As a result, he would often be criticized for "saying out of consideration for the Constitution that Japan would not rearm but in fact was doing so at that very minute at America's urging." This criticism was heard not just among the general public but was seen within our own party as well. Many in the party did not understand what Yoshida was in fact doing, believing that he was just hiding the fact that rearmament was taking place and did not want to publicly talk about it. This level of understanding—rather it was a misunderstanding of what he was saying—was shared by many, in fact more than half of the party members.

The election this time saw attacks from both sides. On the one side were the Socialists and on the other were the Hatoyama faction and Progressive Party. Within the party, the number of those who came to better understand Yoshida's true thinking increased. Namely, Yoshida believed "Rearmament is something that Japan is no position to do right now at all. Moreover, the public is not supportive of it. Nor was it the role of the government to force it upon the people. In any case, rearmament will probably eventually come about naturally when the lives of the people have improved sufficiently. While it might seem cunning, for the time being we should let America [be responsible for Japan's defense]. The Constitution's forbidding a military is a true blessing. If America says anything, we just show the Constitution. Politicians calling for its revision are complete fools." While the language used to explain this was quite rough, this was Yoshida's unchanging thinking on the subject. For obvious reasons, particularly from a diplomatic perspective, Yoshida could not publicly say this in Diet questioning.

The following year, we went to Washington to represent these feelings on behalf of Yoshida. Looking at only this point, it may appear from the perspective of prewar politicians that the Yoshida government was weak-willed, but from the perspective of politicians dealing with the realities of daily politics in the postwar period, we become impatient with the incomprehensible thinking of the prewar politicians who believe it necessary to excite the patriotic spirit of the people and save their money in the hope of having a military as soon as possible.

On September 29, the eve of the October 1 election, President of the Liberal Party Yoshida decided to expel Ishibashi [Tanzan] and Kono [Ichiro] from the party as they were seen as the leaders of those leading the divisive forces within it, leading Yoshida and Hatoyama to fight even more. The opinion that it was necessary to kick them out had been building for some time but this had been kept in check by the older leaders in the party. However, on September 25, Hirokawa, who was seen as the person closest to Yoshida, visited Finance Minister Ikeda. Other movements began to be seen around this time as well, suggesting that something big was afoot.

September 25 was a day that for another reason I remembered several years later as being an important day. It is a side story, but let me introduce it here. That morning, I went to the private home of Finance Minister Ikeda earlier than usual. Agriculture Minister Hirokawa finally came by and I went into a room off of the guest room. Through a screen, I saw that Hirokawa had brought someone along whom I had never met before. The three of them spoke for a minute or two about something, and then Hirokawa told the other visitor to "go wait somewhere." Hirokawa and Ikeda were now alone. The whole time they spoke about Ishibashi and Kono, and their removal from the party, and I heard their names specifically mentioned several times. Thereafter, Hirokawa left with the other visitor who had been waiting in another room.

The person I did not recognize and would not know about until much later turned out to be Ito Jufuku of the Hozen Keizaikai, a shady business that caused some problems shortly thereafter. When the scandal it caused became public [in early 1954], Ito had apparently told investigators, "On that day he went along with Hirokawa to visit Finance Minister Ikeda to request the regulation of Hozen Keizaikai and to thank Ikeda through Hirokawa for his efforts." For me, who witnessed the conversation through a screen in another room, when I heard Ito had made this statement, I tried to recall the scene. No payment was made during that one or two minutes that they were talking. Ito himself apparently told investigators that he simply assumed Hirokawa had made the necessary arrangements. Moreover, the discussion between Ikeda and Hirokawa seem to focus exclusively on the issue of expulsion from the party. The only guess is that Ito, who was asked to wait outside in another room, assumed the discussion between Hirokawa and Ikeda had to do with the expression of thanks. I do not know if this is true or not, but it seems likely and this is what I imagined to be the case when the problem emerged years later. I have really gotten off track with this story, but on this morning, it appears that Ishibashi and Kono were kicked out of the party.

NOTES

1. In addition to the fact that Fukunaga was close to Yoshida, he was also a freshman representative, which may have bothered some party members. For more, see Masumi Junnosuke, *Postwar Politics in Japan, 1945–1955* (Berkeley: University of California Press, 1985), 282–83.

2. Nasu Imperial Villa, located in the town of Nasu in Tochigi Prefecture, was built in 1926 and served as the summer palace for the Emperor.

3. Article 7 reads, "The Emperor, with the advice and approval of the Cabinet, shall perform the following acts in matters of state on behalf of the people. . . . Dissolution of the House of Representatives." Nine other acts are proscribed but not included here.

4. The Tadamigawa River is located in the southwestern part of Fukushima Prefecture.

5. Tsushima was Miyazawa's boss after the war in 1945 when he served as Finance Minister in the Higashikuni Naruhiko Cabinet.

Chapter Five

The Ikeda-Robertson Talks in Washington, 1953

RESILIENCE

Intraparty fighting within the Liberal Party at the time of the general elections in October the year before was followed by problems in choosing the party leadership subsequently. Although the Liberal Party did not actually break up, it was no longer functioning as one party and Yoshida's ability to govern the party was at an all-time low.

Namely, Miki Bukichi, who had supported Hatoyama since the time of the general elections the year before in order to bring down Yoshida, now, as Chairman of the Executive Council for the party which allowed him to take charge of a group of concealed, like-minded people in the party, tried to oppose Secretary General Sato [Eisaku] of the Yoshida faction. Moreover, Agriculture Minister Hirokawa, who until last year had been widely recognized as someone close to Yoshida (and he himself admitted it), began to openly oppose Yoshida over frustration with choosing the party leadership.

On the other hand, Ikeda, who since 1949 had assumed a leading role in the party, had to leave it due to his second slip of the tongue, which invited a motion of no-confidence in the Lower House in November last year. He was replaced as Finance Minister by Mukai Tadaharu, with Ogata Taketora assuming the role of Chief Cabinet Secretary. It was around this time that some people began to predict that Ogata would succeed Yoshida.

In any case, Chairman Miki's anti-Yoshida stance was quite clear. Using the council as a base of operations, Miki sought to have Yoshida and others purged from the party while expanding the relationship with Shigemitsu's Progressive Party. In addition, Miki no longer attempted to hide that he was working with the Hirokawa faction and began planning for the overthrow of the Yoshida administration if the timing was right and create a Hatoyama-led government.

In addition, Hirokawa's openly challenging Yoshida while still serving as Agricultural Minister invited discussion within the party that he should be removed from the cabinet. When photos of him with Kodama Yoshio, the right wing underworld figure, at the latter's home, appeared in a newspaper, Yoshida had had enough and began to consider relieving him of his duties. It was becoming apparent in many people's eyes that Yoshida could no longer govern, in light of his Liberal Party and the cabinet, being divided as they both were.

Deliberations in the Diet began to focus primarily on the rearmament issue from about this time. When the two wings of the Socialist Party pursued it and its connection to Article 9, the Progressive Party opened a party congress and agreed to seek the establishment of a self-defense army. In a speech at the time, party president Shigemitsu, arguing his party's pro-rearmament position quite strongly, stated, "it was necessary for Japan to cooperate as a member of the democracies. It is necessary for Japan to maintain self-defense forces commensurate with its national power . . . and for the government to make its views honestly known to the people. Politics of deceit are a crime."

Moreover around this time, relating to Japan, President Eisenhower called upon the Congress to "pass a resolution annulling the secret provisions of the Yalta Accord." In a related question in the Diet on Chishima and the other territories, Prime Minister Yoshida answered that "he would work hard toward seeing Chishima and the other former territories of Japan returned."

The Diet session continued until the end of February when during an explanation in a meeting of the Budget Committee, Yoshida let slip a personal remark, "You stupid fool," which threw the meeting and Diet session into chaos. As if waiting for precisely something like this to happen, a motion to censure Yoshida in the Diet passed due to the absence of Miki Bukichi and others from the *Mindoha*,[1] and Hirokawa's group. Immediately after this, Hirokawa was removed as Minister of Agriculture and Yoshida asked rhetorically to those of us close to him "whether one bullet was really enough to take him down," citing [Georges] Clemenceau, and showing that he was ready for a fight. However, much of his body was already covered with wounds.

The end result of this was a motion of no confidence against the Cabinet. Yoshida made it known that he was prepared to dissolve the Diet if the motion passed. Nevertheless, in the evening of February 14, it passed by twenty-one votes and the Diet was dissolved again. Prior to this, twenty-two members, including Miki, Ishibashi, and Kono left the Liberal Party (technically, they created a breakaway party or "bunto"). Several days later, Hirokawa's group joined with them and created a new party with Hatoyama as its head. As a result, the Yoshida Cabinet, which enjoyed a large majority, had to face the general elections as a minority party.

REARMAMENT AS A POLITICAL ISSUE

The biggest issue of this election was the rearmament problem. As was mentioned several times already and increasingly being debated in the Diet, the Left Wing of the Socialist Party was clearly against it, calling for "opposition to rearmament, dissolution of the Safety Forces." When asked how a neutral, unarmed Japan would defend itself, Nomizo [Masaru], Secretary General of the right wing of the Socialist Party said Japan should "sign non-aggression pacts with each country."

Bunjito (the name of the breakaway group under Hatoyama at the time) and the Progressive Party, as described above, were in favor of rearmament. Of the two, Bunjito called for rearmament after revising the constitution, while the Progressive Party was divided on the need for constitutional revision. The Yoshida Liberal Party, as has also been explained, argued that the "expansion in self-defense capabilities should be done gradually in response to the increase in national strength." This opinion was criticized, however, as unclear. The Right Wing of the Socialist Party stated that it "recognized the right of self-defense. However, the Safety Forces are now a military and should be returned to the level of the Police Reserves."

As the elections were heating up, on the Korean Peninsula, an agreement was reached after a long delay on the exchange of prisoners. After the signing of that agreement, the hostilities in Korea essentially came to end. Related to this, the U.S. government quickly came out and said, "Even if a truce were realized in Korea, procurements in Japan would likely continue. The U.S. government would not reduce disbursements to Japan for at least three years." This statement was probably made to calm the fears of the business community and to strengthen the position of the ruling party in the elections. However, as is too often the case, the American attempt was off the mark and did not lead to the results desired in Washington.

The results of the elections were that the Liberal Party gained nearly two hundred seats coming in first place. The Left Wing of the Socialist Party surpassed the Right Wing, and surprisingly, few votes went to the Bunjito and Progressive Party. An editorial in the Asahi Shimbun around this time appraised the results in the following way: "The parties supporting rearmament, namely the Progressive Party and Bunjito, did not do well. The Liberal Party, which did not support rearmament, at least on the surface, generally retained its lead. The fact that those opposing rearmament, namely the Left and Right Wings of the Socialist Party, and especially the Left Wing, which was strongly opposed, made large gains showed the feelings of the people toward rearmament. In addition, the fact that many of the big-known candidates, who generally belong to the prewar school, lost one after the other suggests that the time has come for a generational shift in our political world."

THE BASE PROBLEM

In this way, around the time the rearmament issue was gaining attention of the general public, the so-called "base problem" that is discussed today began to also get the attention of the people. As a result of the 1951 Security Treaty between Japan and the United States and the related 1952 Administrative Agreement, the Japan-U.S. Joint Committee was created in 1952 for representatives of both countries to discuss issues arising from the provision of areas and facilities to the U.S. military, and a year had almost gone by since its establishment.

Generally speaking, complaints by local authorities with regard to the use of the bases (the government does not like this word; it prefers to use "areas and facilities") and problems in discipline of U.S. forces and the effect on public morals were being heatedly debated at the time. One thing that further complicated the situation was the fact that air bases were larger than ever with the use of jet aircraft and related communications facilities had to be similarly increased. In some cases, it seemed that the bases were taking up an even larger amount of land than during the Occupation period and the number of people directly affected by this was actually increasing and thus the situation was even worse than during the Occupation.

Some specific base problems that emerged just during this first year included complaints in Tachikawa City on health issues due to the fact that aircraft fuel had leaked into the water supply thus making the water undrinkable and opposition to the ruining of tourist places such as Nara City and Fuji-san. In addition, the discovery of what became known as "Sasebo Bacteria" in Sasebo caused an overreaction of the U.S. military in preventing sexually transmitted diseases. There were numerous cases where female employees working for the U.S. military were forced to get an examination, which probably led to a cleaning-up of the problem.

Among these problems was that of Uchinada in Ishikawa Prefecture. If Japan did not quickly make available the training range for live fire training, $100 million in procurements for shells would be lost. Because of this aspect, the problem would become very complex. Thus, one characteristic of these types of problems was that as the standoff between the central government and the local authorities grew more and more severe, politicians representing the local interests had to take the side of the local communities. A pattern emerged in which even if a politician had the courage to say that, from the position of the security treaty and peace treaty, someone had to provide the bases, when problems like those emerged, it would inflame the situation and rational explanations would no longer be listened to.

This situation all played well into the hands of, for example, the Communist Party. A sort of underground resistance began to emerge. In Chitose, Hokkaido, for example, in a bar frequented by American soldiers, someone placed a piece of paper with "Yankee Go Home" written on it in a matchbox.

Of course, there were examples around the country where the U.S. military was working well with the local communities, listening to their complaints. There is the case of where, in Gunma Prefecture, U.S. authorities accepted the request by locals "not to kiss in public" and immediately after this a directive went out to troops in the area to not do so. Similarly, as seen in Kokura City[2] in Kyushu in which U.S. troops coming on R&R from the Korean War are serviced by some four thousand ladies of the night and spend about 200 million yen per month, or in Yokosuka City where U.S. troops drink on average of a million bottles of beer a month in the summer, which incidentally represents the annual consumption of the entire prefecture of Nagano, there are many communities who believe that for the time being it is better to have U.S. forces in Japan.

Nevertheless, nationally speaking, the above issues, in other words the base problem, is becoming a latent hotbed of anti-Americanism, and sometimes it becomes entangled with the criticism toward the government that it is secretly pursuing "rearmament step by step." Public opinion is being affected in a way that was not predicted a mere one and a half years at the time of the San Francisco Peace Treaty.

EVENTS LEADING UP TO ACCEPTANCE OF MSA

Going into May, on the eve of the new American fiscal year (beginning on July 1 and ending on June 30 the next year), a quiet debate emerged in the government and conservative parties about whether to accept military aid from the United States, which was called Mutual Security Assistance there. Apparently, the United States was willing to provide a lot of aid, particularly in military assistance, to Japan.

It was clear that the Socialist Party, especially its Left Wing, would "oppose" it, as mentioned earlier. The Progressive Party and the Hatoyama Liberal Party, on the other hand, welcomed discussions with the United States on this question, actively hoping to see the acceptance of the latest weapons as Japan was in the process at this time of establishing a long-term defense policy.

Many of us had predicted that this issue would come up, particularly due to the fact that Treasury Secretary Snyder and Advisor to the Secretary of State Dodge had spoken of this assistance in September the year before. Moreover, as a result of the ceasefire on the Korean Peninsula, a lot of money and weaponry was left over and the Army Department hoped to give it to Japan, something that we were also aware of. Yoshida's view was that Japan's defense capabilities would be gradually increased as long as it did not negatively affect the economy. It made sense on first glance, therefore, to receive the latest weaponry from the United States. However, if too many weapons were accepted, then a military organization larger than originally needed or planned would emerge and this could be dangerous. Moreover, it was quite possible that a great deal of money would be needed in the coming couple of years to fix these weapons, creating a financial strain.

Furthermore, the biggest issue had to do with the fact that MSA required the country receiving weapons to assume some level of military responsibilities. If that level was within the already defined scope of the Japan-U.S. Security Treaty then fine, but if it required a new level beyond that, then a constitutional problem could emerge.

In addition, it was likely that in sending the weapons, the United States was not doing it on a one-time basis without planning, but rather would continue to be planning over the coming years, and thus would likely require the receiving country to establish a long-term defense plan for several years as well. Regarding our own country, the Yoshida Cabinet had stated that it would gradually increase the strength of Japan's defense capabilities and for this some planning of course was probably necessary. However, it was clear that it would not meet the expectations of the United States on the one hand, and on the other, we had to be careful that the planning did not get too large.

We had these issues in our mind in May when the acronym MSA began to be used in Japan. Incidentally, leaving aside the political considerations for a moment, the business community was quite sensitive to the MSA issue, strongly hoping that it would be accepted to replace the demands for procurement that would dry up as a result of the end of the Korean War. It appeared that the *Keidanren* (Federation of Economic Organizations) would start pushing the issue shortly. The business community is probably traditionally in favor of military preparedness based on its political convictions. But it is also probably true that by laying the tracks for accepting MSA and rearmament, they were also hoping to see the expansion of military procurements and industry as a whole.

No matter how he would eventually decide, Yoshida, it seems, felt it necessary to know exactly what officials in Washington were thinking about MSA. This being right before the elections, I asked him if he had any intentions of sending Ikeda to the U.S. Yoshida was in favor of it because first of all because he wanted Ikeda to spread his wings and see another country especially following his removal from the Cabinet as Minister of International Trade and Industry for a second inappropriate comment, and with the issue of MSA. However, from Ikeda's point view, if he went to Washington he would no doubt be asked about Japan's intentions regarding defense and in light of the political situation it was quite clear that no one could really speak with confidence that "Japan will do this or that," which made him uncomfortable.

In light of this, Yoshida instead directed Ambassador Araki [Eikichi] directly to find out about the following points:

1. Why did Dulles announce (at a May 5 press conference) that the U.S. is prepared to give assistance to Japan when Japan has not even requested MSA?
2. In the case of this assistance to Japan, is MSA limited to simple military items, or does it include other-than-military procurements?
3. Does Japan have to accept any new military responsibilities in order to receive MSA, or is the scope of the current Security Treaty enough? Regarding the increase in the National Safety Force, is a long-term commitment necessary? If so, what level is the U.S. looking for?
4. How much is the amount of aid?

The reason the entire contents of the message are included here is to introduce as a whole everything that we wanted to learn on this occasion. Let's look at the domestic political situation once again.

The election was over and the Liberal Party came in first. However, it did not win a majority. An extraordinary session of the Diet was scheduled to meet on May 18. During the two weeks between the election and that day, the Progressive Party and the Hatoyama Liberal Party began to increase their expanding relationship, and since both the Right and Left wings of the Socialist Party sought the downfall of the Yoshida government, the four opposition parties started to work together more. The opposition thought that if they could succeed in having an opposition member named as Speaker of the Lower House, then they could get Shigemitsu named as Prime Minister, and began to move in that direction.

In response, the Liberal Party believed that if the Speaker of the House was from the opposition party, the management of Diet affairs would become extremely difficult, and if that were the case, the argument went, it was probably better to go into the opposition. However, another opinion was that before a situation like that happened, Yoshida should meet with Shigemitsu, President of the Progressive Party.

I was not involved in the efforts at this time for the Yoshida-Shigemitsu meeting and thus do not directly know all the details. However, my reason in introducing what I have heard about the meeting is because I was involved in events about four months after it at the end of September, and at the early stages of the planning the meeting, and thus I would like to inform the reader about the atmosphere at the time of the first attempt to hold such a meeting.

The senior leadership of the Liberal Party came to the conclusion that the only way to break the impasse was to have a meeting between Yoshida and Shigemitsu. Secretary General Sato and Vice President Ogata relayed this recommendation to Prime Minister Yoshida at Oiso.[3] As expected, Yoshida made a sour face, but eventually agreed if that were the way to proceed, he would write a letter and have Sato deliver it. On the same day, watching these movements of the Liberal Party, Secretary General Kiyose [Ichiro] of the Progressive Party announced that even if Prime Minister Yoshida requested a meeting, if it did not lead to the naming of Shigemitsu as Prime Minister, then Shigemitsu would not attend.

The letter Yoshida wrote that was left in Sato's care to deliver to Shigemitsu was a bizarre one, symbolic of his reluctance in writing it. The important points are captured here.

> Greetings. I hope this finds you in good health. There are strong voices in and outside of the party calling for talks between the two conservative parties in order to stabilize the political situation and improve the running of the Diet. I believe this to be necessary too, and that it would be problematic to leave the situation as it is. For this reason, I have decided to send Secretary General Sato as my representative to hear the views of your Party. I would be grateful if you would meet with him.

In short, this was not a letter that said, "Let's meet." Yet, Yoshida was asking that Shigemitsu let his envoy know what he was thinking with regard to the political situation. By doing this, he tried to maintain his sense of pride.

Secretary General Sato passed this letter to Shigemitsu. Sato explained that he was acting as the Prime Minister's envoy and orally relayed that the Prime Minister would like to meet and wished to know his schedule. Shigemitsu reportedly responded in the following way: "The situation is quite grave. (Author's note: Shigemitsu had a tendency to use this phrase often.) I do not hesitate to meet with you. However, in order not to create any misunderstandings, I will respond to your letter with a letter."

The following day, Secretary General Kiyose passed the letter from President Shigemitsu to Prime Minister Yoshida through Sato. After expressing his "hopes that the letter found him in good health," Shigemitsu wrote that he "believes he is familiar with the decision of the party [that Yoshida would have to agree that Shigemitsu be nominated as Prime Minister as a precondition for the meeting]." The Liberal Party decided that in light of the letter, there was no point in having the two leaders meet. In addition, because the Progressive Party released to the public a part of the exchanges, the meeting in the end was not held. Yoshida went ahead and relayed this decision to Shigemitsu: "According to your letter, your Party has already decided not to support our meeting. Because there is no chance for a meeting, let's call it off. If the opportunity presents itself at an appropriate time in the future let us meet then." At the time, Yoshida felt quite relieved, and told one of the leaders of the Liberal Party that had recommended the meeting in the first place, teasingly, "it looks like my intuition was much better."

In fact, it was apparently the group headed by Kishi Nobusuke, leader of the *Saiken Renmei* (Japan Reconstruction League), who initially sought to have the two party presidents shake hands. Kishi had been close with Shigemitsu since the hard days spent at Sugamo Prison together. It was Chief Cabinet Secretary Ogata and Secretary General Kishi, who because of their positions, got this idea.

However, their first miscalculation was related to the situation within the Progressive Party, namely their misunderstanding that if Shigemitsu agreed to the idea then it would happen. They underestimated the influence of the Ashida faction within the party which was strongly opposed to the move. The second miscalculation was their having proceeded without Mr. "O"[4] from the Progressive Party being involved and as a result he did not lend his help. These two tactical errors were the largest reason for the failure. In fact, the role of Mr. "O" was not overlooked, but the decision was made that it would not be appropriate to ignore Secretary General Kiyose as the main channel.

In the end, Yoshida's stubbornness won out. While the position of the Speaker of the House went to the Progressive Party (Mr. Tsutsumi [Yasujiro]), Yoshida ended up remaining as Prime Minister when the Right and Left Wings of the Socialist Party abstained in the vote for Shigemitsu.

At this point, in forming the cabinet Yoshida decided to ask the Progressive Party for its cooperation and visited Shigemitsu in Kamakura. The reason why he was so reluctant to do so the last time was because it would appear that he was asking Shigemitsu "to let him be Prime Minister" and he definitely did not want to do that. However, now he was simply asking for Shigemitsu's help in forming the cabinet, which he would have to do in any case. So, it was the same meeting, but in Yoshida's eyes it had completely different connotations.

The Yoshida Cabinet was formed on May 21. Ikeda, who had been on the outside for some time, came back as Chairman of the Policy Research Council. This was done for two reasons. On the one hand, it would be necessary to discuss policy issues with the Progressive Party, and on the other hand, it would be necessary to resolve the problem of the MSA from a broad perspective. Yoshida likely had these two intentions in mind when appointing Ikeda.

The debate in the Diet session ended up focusing on the MSA. The media, too, was asking the opinions of the U.S. side on this question, meeting with newly arrived U.S. Ambassador Allison and those from the Congress who arrived in Japan to look into the MSA issue, namely Democratic Senator [Warren G.] Magnasun and Republican Senator [Everett M.] Dirksen.

The focus of the interest centered on the question, "If the government accepts military aid of the MSA, would it have to increase the strength of the Safety Forces in return?" To this, the government responded with the following answers, based on the report that Ambassador Araki had sent back after the initial inquiries: "No new military responsibilities would emerge [from accepting the aid]," "the aid Japan receives won't require repayment," "the amount of aid received can be determined during negotiations," "although the U.S. Fiscal Year begins on July 1, there is no need to give an answer before then." To deflect further questioning, other answers given by the Prime Minister and Foreign Minister were that the issue was still being studied, and that negotiations had not yet begun. In addition, at the first press conference after the formation of the cabinet, Yoshida stated, "the Safety Forces would not be strengthened now. We are committed to reducing taxes, and thus we cannot increase them. Moreover, it will be enough [the level of the Safety Forces] is relative to national strength. America won't make us do anything unnecessary beyond that."

THE WELCOME OF THE
NATIONAL SAFETY AGENCY DIRECTOR

Around this time, a great stir emerged just as public opinion began to get shrill on the question of rearmament and MSA. This was the reported announcement by Director of the National Safety Agency Kimura [Tokutaro] during a trip of a "Police Forces Five-Year Draft Plan" that he had been working on and had brought together (Kimura himself denied the media reports).

Of course, the National Safety Agency is one that is permitted to study precisely this sort of issue. Likewise, for the reasons already explained, if the MSA were to be accepted, it was necessary for the Japanese government to have a somewhat long-term defense plan of its own. Moreover, also as explained earlier, when Yoshida suggested that he was going to send Ikeda to the U.S., Ikeda believed that he might be taken advantage of there if Japan had not made up its mind as to what it wanted to do. As seen from these concerns, it can be understood therefore that it was important for Japan to have a target of some kind.

Yet as alluded to before, the problem exists that when an organization is created to fulfill a certain role, it is easy for that organization to think its work the most important. With the Safety Agency created and studying a defense plan, it was nearly certain that it would attempt to create the best plan based on this thinking and divorced from national policy, public opinion, the national economy, and diplomatic stance. In particular, with the case of the Safety Agency, because the policy of the Cabinet was such, it was easy to be treated as an unwanted child, and as a result if the opportunity presented itself, they would want to speak out in a big voice to show their presence. On top of that, one more special consideration was because since the time of the National Police Reserves, the U.S. military advisory group showed favoritism toward the Safety Agency and through this relationship, information from Washington, including the atmosphere there, came in directly, there was a tendency of the Safety Agency to forget the issues peculiar to Japan. To this unique situation came the outspoken Kimura as Director General.

The "Police Forces Five-Year Plan" announced by Kimura as reported in the press was premised on approximately 2 million dollars of aid initially but with the defense burden decreasing year-by-year. Due to this, the Safety Agency's expenses would likely increase, according to this logic. In addition, in Fiscal Year 1957, the Safety Forces would have 210,000 personnel, and 145,000 tons of ships, and 400 planes, of which about half would be jets.

It should be pointed out that in light of the various circumstances mentioned above, the Safety Agency showed self-restraint in this plan. For example, the plan was by far smaller than the "Six-Year Defense Plan" of *Keidanren* and others. Nevertheless, it was an issue of great interest to the public. Much examination in the Cabinet from different perspectives would be necessary. The reporting of its release before such a study had been undertaken likely caused problems for Prime Minister Yoshida.

In the middle of this controversy, recently arrived Ambassador Allison gave a speech in which he said, "the United States has no intention to force MSA on Japan. It is up to Japan whether to accept it or not. Moreover, even if Japan does accept it, there will be no demand that it do more than what it is economically capable. In addition, Eisenhower has confirmed that to the effect that there will be no asking that the Safety Forces be dispatched abroad." He added that there seemed to be misunderstandings in Japan on these points.

There was a meaning behind the comment, "Japan has the right to decide everything [with regard the terms of MSA]," in Allison's speech. Just at this time, the Foreign Ministry was entering in discussions with the U.S. Embassy on MSA aid. And on June 6, Foreign Minister Okazaki in his speech to the Diet stated "Regarding the aid based on the MSA, if it is beneficial to strengthening our self-defense capabilities and contributes economically to the people, then it might be good to accept it. We hope to reexamine the contents and make a decision with no regrets." With this, the government had officially announced that it had made up its mind.

In order to further amplify the point, the Foreign Ministry's Cultural Information Division published a brochure explaining the MSA in which the points already previously stated by the government were introduced in one document. In it, the government took the position that if there were no additional special requests made by the U.S. government, it would go ahead and accept MSA. The main points were as follows:

1. The aid would most likely be limited to military-related items;
2. Japan would face no new military responsibilities and thus no problems would emerge with the constitution;
3. The business community would experience a positive impact because MSA would last longer and be a more stable revenue than procurements for the Korean War.

Because things had come to this point, the government decided that it was necessary to exchange official documents summarizing everything that had been discussed informally, which would serve as the basis for negotiations in the future. On June 24, the government officially sent questions to the U.S. Embassy, and received answers based on a telegrammed response on the 26th, which it made public. Its main points—those that Japan asked about— were as follows:

1. Will the objectives of MSA be seen as fulfilled if Japan is able to secure its internal stability and defense? (For example, this meant that Japan would not be responsible for sending its forces abroad.)
2. When thinking about Japan's defense, the Japanese government views the stability and development of the economy as a priority. Is this correct?
3. Military responsibilities relating to MSA fall within the scope of the security treaty. Is this correct?

4. By the "Increase and Maintenance of [Japan's] Defense Capability" as cited in the MSA, the government of Japan understands this to mean that in the case of Japan, it would not be done at the expense of Japan's political and economic stability. Is this correct?

In response to this request for clarification on these and other points, the U.S. government answered in the affirmative. As a result, it decided to officially enter detailed negotiations.

YOSHIDA DRIVES DULLES CRAZY

Prime Minister Yoshida had for some time wanted to send an appropriate person to the United States in order to discuss all of the unresolved economic issues left over from the time of the Occupation to the present, namely the introduction of foreign currency into Japan, leases to the United States, and the repayment of loans from the United States (GARIOA). Former Finance Minister Ikeda had been asked about this question sometime before, but as mentioned above, he believed that it was not the time.

In July after the government had decided to accept MSA and began to study it in detail and the Safety Agency had a long-term plan drafted, the Prime Minister once again asked Ikeda to consider going to the United States after the end of the Diet session. At the time, I heard from Ikeda that request, and asked him, "what did he say for you to go and do?" Ikeda responded, "Well, it's just like it always is; he does not specifically say. As usual, however, the topic of the introduction of foreign currency came up."

It is true that Yoshida was not the type of person who would give detailed instructions on each issue. Yoshida would explain that he was not knowledgeable about the economy and therefore could not speak intelligently about it, but he had an innate ability to decide what was best when the time came.

When I heard what Yoshida had said from Ikeda, I thought it was problematic. If he went abroad at this point, it was clear that the discussions would focus on defense issues. Also the U.S. would present all sorts of demands. We had just finished limiting the demands from MSA to the greatest extent possible. Indeed, for the most part, MSA was not popular in Japan. If we were to refuse MSA, the Socialist Party might praise us, but it would take us away from the course that we believed was most in Japan's interests. In either case, it was not an easy task ahead of him. I asked Ikeda "if there was some hope [Yoshida would reconsider]" but Ikeda, who held essentially the same view, had the look on his face like his turn had come and it could not be helped. As a result, we decided to find time in between Diet meetings to listen to experts from the Safety Agency on defense issues.

However, just about this time, the press reported that Secretary of State Dulles gave testimony before the Finance Committee of the Senate in which he said he thought "the Japanese Safety Forces would increase their strength to the goal of ten brigades." Because this caused some misunderstanding, Dulles held a subsequent press conference where he stated, "the United States has a provisional plan in which the Safety Forces, for the preservation of domestic peace and for self-defense, would increase their strength to a final goal of about 350,000, or by U.S. standards, ten brigades. Of course, this is an issue for the Japanese government and people to decide."

To be honest, the number 350,000 was one that we had heard in the past. As was mentioned before, we did not easily forget the number 350,000 that suddenly came out of the mouth of an official representing the Defense Department in September of the year before in Mexico City when we met with Dodge. With Dulles' statement this time, we had a good idea about what to expect if we were to go Washington.

There was a fair amount of concern already that if Japan accepted MSA, America would unreasonably force the Safety Force to expand. Dulles' comments threw oil on the fire. No matter what the Japanese government said in its explanations, domestically the debate began to see the MSA and 350,000 as one in the same.

Secretary of State Dulles visited Japan on the way back from a trip to Korea where he signed the U.S.-South Korean Mutual Defense Treaty after the truce in the Korean War. The visit took place on August 8. Two or three days before that, Prime Minister Yoshida requested Policy Research Council Chairman Ikeda to prepare talking points and background materials for his meeting with Dulles. We listed up the different outstanding issues in bilateral relations, and prepared speaking points on the outlook for the Japanese economy and budget. Using this, we explained that it would be a real problem if the increase in force levels went ahead as expected, that numerous difficulties would emerge, and that there were a host of demerits working against the idea. (These points will be looked at more in the discussion of the Ikeda-Robertson talks).

The Prime Minister met with Secretary Dulles for about thirty minutes prior to a reception at the U.S. Embassy. According to what I heard later, as expected, Dulles spoke of Japan's defense, reportedly saying: "I want Japan to do more in the area of defense as a key country in Southeast Asia. Italy, which is much farther away from a communist country than is Japan, is contributing 7 percent of its GDP to defense, while Japan is only giving 2 to 3 percent." This was a figure that we always heard when we went to Washington. Probably Dulles had memorized the notes his staff had prepared. (Or, the comparison in figures was something used by Dulles in testimony to the Congress.)

In response, Prime Minister Yoshida spoke about Japan's relative national strength and the constitutional issue, and pointed out that while it was easy to talk about rearmament, doing it was much harder, explaining even if the Safety Forces were increased, it would only be by 20,000 to 30,000.

Dulles, after having a successful visit to Korea with President Syngman Rhee on the Korea Defense Treaty, seems to have left Japan less than satisfied. This was what the veteran correspondent of the *New York Times* James Reston, who had stopped over in Japan at the time, wrote in a story later.

Reston met with Yoshida the day before the Yoshida-Dulles meeting took place, and spoke with Yoshida on a number of things. Prime Minister Yoshida told Reston that, of course, defense was important, but Japan did not have that ability. "Only by strengthening the economy of this country and the authority of its government at home will Japan be able to increase her responsibilities. Our independence must eventually be defended by our own hand. That is a basic principle. But it is impossible to do that now."[5] Reston said later that Yoshida told him a future problem will be the fact that "amendment of the Japanese Constitution was the 'only legal way' in which Japan could hope to participate in a major rearmament program. . . . [However, the Constitution also] gave the women the vote for the first time and they are reported to be very much against a rearmament amendment."

THE MEMO PREPARED FOR
THE YOSHIDA-SHIGEMITSU TALKS

Shortly after Dulles left Japan clearly frustrated, Shigemitsu, president of the Progressive Party, suddenly clarified his stance, attacking the lack of progress in Yoshida's foreign policy. I read with great displeasure the news of his speeches while traveling around the country in which he said, "Dulles has blamed Japan for not living up to its promises regarding defense. A great concern has been interjected in Japan-U.S. relations and for this we can only say [Yoshida's] diplomacy has failed." Heavily criticizing other politicians is a fact of life, but using Dulles's dissatisfaction as a way to declare victory was improper in my opinion.

Just before this Diet session began, when Prime Minister Yoshida visited Shigemitsu in Kamakura and requested his cooperation in forming a cabinet, regardless of what the results were, Shigemitsu did not appear to have any strong disliking of Yoshida. Nevertheless, what made Shigemitsu become aggressive in attacking Yoshida involved two things. First, when Ashida questioned Prime Minister Yoshida in the Budget Committee on the question of defense issues, the Prime Minister did not budge on his views to date and completely rejected the proactive defense views of Ashida, and in turn, Shigemitsu. Second, Shigemitsu likely realized that in the end, if he kept quiet, the chance to head the government would never come.

By the way, we had a reason as to why we were even more concerned than usual about Shigemitsu's actions. This is because if Ikeda were to go to the United States, he would be asked about defense plans. It was necessary to study what sort of answer we would provide. In order to do this, we were meeting every day with officials from the Safety Agency, as was mentioned before. Whatever answer we gave, we would have to explain the future prospects and the policy of the Cabinet. And at that point, even if we explained the views of Prime Minister Yoshida, State Department officials familiar with the political situation in Japan would be far from satisfied. It was well known that the current Yoshida Cabinet was not as strong as his previous administrations. As proof of this, in the current Diet session, the government was forced to greatly revise its budget at the demand of the Progressive Party. Therefore, if we were to go to America and assume even a strong position on issues, it was necessary to have at least a shared position between the Liberal Party and the Progressive Party.

The proper way to go about coming up with a policy agreement between the parties is to work at it from the bottom, but because of the above situation and the fact that nothing was moving quickly, an agreement could not be had in time from below. If that were the case, then the only course left was for both party leaders, Yoshida and Shigemitsu, to talk directly and come to an agreement on this issue. We concluded that this approach was the only option.

We wondered how we could make this meeting a reality, and around this time, began to sound out someone in the business community who was close to Shigemitsu. At the introduction of this person, Mr. "H," Ikeda met with President Shigemitsu in a building in Hibiya owned by Mr. "H" for the first time on August 23.[6] Shigemitsu was extremely cautious, but we proceeded to meet several times at that location. Shigemitsu stated in the abstract that now was an important time and explained his position in a way that convinced us, but we did move on to specific steps on how to proceed. Occasionally, we asked two senior leaders of the business community, Mr. "K" and Mr. "A," to attend and help move the discussions along.[7]

At one point, in order to find out Shigemitsu's thinking we also had Mr. "A" meet Mr. "O," a senior member of the Progressive Party, and prod him too. During this time, Mr. "O" said several times that Shigemitsu would not budge until he had a written promise from Yoshida that there would be a change in government.

As has been stated many times so far, the main point Shigemitsu attacked Yoshida on was his lack of a proactive defense posture. As a result, we began to consider a formula by which the Liberal Party could come closer on paper to Shigemitsu, while not sacrificing its principles.

Because Shigemitsu's position within the party was delicate, we took extreme caution to prevent any of this from getting out. The meetings at the building in Hibiya continued for nearly a month. We were able to prepare a statement that served as a draft new policy agreement for Yoshida and Shigemitsu. It comprised the following points:

1. It is necessary at this time to formulate a long-range defense program and to clarify the policy of strengthening the self-defense power;
2. Change the name of the National Safety Force to a self-defense force and give it the duty of defense against direct aggression;
3. If the constitutional issue comes up as a result, it should be discussed separately; and
4. In the economic sphere, discuss policies for long-term rebuilding of the economy

After several meetings to find out if this was acceptable to Shigemitsu, we learned that it in fact was and set out to convince Yoshida. When it became time for Ikeda to bring a copy of this statement to Yoshida, I had known that Yoshida was not much interested in meeting with Shigemitsu, and that he would probably not agree with the phrases "defense against direct aggression" and "discussing the constitutional issue separately." Ikeda similarly believed so. When Yoshida responded, "This looks good," Ikeda was quite surprised and said, "you really make a quick decision when you want to." Prime Minister Yoshida replied, "Even I am not such a grudging person." As a result, the stage was set to show the statement to Shigemitsu.

Surprisingly, Shigemitsu requested that the two phrases, "discussing the constitutional issue separately" and on "economic policy" be deleted. In fact, we were quite grateful about this request and agreed immediately. However, when thinking about the reason behind his requests, we imagined that Shigemitsu did not wish to get involved in the problem of the constitutional issue as there was a division within his party between the view, known as the "Kiyose Theory," which argued that it was possible to possess a military without revising the Constitution, and the opinion that Japan could not possess a military without revising the Constitution. The deletion of the phrase on economic policy had to do with the fact that the Progressive Party was essentially one in which different factions espousing capitalism, revisionist capitalism, and cooperativism all lived together under one roof. It appeared that Shigemitsu did not want to cause a debate to erupt on economic policy.

Since we came this far, we thought that consultations could now begin, but it still took some time. The issue was the timing, when Shigemitsu would meet with the Prime Minister. After several days, there was still no answer. Even asking Mr. "H" from the business community to prod Shigemitsu along produced no answer. I, being impatient, thought that if that were the case, then we would have Yoshida send Shigemitsu the proposal by letter and ask for an appointment to discuss it. A messenger would bring the letter to the front door of Shigemitsu's residence. A reporter would surely notice this and the resulting press speculation would likely make it easy for Shigemitsu to decide. Ikeda rebuked me, however.

We came to know the reason for the delay a few days later. Mr. "A" from the business community visited with Mr. "O," an elder statesman of the Progressive Party, and was told in a roundabout way that "the other day, the President (Shigemitsu) was shown some sort of policy proposal, which he proceeded to immediately put in his pocket and said he could not be responsible for it." With this, the mystery came to an end for us. Ikeda met with Mr. "O" again and when he showed him the same proposal, Mr. "O" was apparently quite happy. Because Prime Minister Yoshida lent his agreement to visit Shigemitsu in Kamakura on Sunday, September 29, the only job left was to inform the leadership in the government and the party but without letting it leak out. Ikeda did so by informing the necessary people on Saturday afternoon. However, if he did so, reporters would no doubt find out during the evening and the story would appear in the morning newspapers. Ikeda asked Yoshida that if the story did appear that he not become angry and change his decision to meet.

Prime Minister Yoshida visited Shigemitsu on Sunday morning and left after speaking with him for about one hour. Both men agreed at that time to the previously prepared statement. The final draft was the one introduced above, with some sentences added to it:

> In view of the current international situation and the rising spirit of racial independence within the country, it is necessary at this time to clarify the policy of strengthening the self-defense power and to formulate a long-range defense program which is in keeping with the nation's strength and which will keep step with the gradual reduction in the U.S. security forces. In accordance with the above, the National Safety Law will be immediately amended to convert the National Safety Force to a self-defense force and to give it the duty of defense against direct aggression.

With this, the Secretaries General of both parties were to discuss how to actualize the above statement. One of the midwives of this event, Mr. "H" from the business community, lived next to Shigemitsu in Kamakura, and around 10:30 of the day of the meeting between Shigemitsu and Yoshida, he called my home to let me know that Yoshida had arrived around 10:00 and that they were engaged in talks at that moment. A lot of cameramen had shown up, damaging the walls and causing a lot of destruction, he said, although his voice sounded happy. Having the meeting a couple of days before we departed for Washington on the 29th was just in time.

IKEDA-ROBERTSON TALKS IN WASHINGTON

Among the members of the delegation, Ikeda and I, due to Diet provisions, could not represent the government as we were also members of the Diet. Ikeda, who led the delegation, went as the personal emissary of Prime Minister Yoshida, with Finance Vice Minister Aichi [Kiichi] representing the government. Finance Counselor Suzuki [Gengo] and Chief Accountant Murakami [Kotaro] also joined later.

It took a long time to get ready for the mission. First, we prepared analysis of the economy, which was showing signs of inflation, and of its future prospects. Next, we prepared documents on the use of foreign investment for reclaimed land and road construction as well as plans for the use of counterpart funds from surplus agricultural goods. We also prepared documentation on other issues, but because the main purpose in the negotiations was over Japan's defense program, we developed an idea for Japan's defense that would require the least possible commitment over the longest time, after having studied the issue intensely from the perspective of finance over several weeks with specialists from the National Safety Agency.

As explained before, the National Safety Agency had prepared a five-year program in which ground forces numbered around 210,000. We thought that this number could be reduced. On the other hand, Dulles had already made public his desire to see a force of 350,000. The upcoming discussions would likely focus on what to do between these two figures. However, we did not put our defense plan to paper at all. To be honest, this was because we did not want our final position to be known to Washington ahead of time, especially in light of the fact that the Safety Agency at the time and Washington were in regular contact. Not only this, but more accurately, Ikeda planned to feel out the U.S. side before deciding our final position. We did not know in fact about where Ikeda would finally drawn the line until partway through.

In any case, this mission was being interpreted by the public as deciding the basics of Japan-U.S. relations for the future, and indeed, we believed this to be the case as well. Moreover, several days before we left for the United

States, we spoke with Ambassador Allison for about an hour, who told us that he sent his Economics Minister, [William W.] Diehl, on ahead to Washington where he would be speaking with Assistant Secretary of State Robertson, Director of the Budget Office Dodge, and two or three other cabinet secretaries about participating in the meetings if time allowed.

Our group arrived in Washington around 10:00 p.m. on October 1. We were met by many people, including Ambassador Araki from Japan and several from the U.S. side, including Director of the Budget Office Dodge and his wife, and Assistant Secretary of State Robertson. The next morning at the Japanese Embassy, we met with Ambassador Araki, Ministers Takeuchi [Ryuji] and Watanabe [Takeshi]. Emissary Ikeda discussed the domestic situation back home in Japan and his thinking with regard to the upcoming negotiations, and the Ambassador and his staff explained the current thinking within the U.S. government. We received a great deal of cooperation from the Ambassador and his staff in these negotiations.

In the afternoon, we first paid a courtesy call to the Director of the Budget Office Dodge, followed by a one-hour meeting with Assistant Secretary Robertson, where we discussed the schedule for the talks and the agenda, as well as examining the arrival statement of the delegation to be released by the State Department. As for the agenda, which was not publicized of course, we confirmed the following simple one:

1. Japan's defense and U.S. aid
2. Economic cooperation with Southeast Asia and reparations
3. Trade with Communist China
4. GARIOA (money incurred during the Occupation by Japan to the United States)
5. Foreign investment into Japan and loans
6. Other domestic concerns in Japan

However, some discussion emerged early on between the two countries on the content of the press release for Ikeda's visit to the United States. This was because the State Department's draft stated, "Ikeda and Robertson agreed that the agenda of the meetings to be held over the next two weeks between the two sides will be about Japanese defense plans and U.S. assistance, as well as problems relating to Japan's economy."

With the start of the meeting this time, the strategy (not really an appropriate word) of the State Department officials, as we were able to surmise, was to hear out Ikeda over the first couple of days to find out Japan's true intentions with regard to defense. Following this, it seems, during the break of a couple of days, the American side would firm up its position after speaking with other departments in the U.S. government and then after the recess, produce its position to the Japanese side. (I write "it seems," but really it was "in fact," but because it was an apparent situation, I will leave it as is.) Because of these considerations, the U.S. side's draft press release included—out of the blue—"defense plans." This was problematic for us, so we opposed it. Our thinking was as follows. We took the opposite approach to the State Department's negotiating strategy. First, we explained the situation with regard to Japan's economy and social climate, arguing that large-scale defense plans were completely impossible. Next, we asked how much and what kind of financial assistance the United States was prepared to give, and added that without knowing how much aid was coming, it would be difficult to make any defense plans. In addition, we explained our firm belief that if "defense plans" was the only item said to be discussed in the press release, it was likely that opposition would emerge in Japan over the talks. What was planned to be a meeting only for coordination purposes turned out to take more than one hour due to the need to revise the draft press release. The final version of it used the phrase, "Problems regarding Japan's economy."

As it was the weekend, the first meeting was held a couple of days later on Monday, October 5, for two-and-a-half hours from 10:30 a.m. in a conference room at the State Department. Assistant Secretary Robertson chaired the meeting, attended by some twenty representatives from the U.S. side, including Budget Director Dodge, Assistant Secretary of Commerce [Samuel W.] Anderson, and others from the State Department, Defense Department, Treasury Department, Foreign Assistance Office, Commerce Department, and Budget Office. The meeting room was a little warm that early October day in Washington.

Special Emissary Ikeda began the meeting by handing out a document entitled "The Situation Today of the Japanese Economy and Problems Facing It," which was prepared before he departed Japan as a summarized version of a Economic White Paper, and some economic statements, which he proceeded to explain. This explanation took a full hour. While the U.S. side did not probably expect "defense plans" to be suddenly raised, there was a look of disappointment on the faces of some from the Defense Department, although not on Dodge and the State Department representatives. However, I was impressed with the good training of American officials in how they listened with great interest throughout the entire discussion.

YOSHIDA'S OPINION PAPER TO DULLES

And then, we distributed the opinion paper that had been given to Dulles at the time of his meeting on August 11 with Yoshida when he visited Japan, as mentioned earlier. Both Dulles and Robertson, who was traveling with him at the time, were familiar with its contents because they had likely read it already, but below is a summary of it.

1. With the cessation of hostilities on the Korean Peninsula, the situation in East Asia has entered a new stage. However, it is difficult to think that Communist aggression will completely stop. Likewise, Japan's own prosperity cannot be detached from the prosperity of the countries of Southeast Asia. Through the payment of reparations and economic cooperation, Japan hopes to contribute to the strengthening of the independence and economic prosperity of the countries of Southeast Asia. Moreover, in response to these situations, the time is coming that Japan consider a fairly long-term plan to gradually increase its defense capabilities.

2. In order for the Japanese economy to grow, it is necessary to modernize the electrical, coal, shipbuilding, steel, and other major industries. However, the capital to do so is lacking, and in modernizing, the problem of unemployment is linked. In addition, the impact of the war is still seen in different areas, with roads and transportation still poor. The disruption in agriculture is another result. In light of this situation, Japan must increase its population and increase exports. Trade with China is also restricted. Compared to the prewar, Japan must get its natural resources from far away, which is more costly. The countries of South Asia are likely not willing to be providers of natural resources until the problem of reparations is taken care of.

3. The people of Japan are definitely not Anti-American, but the feeling of independence has grown after the long occupation following the end of the war, and it is a fact that it is exclusionary. Moreover, considering the current standards of living in Japan, there is a danger for Communism to take hold here. In light of this political situation, it will be very difficult if the feelings of the people are not carefully guided in the future.

4. In looking at the Japanese situation in light of the above points, it is desirous that the issues pending between our two countries be studied and the road to cooperation on expanded. At that time, the following issues to be studies are:

   a. Japanese Defense. We have begun to study how to gradually increase Japan's defense. However, it would be difficult to decide this issue in isolation as it is related to Japan's economic power, reparations, and other considerations.

   b. Reparations. The responsibility for reparations was reduced to the greatest extent possible in the San Francisco Peace Treaty, but we hope to resolve these issues as quickly as possible in order to promote friendly relations with the countries of Southeast Asia.

   c. GARIOA (financial obligations to repay the United States for aid to Japan during the Occupation). There is an argument in Japan that since this aid was not a loan it does not have to be repaid, but I consider it to be a loan to be repaid. However, it is difficult too for Japan today to repay it in light of the problems with other foreign loans and reparations.

    d. MSA. As a result of the ceasefire in Korea, demand has dropped dramat-
       ically and Japan's foreign exchange holdings are dangerously low. There-
       fore, with MSA, procurement should be large enough to assist in the lack
       of dollars.
    e. Loans. Japan has applied for a loan from the World Bank in the amount of
       40 million dollars for a thermal power plant and hopes the United States
       will assist in expediting this request.
    f. Relations with Southeast Asia. The views of Japan on this matter as well
       as its connection with reparations have been stated above. We strongly
       desire the assistance of the United States economic and diplomatic or-
       ganizations in this regard for the sake of Southeast Asia's economic pros-
       perity.
    g. COCOM. Regarding COCOM and CHINCOM, which places restrictions
       on items exported to Communist China, we have the right to have the re-
       strictions on our exports reduced to the level of the UK.
    h. Territorial Issues. Regarding the Ryukyu Islands, we desire the early re-
       turn of administrative rights. Regarding the return of the Bonin islanders
       to Ogasawara, we desire this too as early as possible.
5. In order to resolve these issues, I desire for the United States to begin preparations for discussions, which I hope we can have in the near future.

Instead of going to the trouble of explaining that the mission came here to
represent Yoshida's views, we simply distributed this memo to the U.S. side.
It included all the issues at hand between the two countries.

PUSHING THE "DEFENSE ISSUE"
TO THE BACK BURNER

After this, Ikeda stated that he:

understood the U.S. side desired to discuss many things with the Japanese delegation regarding Japan's defense. We also hope to. However, as was just stated,
the Japanese economy is still weak, and there is also the very difficult issue of
the "Constitutional Problem." Moreover, without a detailed and comprehensive
study of U.S. plans to withdraw its military presence and the prospects for U.S.
assistance to Japan in light of U.S. policy in the Far East, especially the resolution of the Korean War and the problem of Communist China, Japan cannot develop its own plans. As a result, in the first stage of our talks now, we would like
to request the support of the related departments and agencies on this point.

We outmaneuvered the State Department in its original strategy to raise defense issues first, but they did not raise any objections. The participants in the
meeting from the U.S. side did, however, ask a number of questions.

The first question was from Assistant Secretary of State Robertson, who surprisingly asked about GARIOA, and Japan's position on the repayment of the loan. We were aware that at the time, Robertson was being grilled by the U.S. Congress on this issue. Ikeda responded, "the Japanese government believes that it is of course a loan that must be returned, but it is necessary to discuss with you the amount and method of repayment. In addition, there is the relationship to Japan's economic power, especially the problem of foreign currency and reparations."

In fact, the problem of GARIOA was an issue in which there was a difference of opinion, or perhaps better stated, opinion, for a long time between the prime minister and us. We believed that while of course we could not withhold repayment of it at this point, we did not want to touch the issue for the time being because of the opinion in Japan that GARIOA was not a loan but a gift and the fact that it was a problematic and technical one. Nevertheless, immediately before our departure, Prime Minister Yoshida called us to meet with him. "You both are originally from the Ministry of Finance and probably always think about bargaining over money borrowed. But don't do that with GARIOA, please. I have promised Dulles on several occasions that we would repay it. Japan, after all, is a samurai nation. However, in order to repay it, I have also asked on occasion for a new loan," Yoshida told us, grinning. Yoshida held this opinion from beginning to end, and thus we could not do anything in the matter but go along with his wishes. That is why GARIOA was specifically raised in the memorandum handed to Dulles, as explained above.

In the period between 1945 and 1947–1948, Japan did not have any food or clothing, and asked the United States for anything it had. The Japanese government seemed to have no role other than requesting this aid during those years. Yoshida, as Japan's leader at the time, likely felt that he could not now act ungrateful. Next, Robertson asked about reparations to Southeast Asia. Ikeda explained that reparations were linked to future friendly relations and trade, and thus he hoped to have them taken care of as soon as possible. When Ikeda explained that Foreign Minister Okazaki was at that very moment visiting those countries to talk about this matter, Budget Director Dodge opened his mouth and said,

> In my experiences with traveling to Japan, the Japanese appear to have forgotten all of the relief supplies America sent Japan during the Occupation period. Even now on defense issues, it really should be Japan itself paying for new defense capabilities. For those that supposedly understand the issue, even they think that it is normal for Japan to be asking the United States to loan or give aircraft or destroyers, the most expensive things to make, to Japan. For others, there is a tendency to view it as representing America's evil ambitions. I just can't understand it.

For Dodge, this was a reasonable explanation. At the time of the San Francisco Peace Conference, GARIOA was the first thing he raised, as he did in Mexico. As discussed earlier, according to the decision of the Far Eastern Committee during the Occupation, the first obligation of Japan was to pay back the GARIOA, followed by reparations if there were any ability to pay left.

Moreover, America provided these loans in dollars, but there did not appear to be any discussion as to how to pay them back. Wasn't there a plan to pay back part of the loans in yen, to be used toward the stationing of U.S. forces in Japan or to the State Department's representation in Japan, in which a part of the money would be used in Japan and reinvested there? If such a plan existed, when the Defense budget got cut, the government could explain that the money was that which was being repaid by Japan in any case and did not represent a new program. I assumed that some sort of arrangement existed from that time along these lines.

[Charles A.] Sullivan, representing the Department of Defense, asked the following question:

In Japan, there is the argument that rearming is against the Constitution. In addition, you yourself Mr. Ikeda appear to hold the opinion that a Self Defense force that goes beyond a defensive nature gets into constitutional questions. However, I have heard that Prime Minister Yoshida and Progressive Party President Shigemitsu recently met and agreement was reached on the need to increase Japan's defense capabilities. If this is correct, won't Japan's views on this matter change as a result of the meeting between Yoshida and Shigemitsu?

IKEDA-ROBERTSON EXCHANGE
ON "WAR POTENTIAL"

The reason our mission planned to come to the United States after the Yoshida-Shigemitsu meeting was that when the mission explained the future of the problem of defense to the American side and we were asked to explain why we could not handle any additional responsibilities, it was necessary to have the support of the Progressive Party as well because the strength of the Yoshida Cabinet alone was not enough. In other words, it was necessary to convince the U.S. side that this was truly Japan's position. However, I must be honest in saying that we did have a trick up our sleeves. In other words, if both men were to meet and come to an agreement on a statement, then in the world of Japanese journalism, the simple fact that they met would create a huge stir. For those Americans in Washington dealing with Japan, it would be reported that as a very rare meeting.[8] Even if it was learned later that the substance of the discussions was not anything important (I am not making light of this meeting because it in fact lead to the approach and eventual merger of the two parties), for the time being it was understood to be significant. I would not be telling the truth if I were to say that we did not think of the symbolic effect that it would have.

Thus, of course Sullivan's question arose, and in America the strong desire existed that "Japan was finally about to get serious on defense." But we hoped to use the opposition to "an unacceptable and impossible defense program" to support our position. In response to Sullivan, Ikeda stated:

> At the Yoshida-Shigemitsu meeting, it was promised that a "long-term defense plan" would be prepared. It seems that you think Liberal Party President Yoshida accepted the Progressive Party's interpretation of changing the Safety Force to a Self Defense Force to mean "war potential," but no where has Yoshida made such a promise. The Liberal Party's position is that anything approaching "war potential" is a constitutional issue, and that changing the name of the Safety Force to the Self Defense Force still requires it to be below the level of "war potential."

However, even Japanese would question this interesting explanation. Because we were in the middle of the debate, we believed what we were saying, but the American side did not seem to understand our explanation. It could not be helped if they did not understand it, I thought. Because of this, Robertson continued by stating, "It can not be war potential, but it is okay if it is below war potential. Just where exactly do you draw the line? If 100,000 are okay, but 300,000 is bad, why? Maybe, you will say that now, 100,000 is all that is possible, and a couple of years from now, 'well, perhaps up to 300,000 is permissible.' It is like a rainbow. If you go to the end of it, you think you will find what you are looking for when in fact you won't." His analogy was quite interesting. Ikeda responded:

> In China there is a saying about fifty steps and one hundred steps, which means there is not a big difference in things. It is a vague, but in real world politics, the difference between one hundred steps and fifty is fifty steps, a big difference. Actual problems are not cleanly divided between "quantity" and "quality." At some point, the problem of "quantity" changes to one of "quality." In addition to the feelings among the people and our actual economic level is the Constitution. There is a point to which certain things are permitted, but after which, they are not. I have been Finance Minister for a number of years and have been involved in providing funds from the budget. I have often told people that I will give say a certain amount of money for something, but not any more. In discussing this with you, you might ask why not approve 10 million dollars? If that is the case then no decision can be reached. As you are aware, Director Dodge, who is involved in forming budgets, is present here.

With this everyone laughed. The exchange continued. Robertson asked Ikeda, "Does this mean that if Japan does not revise its Constitution, it can not pursue full-scale rearmament?" Ikeda answered, "I myself interpret it that way. In any case, constitutional revision is not a problem that can be discussed so lightly." Next, Robertson asked, "How many years do you think it will be before the Constitution can be revised?" Ikeda said, "I do not think the Constitution can easily be revised. Even if the Lower House was interested, the term of the Upper House is six years, and for the next two-and-a-half years, the issue absolutely won't come up. Even if an election is called two-and-a-half years from now, we still won't know what will happen. So, the only way to go about increasing Japan's defense capabilities is by limited, provisional planning." Robertson then asked, "The principle of defending a country by oneself is one that I do not think the current Cabinet of Japan rejects. Is Japan conducting any public relations to get the people to gradually accept this idea?" Ikeda replied,

We have no objection to that principle. Recently, the most effective enlightenment regarding this principle was when President Rhee of South Korea illegally occupied Takeshima. Seeing this, many people in Japan likely realized the need for self-defense. But what must not be done is undercutting the standard of living by pushing defense. This would be unacceptable. Japan just does not have the means to do so right now. Instead, it is necessary to raise the standard of living through which people would come to recognize that there is something worth protecting. This would be effective in developing a healthy defense consciousness among the people.

Dodge and Robertson then asked about Japan's economic situation, including a question about trade with India. We did not get into a deep discussion about India, but as mentioned earlier, President Black of the World Bank had asked about India's furnaces last year in Mexico.[9] Over the past two or three years, India had become a source of constant concern for the United States (as it is now). Robertson next mentioned that "Japan is very much concerned with introducing foreign investment, and has even created new laws for it. Despite this, whenever an actual opportunity arises, Japan always talks about the negative effects on its domestic industry or says that its shares are not enough," and asked, "Why is this?"

This was a question that we did not want to have to answer. When Prime Minister Yoshida went to the United States the next year, he was asked the same question, and Minister for International Trade and Industry Aichi was asked the same thing by the Commerce Department, as is discussed later. From my vantage point, the issue of bringing in foreign currency was something that only Prime Minister Yoshida was interested in. Even Ikeda and

Aichi, two of Yoshida's most trusted lieutenants, were not truly enthusiastic about.

From my subjective point of view, I think Prime Minister Yoshida was the only one who was so bold in his thinking on this issue at the time. Yoshida's belief was that if Americans brought money to Japan, they would use Japanese labor to do the work. There was nothing wrong with that. Moreover, if the products made were then shipped to Southeast Asia, Japan would be at the center of this trading framework for the region. While it would be problematic if some items produced were harmful to the people of Japan, but this would hardly happen. Without this type of trade and foreign investment, the only things Japan could produce would be those items that really did not make too much of a difference, such as orange juice. For industries that would be unduly affected by foreign currency, special provisions could be made. Some voices of opposition emerge arguing that the Japanese enterprises won't be able to compete if more technical or well-known brands are introduced into Japan, but that is like saying it is necessary to ban the importation of cars to protect the rickshaw businesses.

This was essentially Yoshida's thinking, and why each of his cabinets always included "the introduction of foreign investment" in its policies. Even Ikeda and Aichi could not really oppose it. Both of them had served as Ministers of Trade and Industry and were familiar with just how weak Japanese industries were and what the effect would be on them if the gateways to Japan were to open. This perspective, the need to protect Japanese industries, is probably the reason why they could not go along with Yoshida on this issue.

From America's point of view, that way of thinking—protecting domestic industries—was "protectionism." The U.S. side would regularly criticize this saying, your country's Prime Minister is not pursuing protectionism, and your domestic laws were not written that way. Every time I heard this I thought to myself, what America says is correct. Either we need to align the actual contents with the official policy, or we need to drop the official policy (incidentally, whenever this issue came up in the Diet, the position of the Diet was, and is now, protectionist).

Toward the end of the discussion, the U.S. side inquired, "Based on your explanation it would be impossible to undertake full rearmament due to the connection with the constitution, but you are prepared to have detailed discussions on a 'Gradual Defense Program (*Zanshinteki Boei Keikaku*)' that would not go as far as that?" To this, Ikeda carefully answered, "We would like to study the possibility after considering in the future the various proposals for MSA and procurement from Japan." In other words, Ikeda was saying that it was necessary for us to see their hand first. The conference ended for the day on this note.

THE DULLES-IKEDA MEETING

At 4:00 p.m., Ambassador Araki led us to the State Department for a meeting with Secretary of State Dulles. Ikeda stated:

As a Japanese, I would like to express my deep appreciation for the show of friendliness that the Crown Prince received from the citizens of the United States during his recent visit to America. On this trip, I have come to exchange opinions on some issues of concern between Japan and the United States as a private representative of Prime Minister Yoshida. In particular, on the problem of increasing its self-defense strength, just before we departed Yoshida and Shigemitsu met as you probably know.

Dulles replied, "When I met with Prime Minister Yoshida recently in Tokyo, I understood he was thinking of visiting the United States and I told him we would welcome it. In particular, it would be even better if he had a strong conservative coalition supporting him when he came." (This seems to suggest that he desired a conservative merger.) To this, Ikeda responded, "I will encourage him to come after my talks here finish and the political situation stabilizes in Japan." Dulles then noted,

My job has taken me all around the world. I have seen in many countries that when a government does not have a majority in its parliament, its leaders have to use their heads and energy toward lining up enough support on crucial votes. This is one of the weaknesses of democracy, but lining up votes is the job of a politician, not that of a statesman. I look forward to the day when the political situation in Japan stabilizes and Prime Minister Yoshida can come here as a true statesman.

He continued, "My relationship with Japan is deep, from around the time of the peace treaty and I believe the Japanese to be an outstanding people. I am eagerly looking forward to when Japan is able to assume a leadership role in the Far East. I may ask a lot of Japan, and appear to be somewhat impatient. But, I want you to understand that this is because I think so highly of Japan." It was unusual for Dulles to be so humble, as his last comment was. This was probably because he realized that his comments, as introduced before, that Japan's defense efforts were not enough and that its Safety Forces should be increased to 350,000 had generated a great deal of outrage in Japan.

The next meeting with Robertson was scheduled for October 8, so on October 7, we were invited to Blair House and asked by Foreign Operations Administration Director [Harold E.] Stassen about India again. On the afternoon of the 8th, we visited Acting Secretary of the Treasury [W. Randolph] Burgess. Burgess had been Chairman of National City Bank, and was one of America's most prominent bankers. He had been asked by President Eisenhower to help Treasury Secretary [George M.] Humphrey. The question of the recovery of the convertibility of the British pound came up. Apparently there was much interest worldwide in America's granting 4 billion dollars in credit to Sir [John Maynard] Keynes' Britain. The subject of the Japanese yen convertibility also came up, but the Japanese economy at the time was experiencing inflation from the effects of the Korean War, and unlike today, there was no guarantee that the yen would be convertible in the future. As Dodge pointed out at a meeting some days later, the exchange rate for yen on the black market in Hong Kong was 20 percent higher (360 yen to the dollar versus 442 yen to the dollar at the official rate). Compared to the 390 yen of exactly a year before, it was a time of miserable performance even in the black market.

THE OCTOBER 8, 1953, MEMORANDUM

As a result of our internal discussions about how to proceed with our meetings after October 8, we agreed "defense" should be the last issue taken up, with economic issues introduced first as we discussed in the past in order to bring the other side into our way of thinking. In order to do so, we prepared one document. This memo was meant to confirm the thinking of the U.S. side with regard to economic issues, and was subsequently named the October 8, 1953, memorandum.

Japan's Memo of October 8, 1953

A summary of the memo is introduced below. (In response, the United States prepared a detailed memorandum, which is introduced later.)

1. It is necessary to examine what sort of fiscal problems will emerge in the future if Japan were to develop a long-term defense program. The biggest one will likely be reparations. Reparations are directly related to the future prosperity of Southeast Asia, and as such, Japan is interested in the U.S. opinion.
2. The main countries calling for reparations are the Philippines, Indonesia, and Burma. They are requesting a large figure and appear not to be aware of the limitations in Article 14 (Reparations) of the San Francisco Peace Treaty.
3. Relating to this reparations problem,
   a. The possibility of matching U.S. aid to Southeast Asia with reparations.
   b. If the United States is the key point in developing Southeast Asia, Japan would like the U.S. to recognize Japanese financial participation.
   c. If either Japan or a country in Southeast Asia were to establish a joint venture, would the United States be willing to participate?

4. We would like Japan's economic participation be considered in the rebuilding of South Korea.
5. We are still grateful for the GARIOA aid, but we currently have and will have in the future several financial obligations in the future that we must give priority to. This is more so in light of the current discussion on the defense problem.
6. Regarding MSA aid,
   a. Will MSA aid to Japan included more than just finished items (so-called end item) such as destroyers and jets, such as that which "is not directly related to defense," as seen in the aid given to countries in Europe?
   b. The Defense Department and Foreign Operations Administration is expected to undergo structural changes shortly. Is it all right to assume that MSA aid will not be suddenly cut off?
7. Japan is attempting many ways to increase domestic savings, but it does not seem to be enough to allow for the modernization of facilities and the improvement in productivity. As a result, the provision of capital to Japan— whether by direct investment or loans—is desired. Moreover, we hope that the United States will encourage the Import-Export Bank and World Bank located in Washington, D.C., to do the same.

The U.S. side clearly wanted to jump into discussions on defense planning, and looking at the memo now, it reeks of being an attempt to beat around the bush. Especially on the issue of GARIOA, the attempt to explain the need to not pay it in order to make funds available for defense likely really annoyed the other side. This document was passed out at the meeting on October 8. A large part of the meeting focused mostly on military matters, as originally planned.

Assistant Secretary of Defense [Frank C.] Nash explained the American military's view of the situation in the Far East. He was full of confidence and energy, giving his audience the somewhat strange feeling of being on a jet.

HOW WOULD THE SOVIET UNION INVADE JAPAN?

According to Nash,

The Soviet Union has between 500,000 and 600,000 ground troops in the Far East, and 5,000 to 6,000 warplanes, including MIG fighters as well as TU4 and IL24 bombers. For the Soviet Union today, if bombers were launched from the area of Siberia, MIG fighter escort support would be difficult. For a long time, this has been one of the headaches for Soviet strategy toward Japan. For this reason it is likely the Soviet Union would open hostilities on the Korean peninsula and invade South Korea. By doing so, they would be able to establish a forward air base for their MIG fighters, from which they could launch raids into at least the heart of western Japan. If the Soviet Union started a war with Japan, it would likely be executed like Hitler's blitzkrieg. First, the Soviet Union would launch an airborne and amphibious attack on Northern Japan, probably Hokkaido, by dropping troops in by parachute, in an attempt to secure an air base. Around the same time, amphibious operations would also be conducted at several locations on the Sea of Japan side. The U.S. has concluded that ten divisions of 325,000 ground troops would be necessary in Japan to protect it against such an attack. For Japan, however, it is difficult to move ground troops capable of railway, road, and bridge building. Moreover, according to the reports of some experts, there are not many roads and bridges on which tanks can move easily. Likewise, it is not easy to move ground forces from Kyushu up to Hokkaido. It would be up to the Soviets to decide where they would land forces on the Japanese coast, and thus it would be necessary to have some defensive force set up. Because of this, and the fact that the coast is long and the sea approaches wide, it will be necessary to place forces at certain places along this wide area.

Nash's explanation was along the above lines, but it was too technical. Moreover, Japan did not have this sort of military intelligence at the time, and so it was like an amateur trying to debate a professional. We basically just let the explanation go on without really paying attention.

After he finished his explanation, [Norman] Paul, an expert on MSA, spoke in general terms the type of military aid planned for Japan. According to his comments, "There are extra funds in this year's fiscal year (the fiscal year runs from July this year to the end of June 1954) that can be used. Unfortunately, those funds can not be applied next year, so if you are going to use it, now is the chance." He continued,

We have provided thirty frigates and fifty landing craft, all of which are on loan. As for aircraft, because U.S. production capabilities are not meeting demand, and the fact that Japan has no trained pilots at the moment, we will send training planes immediately once the actual training begins. Funding for pilot training is already allocated in the MSA budget. Regarding ground forces, this fiscal year we will fully prepare for the initial equipping of the current force, namely 110,000 men (in America, this translates as four divisions), and increase the forces by 70,000. Because we have to transfer the equipment and weapons by the end of this fiscal year, in other words the end of next June, if the term is extended at all, it will require the consent of the Congress. (He added that there was a fear of criticism by Congress if their consent was needed a second time because both South Korea and Taiwan needed a lot of funding, and fast.) We have already begun preparing next year's budget requests, but in order to do it, we need to be able to explain Japan's plans for its defense build-up and where our assistance is to go. Without being able to do so, our requests would not make it past the budget office or the Congress. Therefore, we would like it if the Safety Agency and U.S. forces in Japan could begin consultations immediately. This is not interfering with Japan's internal affairs, as this is how it is done with the countries of Europe and we would like to approach it similarly. If long-term plans could be established, these could be reviewed each year. At that time, the relationship between the defense budget and the overall budget, the proportion between defense spending and national income, revenue and the overall taxation system, the possibility of inflation, and the defense procurement industry could all be examined together. Finally, one thing that our defense officials feel is that Japanese defense efforts, in proportion to its economic power, are not enough. Over the past year, Japan's defense spending was approximately 100 billion yen. This represents only two percent of Japan's Gross National Product. This year as well, it looks to be about the same. The United States government thinks that Japan can currently double the money it is spending on defense. As a result of the Korean War, Japan has experienced a good economy, which makes us believe that Japan is more capable than ever to increase its defense spending. When we approach our Congress to request the funds for assistance to Japan, we have to be in the position to explain that Japan, like other countries, is doing its utmost in the area of defense.

At the end, Robertson kindly discussed in detail the prospects for the ceasefire on the Korean Peninsula and on his talks with South Korean President Rhee, which I will not include here. The conference ended at 4:30 p.m. this day.

THE PENTAGON PLAN

The third conference was held on October 12. Sullivan, representing the Pentagon, explained the U.S. Pentagon-drafted vision of Japan's defense forces. There were many instances when amateurs like us had no idea what was being said.

1. Air forces
Interceptors—9 squadrons/225 planes
All-weather planes—3 squadrons/75 planes
Fighter bombers—6 squadrons/150 planes
Tactical reconnaissance—3 squadrons/54 planes
Transport—6 squadrons/96 planes
Others—200 planes
Total—800 planes
However it would take three to four years for all of these to be ready. Personnel would number 30,000. In the current Fiscal Year, the focus

would be on pilot training. The United States would provide T33s for practice and open a pilot development school.

2. Maritime forces

Frigates—18 ships

Landing craft—50 ships

Minesweepers—40 ships

Personnel would number about 13,500, but the plan was still tentative.

When we asked what would be done about escort destroyers, Sullivan said he thought Japan's shipbuilding capacities would be able to handle it.

3. Ground forces

Nash's statement of 325,000 was planned to take the following shape:

By the end of June 1954, six divisions

By the end of June 1955, eight divisions

By the end of June 1956, ten divisions

However, Sullivan's explanation seemed to have been a simple reiteration of the report of the U.S. military in Tokyo, and quite shaky. In addition, the number 325,000 was not one that was methodically solid, but strongly appeared to be one that was a sort of objective, picked out of the blue. Right around this time, Robertson stated, "Now that the U.S. Defense Department's views have been explained, I would like to invite Mr. Ikeda to present his ideas, if he has any, unofficially if necessary."

By then, we had said what needed to be said, and gained a good idea about what the U.S. side was thinking. If the Defense Department's plan could be so shoddy, we began to think, then if we presented our ideas, we could probably debate them to a draw. "I understand," Ikeda began. "We will submit our ideas by lunchtime tomorrow to Mr. Robertson. But, they would be only my ideas, and I can provide only one copy. I want you, Mr. Robertson, to make only enough copies as you think appropriate." After making this promise, Ikeda left.

In truth, our knowledge of defense issues was superficial at best, and we probably should have brought a specialist from the Safety Agency. However, as mentioned before, the relationship between the Safety Agency and the U.S. military was very close, and a lot of information would get to Washington. Because of this, we decided not to bring anyone along. As a result, in the meetings, we were able to judge on our own for the most part the extent of Defense Department thinking. To help with technical decisions, we brought Murakami of the Legal Section, Budget Bureau, Ministry of Finance, who had been studying defense issues, with us. In many ways, we ended up relying heavily on Financial Commissioner Suzuki and this Murakami.

THE TRUTH ABOUT THE "IKEDA DEFENSE PROGRAM"

Below, I will briefly introduce the "Personal Ideas of Ikeda for Japan's Five-Year Defense Program," which became a very hot topic at the time. This was given to Mr. Robertson on October 13. The study is quite long and technical, looking at strategic scenarios and related weaponry. It stated:

The following is the result of Ikeda Hayato's personal study of Japan's defense program. It reflects recent Japanese government thinking based on information available in Japan, but is not an official study or a final one.

1. **Land forces.** Land forces will be increased to 180,000 over a three-year period, beginning next fiscal year. These will made up of 10 divisions and two artillery and tank groups.
2. **Maritime forces.** Two hundred ten vessels, approximately 156,550 tons, will be built over a five-year period. Of these, 74 will be escort ships and 31 will be minesweepers. Approximately 31,300 personnel will be required.
3. **Air forces.** Over the next five years, 518 aircraft will be maintained. The premier aircraft will be two wings of jet fighter-bombers (150 F84Gs), one wing of jet all-weather fighters (36 F94Cs), and 218 others, as well as 300 trainers. Personnel required would be 7,600.
4. **Air base forces.** Air control and air warning groups (i.e. radar) would be created, as would one air base supply wing. Over a five-year period, 13,000 people would be hired.
5. **Cost:** The cost for the establishment of the above forces would cost approximately 900 billion yen, of which Japan would pay 620 billion yen. The United States would be responsible for the remaining balance of 280 billion. However, the majority of the U.S. balance was in ships, aircraft, and weapons and these were calculated at book price, which came to approximately 800 million dollars.

The above was a brief summary of Ikeda's personal ideas. When compared to the U.S. plan the most different point about it was the fact that we planned for our ground forces to number 180,000 and their plan shows them at 325,000. Of note, both our side and the U.S. side agreed on the need for ten divisions. The key to this problem was that the U.S. side calculated the strength of one division at 32,500, and we believed it to be 18,000. This difference was clear to even laymen like us. Experts from both sides discussed this issue on several occasions. However, frankly speaking, I did not understand all the details. After all, the military today is completely different from the military we saw after the China Incident through the Greater East Asia War.

Yet, I, an amateur in these matters, will try to explain, however, superficially, what was discussed. In order for a combat force to move into a battle zone, large rear area support forces, such as maintenance and supply, as well as artillery, engineering, tank, technical assets, are necessary. Of these, artillery and tanks are of course absolutely vital. However, to give an extreme example, it would be hard to say Coca Cola, which the U.S. military has everywhere it goes, is necessary for the defense of Japan. Moreover, within logistic units, large teams for washing clothes would not be necessary when smaller ones could be used.

In addition, the biggest difference is the fact that each time the U.S. military goes on one of its missions abroad (of course, they have not fought or had to fight an enemy on its shores), it tends to bring everything with it. In the case of our Safety Force, they are not intended to go abroad. If their vehicles were to break, they could just take them to a local repair shop. It would not be necessary to bring a fully equipped maintenance team. In this sense it would be quite possible to do without military-owned and -managed assets and to get the help of the civilian sector if an enemy were to invade Japan. This is the biggest difference between an expeditionary military and that which fights on the home ground. As a result, it is possible to greatly reduce rear area support forces.

In order to resolve the problem over the number of personnel for the division (experts supposedly call this a division slice), it is necessary to understand that of the 32,500 making up a U.S. division, 20,000 are combat troops, whereas a division in the Japanese Safety Forces is comprised of 27,500 persons, of which about 17,000 are combat forces. So, if these were reduced, the size of a Japan Safety Force division could be about 18,000, including rear area support forces. In the North Atlantic Treaty Organization today, the size of a peacetime division is about 18,000. I apologize for this layman's explanation, but this was the essence of our position. It was with this perspective that the number 18,000, which would appear quite often, originated.

We visited Congressman [Walter H.] Judd of Minnesota.[10] This person, who was quite knowledgeable about Asia, said to the effect: "The United States gave the islands nearby Japan to the Soviet Union as part of the Yalta Agreement, and in the postwar, we stripped Japan to the bone by the new Constitution. And now we are telling Japan to 'Stand Up to the Soviet Union,' but we cannot treat Japan like a puppet this way. Rather than the U.S. calling on Japan to do this or do that, it would be better if it helped Japan do what it wants to do."

On the 14th, we met at the State Department with Deputy Undersecretary [Robert D.] Murphy, who was formerly the U.S. Ambassador to Japan. Because Robertson was out on another trip, Dodge led the discussions in the afternoon. At this time, Dodge gave us an eight-part opinion paper entitled "Measures Regarding the Strengthening of the Japanese Economy." It appears that the paper was in response to our memorandum of October 8, as introduced above.

On the morning of October 15, Major General [Lloyd B.] Brown from the Pentagon attended the meeting with three others to discuss from an expert's perspective the memorandum, "Personal Ideas of Ikeda for Japan's Five-Year Defense Program," that was sent to Robertson on the 13th. They seemed to have recognized that the Japanese proposal was well done despite not having spent much money in making it, and expressed the opinions that in addition to the question of the division slice, it was clear that Japan's defense forces were simply for defensive purposes and thus bombers should be reduced and interceptors increased, and that in order to defend industrial areas, it would be necessary to maintain anti-aircraft weapons.

In the afternoon that day, experts on the regulations of MSA met. For the first time since we came to Washington, D.C., I realized the laws surrounding Economic Cooperation Administration (ECA) and MSA were probably quite complicated and officials only knew that which directly related to their own work. If we asked a question, there is a good chance that they would not be able to answer it. Those who knew the laws as a whole were really limited to the few officials actually dealing with it. Other than these officials, the ones that really knew it were the lawyers that were employed by the embassies of other countries receiving MSA. They had really studied the issue.

In the discussions we had that day with the MSA legal specialists, we came to realize that due to the regulations of MSA beginning that year, the only support we could receive was military in nature, mostly things such as battleships and aircraft that would not fill the void in the economy. Indeed, we discovered the need to develop a new bilateral agreement if Japan use any funds from the proceeds of sales of surplus agricultural goods (as per Article 550 of the MSA) "for the strengthening of the basis of Japanese industry." In other words, while the agreement for the sale of surplus agricultural goods fell under the legal structure of the MSA, were some of the proceeds to be used for economic assistance to Japan for other than military matters, then a new agreement would have to be signed. Moreover, this new agreement would not fall under the scope of the purely military nature of MSA, but under the ECA as an economic agreement. We discovered this after groping in the dark for more than an hour.

To tell the truth, I imagine it is quite difficult to understand the issue just from what was written above, but the atmosphere in Washington was that Japan did not need any economic assistance, only military assistance was enough. This opinion had made its way to Japan some months before. However, even if military aid came, it would not have any impact on the economy. Estimates were that the Ikeda Mission would not be able to return with an economic aid package signed. But we also had our reason and we wanted to sign an economic assistance agreement using the route of the ECA. Even if we did not have a set figure in mind, we felt that it was necessary to create the framework to receive such aid because without it we might not be able to receive any "non-military economic assistance." On the other hand, within the Congress in Washington, the strong opinion was being heard that the countries of the world had begun to recover economically and therefore economic aid was no longer necessary. As a result, the feeling was that the government should not sign new economic agreements with countries simply to create such frameworks if there was no need.

At the risk of sounding melodramatic, we went through a great deal of hardship in order to make and sign an agreement on this framework. Around this time, over the past ten days, an outstanding specialist from the Finance Ministry, Suzuki, really worked hard, discovering a recently example of an economic agreement signed in exchange for bases between the United States and Spain's Generalissimo Francisco Franco Bahamonde. Brandishing this "Economic Assistance Agreement," we began discussions on such an economic aid agreement. (As a result these efforts, by February 1954, in addition to an Agricultural Purchase Agreement, a "Bilateral Agreement based on the Economic Agreement based on the Mutual Security Act" was prepared. The reason that this agreement had "As Based on the MSA Law" in its name was because the laws of the ECA, which until then had been the economic assistance law, continued as a part of the MSA Law.)

I have already explained in detail the October 8 memorandum above. On this day, in the evening of October 15, the U.S. side presented a detailed response.

The U.S. Response

I will introduce in short outline form the response of the U.S. side in the order of our questions.

1. **Reparations and cooperative relations between Southeast Asia and Japan.** The U.S. desires a quick resolution to the problem of reparations. (We interpreted this to mean that the U.S. had approved our deviating from the reparations provisions of Article 14 of the Peace Treaty.) However, regarding the request that the payment of Japanese aid be linked as much as possible to the development plans of these countries, we are uncertain as to what role the U.S. can play as the countries are responsible on their own for developing and implementing these plans. Next, regarding the desire to allow Japanese capital and technical involvement in countries where the U.S. is currently giving aid, this has been the U.S. approach for some time and we

have been encouraging these countries to do so. We will continue to do so. If you look at last fiscal year, for example, in the aid that the U.S. gave these countries, some 20 million dollars made it to Japan. Moreover, in the military aid to these countries (not including Korea and Japan itself), some 24 million dollars were paid to Japan. Washington's basic policy is to allow Japanese bidding on projects when there is no problem with Japanese products in quality, price, and availability. Finally, regarding the desire for U.S. investment in joint venture projects between Japan and the countries of Southeast Asia, we would like to hear more about any specific plans.

2. **Regarding the use of Japan in planning for South Korea's reconstruction.** The first goal of the reconstruction of South Korea is seen in its name — the reconstruction of South Korea. As such, what can be procured from South Korea should be procured from there. The U.S. is doing its best in that regard. Of course, sometimes, it is necessary to procure things from Japan, but that amount is unknown (the answer to this question was very short and brusque, and suggested just how much America wanted to avoid the emotional problems between Japan and Korea).

3. **Regarding the repayment of GARIOA.** The argument put forth by the United States was expected, and good. Both your country and the United States recognized at the time of the signing of the peace treaty that this was a financial problem necessitating further discussion. Moreover, both were in agreement about the need to resolve the issue as early as possible. We were aware that Japan had many difficult issues to deal with on the eve of independence and so we did not push the issue any more at the time. However, it has now been more than two years since you (Minister Ikeda) and Dodge spoke on this issue in San Francisco. During these two years, your country has succeeded in dealing with the issue of foreign loans. Moreover, during this time, it is a fact that the procurement from Korean War has directly contributed two billion dollars to Japan's economy. Furthermore, we have already reached an understanding with West Germany with regard to repaying this aid. In light of this, when a solution to this issue gets delayed, our administration gets severely criticized by Congress. Moreover, we believe you fully recognize that we have no way to justify the delay. Even now at this stage, Japan says that it has many obligations and that it wishes to dispose of them first. However, we cannot wait until then. As a result, I (Robertson) desire that by the end of these discussions, an agreement is reached between us on the following two items:
   1. Representatives from our two countries will meet at an appropriate time and place to enter into discussions on GARIOA repayment.
   2. At this time, they will decide the total to be repaid, the interest, and the years to repay.

4. **Regarding the composition of MSA.** The essence of MSA is military in nature, and as you know, it is currently being used to finish production of planes and ships. However, while this has been the case in the past, though the support of the Japanese industrial economy by procurement from Japan of military

items for Japan and other countries, so-called offshore procurement, some $55 million have gone into the Japanese economy. Of this, $24 million worth was for procurement given to countries other than Japan itself. This year, the planning is still being finalized, but the figures are expected to grow dramatically. Within MSA, there was the Contact Clearing House Service, to handle exchanges of information about investment between countries, and the Investment Guarantee Program, a system to protect investments. However, the newest thing about it was the ability to pay for offshore procurement in local currency due to the "Purchasing of Surplus Agriculture," newly created under the Section 550 of the Mutual Security Act. This was to be used entirely or for the most part for military objectives (Author's note: In fact, in our country's case, beginning in the initial fiscal year, up to 20 percent could be used for non-military matters, and in the second fiscal year, in other words, at the time of the Yoshida-Eisenhower Summit meeting, introduced later, up to 60 percent was allowed for non-military items.) in order, I believe, to assist in the wake of the reduction of offshore procurements. In Japan's case, if you desire and are ready to enter into detailed negotiations, it is probably correct to think about the extent of the participation of each country as about $15 million. (Author's note: The result for us was $50 million.)

5. **Introduction of foreign currency and loans.** The view that because yen is lacking in Japan you need to introduce dollars is mistaken, the U.S. side stated. What things that can only be purchased by dollars, such as machinery and facilities, Japan will need to consider loans for. For everything else, it is necessary to work harder at saving money. In general, the World Bank provides long-term loans, and one for $40 million for the thermal plant is to be signed today or so. The Import-Export Bank is expected to come to an agreement on a loan of $60 million for cotton soon. After this, the U.S. side argued that it was necessary for the Japanese government to encourage personal investing and pointed out that the law on the introduction of foreign currency was not being carried out in spirit (as explained in detail earlier). Moreover, it pointed out that "while it appears the Japanese government welcomes foreign investment on technology and infrastructure, it is overly nervous about acquisition of stocks and thus is greatly limiting the desire of investors." In fact, many of these problems remain unresolved today. Finally, the U.S. side stated its desire that with "the Treaty of Friendship, Commerce, and Navigation about to go into force, the problem of the so-called 'national treatment' will emerge. If you truly welcome investment, then you will need to consider what to do."

After the explanation of the document in its entirety, Robertson spoke out and raised the "GARIOA problem" again, strongly urging that a concrete decision be made about where and when in the future, discussions can begin on it. Speaking with officials from the State Department later, Robertson's comment had not been prearranged during their preparatory meetings and therefore the U.S. participants were quite surprised by it. For informational purposes, I learned that Robertson desired to wrap up discussions on the issue by the middle of next February after consultations with the Japanese side.

In response, Ikeda stated that he understood Robertson's desire, and that he had in fact spoken with Dodge on this matter several times since the San Francisco conference. However, this time, he came as the Prime Minister's personal emissary and would have to relay the request to the Japanese government by telegram. However, at this moment, he did not have the authority to respond on behalf of the Japanese government. Robertson's expression did not appear to change, but we learned later that he was very angry.

THE TRUE POSITION OF THE JAPANESE SIDE— THE OCTOBER 19TH MEMORANDUM

Over the past ten or so days, the two countries had said what they wanted to say and heard for the most part what they wanted to learn from each other. For several hours over the next two days, our side met with Ambassador Araki to discuss how we wanted to proceed with the talks. It was too early to write the final version of the joint statement. On all of the points, it was unclear that there had been a final meeting of the minds between the two countries.

From our perspective, on the issue of size of the Safety Forces, neither side won or lost the debate as to whether they should number 325,000 or 180,000. We also learned about how much we could expect in aid from MSA. Moreover, it looked like we could probably sign some sort of "Economic Aid Agreement," as part of the ECA, explained before. We began to think that it looked like we should buy as much surplus agricultural goods as possible if the money earned could be used for non-military items.

As a result of the meetings on the Japanese side, we were able to clarify our understanding gained in the discussions. We decided to include our thoughts and desires in a memorandum to be given to Robertson prior to the next conference. We used the weekend to begin drafting this document. The memorandum was a long one, and below is a synopsis of it. However, before introducing it, I wish to preface it with a few points.

Namely, the final joint statement was based on only the points on which both sides found agreement. The document we prepared and is introduced below concerns only the opinions of the Japanese side.

In addition, in response to this document (which is called the October 19 memorandum), the U.S. side prepared its own response, stating the points it wanted to make. That arrived on October 22, and will also be introduced later. In other words, these two memorandums were in no means official documents and were not "diplomatic documents." As a result, the U.S. side said that it should not be seen representing the official U.S. position. Of course, it goes without saying that we were not the official representatives of the Japanese government either. However, there is no doubt that the memorandum did help to give us an understanding of just what the U.S. position was. The October 19 Japanese Memorandum was handed to Assistant Secretary Robertson that afternoon at 5 p.m., and read as follows:

> During the course of the past several meetings, the positions of both sides have become clear for the most part. This document clarifies what points have been agreed to and those that remain to be worked out, based on the order of the agenda.

I. **Japanese defense and U.S. aid**
  A. The Japanese representatives explained the four restrictions on Japan's fully possessing defense capabilities. Namely, these are legal, political (or social), economic, and physical restrictions.
    1. Legal restrictions, those found in the Constitution such as Article 9, are quite clear. Because amending the Constitution is quite difficult, even if Japan's political leaders saw the need to revise the Constitution, there is little likelihood that this will happen in the near future.
    2. Sociopolitical restrictions are those that resulted from the thorough "peace education" policies adopted during the occupation. Most Japanese are enthused with the idea of "not bearing arms." In particular, those that were educated in this way in their youth are now becoming adults.
    3. Nothing more really needs to be said about the economic limitations. While the proportion of Japan's defense spending is said to be small in comparison to its national income, this is said by people who do not know the Engle Coefficient. The people who lost fathers and sons in the war faced defeat and had to survive on their own. The first step in true defense must be the provision of social protection of these people. However, this requires a great deal of funds. Typhoons and other natural disasters are a regular feature of Japan. With an overall budget of just one trillion yen, Japan already faces 150 billion yen in damage from disasters this year.
    4. Physical limitations relate to the fact that even if we developed a program to increase the numbers of the National Safety Forces, we would not be able to raise such a force. We cannot just let anyone enter the NSF, which is charged with the security of the country. As a result of the peace education described above, there are very few young men who would willingly step forward and join such a force. Moreover, it would be difficult to protect the force against elements harboring inappropriate ideologies. For Communists, there would be

no better place to be able to wield a gun and do their dirty work. If the draft were initiated, this would clearly fly in the face of constitutional restrictions.

B. The representatives of both countries acknowledged these restrictions. As a result:

  1. They agreed that even to maintain the existing level of Japanese defense, a major level of military aid was necessary. Moreover, regarding this, the Japanese side presented a plan to possess a force of approximately this level. In response to this proposal, the U.S. side pointed out it was still too little, but through continued consultations, a conclusion both sides would be happy with was possible. The Japanese side stated it would like to know to what extent and at what point would aid be forthcoming.

  2. The U.S. recognized that as Japan gradually increased its defense capacities, it could also gradually reduce its defense spending.

  3. The Japanese government must work to enlighten the Japanese people in general to accept the fundamental idea that one's country's defense should be done by oneself.

C. However, on the other hand, by expressing friendship to the people of Japan,

  1. America's providing of aid, not military in nature but economic, would be considered an expression of this friendship. We are aware that the ECA, which provided for economic aid, is already being ended. Today, as Japan possesses self-defense capabilities for the first time since the end of the war, the situation is not much different than that of Europe a few years ago and thus we believe Japan should receive the same economic aid.

  2. The so-called "offshore procurements" greatly benefited Japan's economy and the U.S. side said it would do its best in this regard.

  3. The issue of surplus agricultural items was discussed. The Japanese side believes using the proceeds for road repair (which are also necessary strategically) and the development of military-related industries is meaningful and desires $50 million for this.

II. **Trade with Southeast Asia and compensation**
The participation of Japan in the economic relations of Southeast Asia is believed to benefit the prosperity of both Southeast Asia and Japan. For this, a resolution to the reparations problem is necessary. The Japanese side desires the United States to use its diplomatic influence, or, if it has a development plan for the region, to assist in the resolution of the reparations problem and the development of Southeast Asia. According to reports by Foreign Minister Okazaki who is visiting the region now, the attitudes of these countries are particularly inflexible and they appear to be going beyond Article 14 of the Peace Treaty. (Author's note: Article 26 of the San Francisco Peace Treaty includes an "equality clause," and so we explained our reservations to the U.S. side.)[11]

III. **Trade with Communist China**

The U.S. side understood the desire of Japan to be treated on the same par with the countries of Europe in their trade with China.

IV. **GARIOA**

The Japanese representative expressed the opinion that the issue of repayment of GARIOA is related to other fiscal burdens (including defense spending) and thus the problem of balancing these demands make it difficult to separately resolve just one. However, the Japanese side agreed to recommend to the Japanese government the desire of the U.S. side that the representatives of both countries meet at the earliest time possible at an appropriate time and place to discuss this issue and possibly others.

V. **Foreign investment and loans**

The news of the loans of $40 million by the Development Bank and $60 million for cotton is welcome. The U.S. opinion on Japan's policy for foreign investment is well understood. The Japanese side plans to listen to the opinions of the financial community in New York as well.

VI. **Other domestic problems in Japan**

There are worrisome signs of the restarting of inflation in the Japanese economy. There were some recommendations made by the Japanese side on improving the financial system on this matter.

The above is an overview of the October 19 memorandum we drafted. We informally submitted it to [Robert C.] McClurkin, Director of the Office of Northeast Asian Affairs, on the morning of the 19th, and officially presented it to Robertson that evening.

EXCHANGE OF QUESTIONS WITH FOREIGN REPORTERS

On that day, an article on the upcoming meeting appeared in the morning edition of the *New York Times*, in which the following was written: "A reporter (the UP's [M. Stewart] Hensley, I think) who said that the line between 'defense strength' that is desired and 'rearmament' that is barred by the Constitution appeared to be 'too fine for our Occidental minds' sought guidance. Does defense become rearmament when it could be turned to aggressive ends, he asked. 'That definition,' said Mr. Ikeda through his interpreter, 'suits our Oriental minds.'"

It is true that when we meet with foreigners, we not only learn about their preconceived notions, but they learn about ours too. There were several opportunities with foreign reporters around this time, some of who were quite smart and with whom unexpected exchanges took place. Of them, some that I still remember include:

UP: Mr. Ikeda, we've heard that you presented a very modest defense plan at first in order to see the reaction of the U.S. side.

Ikeda: I am an honest person. I would not do so.

INS: If the U.S. were to give Japan nuclear warheads, would Japan be able to effectively use them?

Ikeda: I am not sure what nuclear weapons are so I am not able to answer the question.

UP: Do the Japanese people desire the return of Okinawa, Ogasawara, which are becoming important U.S. bases?

Ikeda: Yes, we definitely desire their return.

INS: What about the Kurile Islands?

Ikeda: Yes, the same. Especially regarding Habomai, Shikotan, there is no difference in opinion.

UP: The U.S. believes that Habomai and Shikotan do not belong to the Kuriles. Japan relinquished rights to the Kuriles and Southern Sakhalin at the Peace Conference, but the Soviet Union did not have the right to take them. Does Japan desire the return of the Kuriles and Southern Sakhalin?

Ikeda: "No comment."

Chicago Sun Times: (The question is two-fold.) You appear to be dragging out the talks. There is a rumor that you are doing so until Prime Minister Yoshida arrives.

Ikeda: I will be here until the talks are over. However, I am not sure if Prime Minister Yoshida will be coming or not.

These were the types of Q&A sessions we had. That evening, around 5:00 p.m., Ikeda brought me along to visit Robertson at the State Department to formally submit to him our October 19 memorandum. At this time, Robertson said rather strongly, "The other day, you said that regarding the question of GARIOA, you are not the representative of the Japanese government and therefore could not make an official commitment. When a comment like that is made on important issue, it becomes a thankless task for someone like me, the person tasked with negotiating as your counterpart." Probably because no one was around, Robertson made this straightforward comment. In response, Ikeda said, "I made very clear from the beginning that I was not the official representative of the Japanese government. I had to say it that way, because officially I am not. Because of this, I was asked to be the Prime Minister's personal representative. This is something I wish you to understand." The both of them went back and forth a couple of times, and in the end, Robertson said that the issue of "GARIOA" would be treated as before as one part of all the other issues on the table.

The following morning, the *Washington Post* had a story on the issue of Japan's defense. Like the *New York Times* the day before, it alluded to the constitutional problem quite a lot. These two leading papers did not simply criticize the lack of efforts in defense by Japan but also mentioned the difficult hurdle that the Constitution represented. We were encouraged that this recognition had begun to set in or that a briefing by Pentagon officials to this effect had done the trick.

THE TRUE POSITION OF THE U.S. SIDE— THE OCTOBER 21ST MEMORANDUM

A meeting was scheduled for 3 p.m. on October 21. We were aware that the U.S. side had held two days of meetings in an effort to prepare a response to our memorandum of October 19. On the 21st, we received a request from the State Department to postpone the meeting as the response had not been completed in time. It finally arrived around noon of the 22nd. Below is the general gist of the response. Because of the circumstances introduced earlier, it is necessary to explain again that this should not be viewed or cited as an official "diplomatic document," but one that responds to the Japanese memorandum of October 19 and should be understood as a whole. The numbers of the paragraphs correspond to those in the Japanese document.

U.S. Government Memorandum of October 21, 1953

    I. A. The United States acknowledges the existence of the four restrictions— legal, political, economic, and physical—preventing Japan from increasing its defense capabilities. In particular, the first and second restrictions are those to be decided by the Japanese themselves, so the U.S. side withholds criticism on these issues.

    B. 1. Regarding the third and fourth restrictions, the U.S. is prepared to provide enough aid, as long as: (a) the U.S. Congress agrees, (b) Japan is willing to gradually increase its defense, and (c) it will depend on the economic situation at the time as to what extent Japanese efforts will be considered enough, but the thinking of the United States is that if Japan does not put forward a defense budget of $20 million in Fiscal Year 1954 and $23.5 million the following year, it would be difficult to convince Congress to approve aid to Japan. As a result, the U.S. side believes that Japan should plan to increase its ground troops of its National Safety Force to 320,000 to 350,000. The U.S. military in Tokyo and the National Safety Agency should discuss how and when this increase could take place. Therefore, the U.S. desires Japan to decide on appropriating $20 million and $23.5 million respectively over the next two fiscal years. Moreover, the U.S. desires that Japan increase its ground troops by 24,000 within this year, 46,000 by next year for a total of 180,000. Regarding maritime forces, as Japan is able to produce its own small and light-weight vessels such as minesweepers and minelayers, the U.S. desires Japan to lease destroyers and other large ships from it. The U.S. has already made clear its intention to provide enough aid for facilities and equipment for Japan if an understanding were reached for the increase in the forces of three services.

2. The U.S. believes that the opinion of Japan of the need to decrease its defense spending as it builds up its forces is appropriate.

3. The U.S. desires the Japanese government to develop within Japan the recognition of the need for self-defense.

4. If the above long-term defense program is developed and Japan's self defense capabilities grow, the U.S. can begin to withdraw its forces.

C. 1. Legally, Japan may be able to receive "economic aid," but the U.S. has no plans right now to do so as it is unable to find any reason to provide such aid in light of the fact that the Korean War procurements had greatly assisted Japan's economy and compared to other countries, Japan's need for such aid is questionable. Moreover, the Japanese view that it is being forced to increase its defense strength beyond the ability of its economy to support it does not reflect the U.S. policy.

2. Regarding offshore procurements, there are different estimates as to how much they will be based on the defense situation, the level of Japan's economy at the time and how it will be able to handle the orders, etc. However, it will probably be approximately $100 million.

3. Regarding Japan's desire to purchase $50 million in surplus agriculture, this is a reasonable estimate. However, this is in addition to normal imports. Of the $50 million or so, the yen equivalent of $40 million will be used for Japan's defense forces and for the purchase of munitions by countries other than Japan. However, more study is required to see if a part of this money can be used to develop Japan's defense industry. Regarding the remaining $10 million, or 36 billion yen, the U.S. has no objection to Japan's using it to expand its industrial base. To do so will require the signing of a special agreement, however.

II. A. The United States will try to assist in the problem of reparations.

B. The United States recognizes that Japan's participation in the development of Southeast Asia would benefit both parties, and would like to study any specific plans Japan has that calls for U.S. participation.

III. The U.S. side believes that until a political ceasefire is reached on the Korean Peninsula, it is still necessary to maintain restrictions on high trade with Communist China. However, the United States understands the desire of Japan to reduce the level of restrictions it faces to those of the countries of Europe, and we are currently studying the list of items Japan presented and others as well. The U.S. has already announced some loosening of the restrictions, and the U.S. Embassy in Tokyo is checking these items with the desires of your government. However, until the U.S. government is able to rest more easily, it believes it is necessary to continue to put economic pressure on China. The U.S. would be grateful if it could get the assistance of the Japanese government in this regard.

IV. The U.S. government believes it extremely important to be able to make an announcement regarding the repayment of the $2 billion in GARIOA aid prior to the start of the Congressional session in January next year. Therefore, the U.S. side wishes to come to a basic agreement along the following lines: The total amount for Japan to pay would be $750 million, at 2.5 percent interest over a period of 35 years. However, this is conditioned on Japan paying for $43 million for surplus agriculture. Regarding this, the U.S. proposes that representatives of the U.S. and Japan meet in Tokyo on November 15 to sign a final agreement.

V. Foreign investment and loans

VI. Japanese economy

The author has chosen to abbreviate the description of the last two issues.

UNSUCCESSFUL ATTEMPTS TO FORGE A COMPROMISE

On October 23, our group, with the exception of Ikeda, visited the Director of the Division of Northeast Asian Affairs, McClurkin, who was the principle drafter of the State Department response, and asked questions for about three hours. This was in part because as we read the response, we thought that if we discussed the issue a little bit more, perhaps the room for agreement would grow. And, we hoped that even if it is not announced publicly, perhaps some unofficial document agreeing on a variety of issues. Then the issues on which agreement could be reached would be used when completing the final joint statement.

The main point of our questions focused on the defense problem. In particular, there was a discussion on the U.S. side's suddenly stressing in their response that the budgetary necessity for 200 billion yen next fiscal year and 235 billion the year after. At the same time, the U.S. side demanded that the ground forces be increased by 24,000 within this fiscal year and 46,000 during the next year. However, the number of personnel and size of the budget requests did not match up. It seemed as if the figures were being used, on the one hand, to argue for the increase in troops by 70,000, as it had to explain to Congress why the Defense Department in this fiscal year had prepared equipment for

180,000 troops when there were only 110,000. On the other hand, regarding the amount of the defense budget, it seemed they were demanding 200 billion yen as a way to respond to the criticism in the Congress that Japan's defense spending was currently only 2 percent of its Gross National Product.

The U.S. side was only able to explain the foundation for the figure 200 billion yen by saying it calculated for the increase in national income, an explanation that was not convincing. We told them that if some sort of explanation were necessary for Congress, Japan would be spending 123 billion yen directly on defense and another 45 billion yen on benefits to the families of veterans. Next year, according to the U.S. plans, ground forces would be increased by 24,000, which means an increase of almost 24 billion yen and the benefits will rise to 70 billion yen. Together, this meant more than 200 billion yen. We suggested that the U.S. side use this for their explanation to Congress instead. However, the U.S. side did not readily accept it.

We then asked the U.S. side whether their figures for the final force levels for ground troops of 325,000 or 350,000 were not erroneous. To this the U.S. side said, "for the time being, the next two years are important. There is a gap of two years. This point is important."

The American proposal:
By the end of March 1954 — 24,000
By the end of March 1955 — 46,000

The Ikeda proposal:
By the end of March 1955 — 24,000
By the end of March 1957 — 46,000

We felt that the problem on the U.S. side was that they were budgeting this for 180,000 troops. The figures of 325,000 and 350,000 were premised on the American idea of what a division slice is (as explained before), and seemed to represent no more than a desire.

We exchanged a lot of opinions on comparisons of the GARIOA between West Germany and that between the U.S. and Japan (In the case of West Germany, the opinion Ikeda told Dodge at the San Francisco Peace Conference was, whether by chance or otherwise, accepted and led to the negotiations reaching a conclusion.) The problem with this was that the records were handled by the Occupation forces. Since it was immediately after the war, the Occupation forces were responsible for receiving the goods sent from America. The records were poorly kept—there was no way of telling whether the accounting was based on the price in the books or the cost at the time, nor whether the items sent were damaged and ready to be disposed of or were new. As the recent problem of the "old engines" suggests, there have been many examples of such items being given as aid, and if a discussion were started on the quality of those goods, there would be no end.

America's explanation is that the discount it gave Japan (from $2 billion to $750 million) is the same as it gave to West Germany, roughly 37.5 percent. However, frankly speaking, a heated debate emerged because of a rumor that the evening before, the figure $750 million was actually $850 million in the U.S. document that was prepared prior to the final decision on the U.S. side.

After meeting with Director of Foreign Operations Stassen for about thirty minutes, our mission departed Washington that evening for discussions with the New York business and banking community. On the flight to New York, I thought about a lot of things. If we could bring the two memorandums of the U.S. and Japan closer together into one thing, it would be welcomed in the future. In particular, we were able to imagine over the past two weeks of meetings and in the explanation earlier that morning by the State Department officials that the figures of 200 billion or 230 billion yen in budgetary matters, or of 325,000 or 350,000 in ground forces used by the U.S. side were not really based on any particular foundation. On the other hand, the number 180,000 put forth by the U.S. side does appear to have had a reason for sticking to this number. Our position from the time we left Japan was that the U.S. would probably push 180,000, so the question was over how many years to make this happen, and there was a two-year gap between the positions of the two sides. It would be in the interest of both countries if we could spread the number 325,000 or 350,00 over a lifetime. I was trying to think if there was a way in which the number 180,000 could be skillfully approached.

As I was thinking about this, I recalled that the U.S. and Japanese fiscal years were different. In the Ikeda plan, 180,000 would be reached by March 1957 (in other words, by the end of FY 1956), and the American proposal, that would be done by March 1955 (or the end of FY 1954). The gap of two years could possibly be filled by speeding up the dates in the Ikeda plan, having the 180,000 reached by the end of June 1956, it would fall within FY 1956, assuming the U.S. could rebudget it the following year (US FY 1956). In Japan, when FY 1956 is mentioned, it will actually be the end of March 1956. While still on the airplane, I explained to Special Emissary Ikeda and Vice Minister Aichi this thought process and got their agreement to raise this possibility when we got back to Washington. I began to draft a new memorandum based on this thinking.

Regarding the surplus agricultural goods, the U.S. had made clear that $10 million of the $50 million could be used freely. As was said much earlier, from the time we departed Japan, there was a desire for funds for the government to use for road repair and land reclamation projects. Because of this we entered into negotiations on the possibility of using another $10 million freely. One more problem was the GARIOA issue. We knew that the U.S. side, especially Robertson, was really being beaten up in the Congress. Nevertheless, in the end this would not be in America's interests. Special Emissary Ikeda tried to talk to Robertson one more time about this.

Special Emissary Ikeda and I returned to Washington late in the evening of the 27th, having had discussions with the New York business community and a luncheon at the invitation of the financial community and [John D.] Rockefeller. On the afternoon of the 27th, Vice Minister Aichi, who returned to Washington a day early, met with officials from the State Department to explain the three points introduced above, namely, the compromise proposal on the timing for increasing the number of ground forces to 180,000, the desire of the Japanese to increase the amount of money to be freely used from the sale of surplus agriculture by another $10 million, and the leaving of the GARIOA problem to a political solution. The State Department agreed to consider these counterproposals. Upon returning to Washington, we were told that in any case, the issue would be taken up directly in the Ikeda-Robertson talks.

Beginning the next morning, we began preparing the joint statement that would be released after the meeting. We had reservations to depart New York for London on the afternoon of the 31st. If agreement on defense issues was reached at the last meeting on the 29th, we would work it into the joint statement. We finished most of the draft joint statement around noon of the 28th.

U.S. STRONGLY URGES BORROWING

Another meeting between Ikeda and Robertson was held that afternoon. We were asked to wait a day for a response on the three points that Aichi raised the day before, so this day was devoted exclusively to a discussion of GARIOA between Ikeda and Robertson.

Robertson: Just within the past couple of days, I heard some strong words from a senator who asked why we did not demand Japan to repay the loans when those with Germany have already been cleaned up. I am sure that the Japanese Diet is the same, but there must be some way to satisfy both sides.

Ikeda: Now is the time to wholeheartedly study whether the Japanese people will accept the figures of 320,000 or 350,000 the U.S. is proposing. Fortunately, you seem to be willing to not ask the impossible. On the other hand, nothing good will come of the GARIOA problem. If, by chance, on behalf of the government I promised to hold a meeting in November or February on this issue and even if the meeting produced an agreement, the government bill (author's note: Diet approval is necessary for paying loans) will most definitely be vetoed by the Diet considering the political situation today. If something like this were to occur, some discord would emerge between the peoples of both countries. I am afraid of this.

Robertson: When was it that Prime Minister Yoshida said he "was aware that GARIOA was considered a loan?"

Ikeda: He has been saying this for three or four years.

Robertson: Prime Minister Yoshida is clearly saying this, and you promised so in San Francisco. I can only say that it is incredulous that Japan has not yet lived up to its promises.

Ikeda: Even if we wanted to do something about it, the situation in the Diet makes it so that it is impossible to do anything about it. I believe you can understand this, as you meet with your Congress on occasion.

The meeting that was scheduled for the 29th was not held. The State Department had called to tell us that internal discussions were continuing on three points regarding our proposal. We received word the next day, the 30th, from the State Department that "we attempted to bring the U.S. and Japanese proposals together but no consensus was reached within the U.S. government. Further discussions would not likely produce agreement today either. As a result, it is clear that there would be no time to restart discussions with Japan. It is best to give up on these points and complete the joint statement." We were left with some reservations but the concerns we had over a "secret agreement" were now gone and we were actually relieved.

At 2:30 that afternoon, Special Emissary Ikeda visited Assistant Secretary Robertson. After expressing his thanks, Ikeda explained in a careful and solemn way that introducing the GARIOA issue would not be in the interest of both countries. Robertson seemed to have been moved by Ikeda's explanation, although he remained quiet the whole time. (I heard the following when I went to Washington the following year with Prime Minister Yoshida. The day before the above meeting, Robertson said of Ikeda, "He is the type of guy who will do it if he says he will. If he says that fiscally or economically it is hard, it must be really hard. Let's not push the GARIOA issue any more this time. I will take responsibility.")

PRIOR TO THE RELEASE OF THE JOINT STATEMENT

After we finished this meeting with Robertson, we returned to the conference room to continue with making the final adjustments to the joint statement. McClurkin told Robertson that "we were unable to agree on the phrase 'at the soonest possible opportunity' in the sentence on the GARIOA issue stating that in Tokyo representatives of both countries would meet in Tokyo 'at the soonest possible opportunity.'" Robertson immediately responded that he "did not think changing the expression to 'opportunity in the future' would be problematic." McClurkin seemed surprised at how dramatically Robertson's position changed, and then looked over at us.

We had expressed our hope that the statement not be called a "communiqué." Our desire was met and it was kept as a simple statement. It was released in English and Japanese simultaneously at 5:00 p.m. by both the State Department and the Japanese Embassy.

I have already written in detail about events leading up to the release of the statement, and thus it would be meaningless and unnecessary to reproduce the full statement here, particularly because it is publicly available. Instead, in an effort to step away from my own subjective views, I will introduce how the Japanese press (*Asahi Shimbun*, October 31, [1953], evening edition) reported the main points of the statement:

1. The U.S. side acknowledged that the rapid increase in Japan's self-defense capabilities that it desires is impossible due to constitutional restrictions, economic, and social reasons.
2. The U.S. agreed to be flexible in its aid for expanding Japanese self-defense.
3. The inclination to open the road to economic aid, and not just military aid, was seen through a bilateral agreement on economic aid for defense.
4. An understanding was reached to supply Japan with goods valued at approximately $50 million based on Article 550 of the Mutual Security Act.
5. Agreement was reached to have any restrictions on articles in trade with Communist China relaxed through diplomatic organizations.
6. Agreement was reached to have representatives of both governments meet in the near future in Tokyo to discuss the GARIOA problem.

In the evening, after Ambassador Araki had Robertson and his staff over to the Embassy for a cocktail party, he had small dinner party for our delegation. Even if it appeared from the outside that we did not achieve anything significant through these talks, we were from that day forward able to do away with the unfortunate impression that the U.S. side with its large numbers was demanding a huge increase in Japanese defense forces.

We departed New York for London the next day with no small feeling of satisfaction, therefore, because we strongly believed this would contribute to the friendly relations of both countries.

NOTES

1. *Mindoha* is the abbreviation for *Minshu Domeika*, or Democratization Movement, within the Democratic Liberal Party, which was an anti-Yoshida movement officially formed on October 24, 1952. See Masumi, *Postwar Politics*, 287.

2. Kokura is now part of the City of Kitakyushu.

3. Oiso, in Kanagawa Prefecture, was the home of Yoshida Shigeru until the time of his death in October 1967.

4. Mr. "O" is Oasa Tadao.

5. The story in the *Asahi Shimbun* Miyazawa cites originally appeared as "U.S. to Return Some Islands to Japanese, Dulles Discloses," *New York Times*, August 9, 1953.

6. Mr. "H" is Hayashi Hikosaburo.

7. Mr. "K" is Kato Takeo and Mr. "A" is Akiyama Konosuke.

8. Miyazawa uses the expression "like princess-weaver Vega seeing the cowherd Altair" to explain this rare meeting. This is from a story that forms the basis for the Japanese Seven Evenings Holidays (Tanabata Matsuri) in early July. After marrying, Vega neglected her weaving and Altair forgot his cows. As punishment, the couple was banished to opposites sides of the River of Heaven (Milky Way) and are allowed to meet on only the seventh day of the seventh month when a bridge is created across the river.

9. See discussion in chapter 4.

10. Judd was a physician with missionary experience in China between 1925–1931, and 1934–1938, accounting for his initial knowledge of Asia. He subsequently was elected to Congress in 1943 and served until 1962, when he was defeated for reelection.

11. Article 26 reads: "Japan will be prepared to conclude with any State which signed or adhered to the United Nations Declaration of January 1, 1942, and which is at war with Japan, or with any State which previously formed a part of the territory of a State named in Article 23, which is not a signatory of the present Treaty, a bilateral Treaty of Peace on the same or substantially the same terms as are provided for in the present Treaty, but this obligation on the part of Japan will expire three years after the first coming into force of the present Treaty. Should Japan make a peace settlement or war claims settlement with any State granting that State greater advantages than those provided by the present Treaty, those same advantages shall be extended to the parties to the present Treaty."

Chapter Six

Yoshida's Last Trip to the United States as Prime Minister, 1954

FINAL STAGES OF THE YOSHIDA CABINET

The political situation in Japan became more and more unstable entering 1954. The people around Prime Minister Yoshida began to seriously think about an opportunity for Yoshida to resign, but the problem was that it was difficult to directly broach this matter with him. We thought that there was no other way to stabilize the political situation than to employ the tool of a meeting between Yoshida and Shigemitsu, similar to the one used just before Yoshida's trip to the U.S. in 1953, by asking once again an elder statesman of the business community to take some action.

It is true that a great deal of scheming was done along these lines. As this is still a relatively recent happening, I cannot write about it in detail here, but because there were several misunderstandings this effort ended unsuccessfully partway through. This was not the only failure. In order to undertake an "equal merger" with Shigemitsu's Progressive Party, there was no choice but to also "dissolve" the Liberal Party. We finally were able to quietly get Prime Minister Yoshida's approval. During this time, Deputy Prime Minister Ogata learned of Yoshida's "willingness to dissolve the Liberal Party" and publicly announced it.

Using this as an opportunity, a movement began openly calling for the "formation of a new conservative party." Having quietly been working behind the scenes on this merger, Ogata's publicly announcing it came as a surprise and was quite unfortunate. We did not doubt his good intentions, but he probably got caught up in an unfortunate misunderstanding. Philosophically speaking, it may have been simple an unpreventable happening in the flow of history.

Viewed from a philosophical perspective, it was probably something that could not be prevented in the flow of history. However, during this time, Prime Minister Yoshida himself did not show that his positive health was failing. As he always said, echoing Clemenceau's fighting attitude, "One blow can't take me down." In fact, when members of the cabinet began to fight over the budget after our country's economy started to show dangerous signs of inflation beginning the year before, Prime Minister Yoshida announced "the budget would not go above one trillion yen." With that one statement, the situation stabilized and the economy in 1954 went beyond forecasts and was a prosperous one. This was probably the last prime ministerial–like thing politically that Yoshida did domestically.

PRIME MINISTER YOSHIDA LEAVES FOR EUROPE AND THE U.S.

Yoshida was very interested in going on a trip to Europe and the United States, something he had been thinking about since the year before. He even began to regularly say "this year, Europe and America; next year, Southeast Asia." In the Lower House, there was a great furor over the police bill and it looked like at one point that he would have to abandon his plans to depart for his trip, but he went ahead with his original plan and left on September 26 out of Haneda. Many people were saying that this was Yoshida's *hanamichi*, or "great departure." If there was anyone who did not see it that way, it was probably only Yoshida himself.

ADVANCE PARTY GOES ON TO WASHINGTON

The Prime Minister was scheduled to land in New York from Europe on November 2, but this was right around the time of the American midterm elections so the arrival was moved to the 7th. We went to the United States some two to three weeks prior to this in order to meet with U.S. government officials. We departed on October 17 from Japan. We intended to work on the issues still unresolved from the Ikeda-Robertson talks the year before to be included in the joint communiqué by Yoshida and Eisenhower, scheduled to be released on November 10, which was when the official state visit of the Prime Minister to America would end.

Minister for International Trade and Industry Aichi headed up the delegation, with a secretary named Tanaka, Takeuchi, Director of the Foreign Ministry's North America and European Division and a former Minister at the

Embassy in Washington, Ohori [Hiromu], Deputy Director of Commerce at MITI, and myself joining. In addition, Tohata [Shiro], Vice Minister from the Ministry of Agriculture and Fisheries, came to Washington later to handle one of the important issues of the surplus agricultural goods, one of the big issues of the meeting came, as did Suzuki, an official from the Finance Ministry, who was already in the United States.

In other words, compared to last year, the composition of the mission was almost the same—Aichi, Takeuchi, Suzuki, and myself. The only difference was that Ikeda, as Secretary General of the Liberal Party, was asked to stay behind and cover for the Prime Minister in the volatile situation in domestic political affairs, and Aichi replaced Ikeda as head of the group.

On October 20, Aichi visited Assistant Secretary of State Robertson to discuss the scheduled talks, explaining that the purpose of our mission this time in the following way: "Because Prime Minister Yoshida will only be in Washington for a few days and there won't be enough time to really address the outstanding questions at hand between our two countries, we have come as an advance party to have discussions along a prepared agenda over the next couple of weeks. Moreover, it is not too early to consider the joint communiqué and thus we would also like to prepare it at the same time."

On this day, the overall agenda for the discussions was agreed upon:

1. Japan's economy and defense issues;
2. Southeast Asia and economic cooperation;
3. Purchase of surplus agricultural goods;
4. Resolution of the GARIOA issue;
5. Introduction of foreign currency and loans;
6. Other political problems—release of war criminals, immigration, and territorial issues.

The first official meeting began in the evening of October 25, with many participants from both sides attending. Similar to last year, the moderator of the meeting was Assistant Secretary Robertson. The meeting began with Aichi reading an opening statement.

AICHI ANGERS ROBERTSON

The opening statement was something that we put great effort into while we were still in Japan. It was a fact that U.S.-Japan relations had been worsening over the past one year. This was in part, as mentioned before, it seems a reaction to the "honeymoon period" around the time of the San Francisco Peace Conference.

It is true that the impression of American officials pressuring Japan on defense matters had receded somewhat since about the time of the Ikeda-Robertson talks. For example, we longer heard statements from the Secretary of State that "Japan's defense efforts were lacking." Moreover, in the wake of the truce on the Korean Peninsula, a mood of neutralism began to grow more strongly in Japan, and the U.S. began to look like a war-monger for its continued tests of nuclear weapons despite the thawing in the Cold War. For example, the incident in which a Japanese fisherman died after the Bikini hydrogen bomb tests deeply etched in the minds of some Japanese the extreme image of the United States as "war-loving."

America's unpopularity was a phenomenon limited not only to Japan. After traveling to Europe the year before, it seems it was a view shared around the world. It was not only we who noticed it. U.S. diplomats stationed abroad had also been quite concerned about this trend. They tried hard to do away with this image, but as long as a true, lasting peace with the Soviet Union had not been created, there was probably a need for military concerns to take priority. If a somewhat extreme view were expressed, we got the impression that the difference between the thinking of the military and diplomats stationed abroad was that on trivial things, the decision was often made in the military's favor. Moreover, I thought the unique personality of Dulles, who led America's diplomats, had something to do with this. I am not proposing to argue a particular "Dulles Theory," nor am I prepared to do so, but his attention to detail, legal thinking, and strong ability to convince others sometimes leaves his counterparts frustrated. By forcing his views on someone, it seemed at least to me that he showed his propensity to believe that an issue was satisfactorily resolved because he so strongly believed in his own views that sometimes he could not understand the other person's true feelings.

We came to believe—and fear—that over the past year, the trend was getting stronger and stronger in which the people of Japan, which had a long history and pride but were truly weak and poor, were reactively starting to be critical of the direction that America was going in, as stated before. It was this reason that Aichi frankly spoke about this point in his opening statement:

> The Japanese government has faithfully implemented the items agreed to at last year's talks between Ikeda and Robertson. The domestic economy has certainly shown signs of improvement, and while it may not be as much as the United States desires, on defense issues, Japan, on its own initiative, has increased its defense capability. This year is the second year of the five-year defense plan. At this point, the Government of Japan is somewhat concerned about the different perceptions in the priorities of "defense" and "economic prosperity." When there

was fighting going on in the Korean Peninsula, military concerns necessarily took priority, but now it is clear that the two—defense or economic prosperity— are intimately connected. In Asia, it is impossible to have a situation in which "an economically weak country being strong militarily." I believe that in Japan, as well as in other countries in Asia, it is impossible to have a strong defense posture without economic recovery. (Author's note: This comment was an indirect criticism of the fact that the United States, in its enthusiasm to create the Southeast Asia Treaty Organization seemed to be overlooking the need to buttress the region economically.)

This was a rare statement for diplomatic discussions, one that was clear and strong in tone. At the time, all twenty-some representatives from the U.S. side let out a collective expression of surprise. As evidence of this, when Minister Aichi was about finished reading his statement, Robertson, in a rage, challenged him, "In your statement just now, I think you said that 'America was too pushy,' but that is absolutely not true. If the people of Japan really think that this is true, then isn't it up to the Government of Japan to say it isn't so?" We found his comment to be too convenient, and on the way home after the meeting we laughed to ourselves thinking "that was precisely the attitude we were criticizing." At the meeting however no more was discussed on this subject.

SURPLUS AGRICULTURAL GOODS

Robertson's opinion at the meeting that day was that henceforth, several working groups should be created based on the agenda. However, of those, we felt some concern with the complete lack of U.S. preparation on the question of the purchase of surplus agricultural products. The biggest reason for this delay was that the top leadership of the government was totally focused on the midterm elections, and because of this, government decisions of all but the most important matters, were temporarily put on hold.

America's bureaucracy was a large and well-running one whose civil servants would perform their tasks even without supervision, but if came to anything beyond that, then they were unable to synthesize and make a decision without an order from above. Moreover, to move a large wheel that a bureaucracy is, it takes ten or in some cases one hundred smaller wheels. Even on the question of next year's surplus agricultural goods, no one seemed to know what the policy was.

As a result, we were forced to go around at a quick pace to the different bureaucrats and request that a resolution be found to this issue prior to the arrival of the Japanese Prime Minister. In the span of only ten days, we visited with Deputy Undersecretary of State Murphy, Secretary of Agriculture [Ezra Taft] Benson, Secretary of Commerce [Sinclair] Wicks, Director of Foreign Operations [Harold E.] Stassen, [Andrew N.] Overby from Commerce, and Clarence Francis, who headed the committee in charge of dealing with the problem of surplus agricultural products as an advisor to the president, to ask them for their support in quickly resolving the issue.

The issue then moved forward quickly—a decision was made to sell next year 400 million dollars of a total of 700 million dollars worth of surplus agricultural goods (to be disposed of over the next three years). Of that, how much Japan would buy, and how much the fourteen other countries which were applying to purchase the goods was still to be decided. The negotiations over surplus agricultural products continued over the next two weeks, even after Prime Minister Yoshida arrived in Washington from New York. However, I am not able to write about these talks in detail here.

Compared to the previous year, the food situation in Japan had gradually improved, and we thought that there were some disadvantages to Japanese farmers if we just bought any surplus agricultural products from the U.S. The conclusion to this problem was two-fold—when choosing which products to buy, we should try to avoid competition with the Japanese agricultural industry, and when using the profits from selling these products, how much can Japan use freely. Quickly summarizing the negotiations, the American side compromised and agreed to a total purchasing price of 85 million yen. However, we greatly resented the proposal of the U.S. side to permit the GOJ to freely decide on the use of only 39 million yen.

However, a problem existed for the other side—even if the State Department wanted to increase the percentage that Japan could use, the other agencies in U.S. government, such as the Army, Department of Agriculture, Directorate of Foreign Operations, all wanted to have a share of that remaining 46 million yen for their own projects in Japan and Southeast Asia and were fighting over the money.

No matter how many meetings were held little progress was made and as a result, one day I blurted out rhetorically and in a loud voice at a meeting, "Is it even worth helping America by buying its extra wheat if we have to go through all this?" When I saw that the Director of the Office of Northeast Asian Affairs McClurkin was about to say something, I immediately said, "Oh, I was just talking to myself." He in turn said, "My fault. I must have been eavesdropping." With this, everyone laughed.

In the end, I remember that we were able to come up with a compromise on the last day when the Prime Minister was about to leave. After our continued requests, the amount of money Japan could use for surplus agricultural products was increased to 50 million yen.

THE ARGUMENT AT THE COCKTAIL PARTY

I have one more memory of Director McClurkin, who is now deceased. At the time of the Ikeda-Robertson talks the year before, the United States promised to use 40 million yen of the 50 million yen in sales of surplus agricultural products for the defense of Japan and other things. The National Safety Agency wanted to build a destroyer and made this desire known to the U.S. side the year before. However, because of the infighting in the U.S. government mentioned above, a response from Washington was not forthcoming and pretty soon a year had gone by. At the meeting this time, the Japanese side expressed its concerns quite strongly. As a result, the two sides got together to discuss the issue. It was this day that the argument took place.

Right around the time that the two sides were meeting, Minister Aichi and I left for an appointment with Secretary Wilson. At first, we planned not to speak too much about work, but a Major General who regularly appeared at our meetings had been extensively briefing Secretary Wilson on the issues involving Japan and thus we thought that the Secretary was well prepared to discuss the issue of the 40 million yen. "The National Safety Agency is trying to build a destroyer but there has been no decision from Washington for more than a year," we told him. "This is really unacceptable." Wilson immediately responded, "You are absolutely correct. The Japanese proposal seems reasonable enough to me. Please go ahead and do so."

By chance, the Major General mentioned a few moments ago sat in on the meeting and heard what was said. We were quite happy that the issue was unexpectedly resolved in this way, and together we went back to the place where the meeting was being held. When we arrived, the representatives of the different agencies on the U.S. side were in the middle of debating whether the destroyer was a good idea or whether using the money in another way to benefit a certain agency might be better. At this point I said, "Sorry to interrupt but we just came from meeting with Secretary of Defense Wilson on precisely this issue. He does not seem to have any objection to Japan's desire to build a destroyer." Silence filled the room. Especially, an Army official of the Defense Department, who had been strongly arguing that the money should be used for an Army unit, looked quite unhappy and immediately went quiet.

The next night, a farewell cocktail party was being thrown for a gentleman named Moyer,[1] who was going to Japan to become Minister at the U.S. Embassy in Japan. I arrived a little late and learned that McClurkin, Director of the Division of Northeast Asian Affairs, was looking for me, so I found him and approached him and asked him, "Do have something to ask me?" He responded, "Well, yes, let's sit and talk. It is about the issue of the destroyer. Was what you said about Secretary of Defense Wilson approving it really true?" I answered, "Of course, it is true. If you have any doubts, please go and ask directly yourself." To which McClurkin stated, "Wilson is a member of the Cabinet, and the most important among them. He would not be familiar with the details of such a small issue. Despite this, you went ahead and raised it with him. That was a little out of line." I objected, "Not true. If Wilson were alone, of course we would have never raised it, but his advisor (I said the name but now have forgotten it) was right there alongside him. What's more, he was given a ten-minute briefing before our meeting with him. With his advisor there, I do not think it was inappropriate at all." McClurkin answered, "Well, the issue was still under discussion by the concerned agencies. If it is true that Wilson spoke in such a way on the issue, we would like it to be forgotten." I told him, "That can't be done. Wilson is an American Cabinet member, and Aichi is a member of the Japanese Cabinet. You can not just withdraw something that has already been talked about by them." (By this point, our voices had gotten very loud. The other guests at the cocktail party began to get concerned, and one of them tried to intervene. Both McClurkin and I told the gentleman that his assistance was not needed. We continued our going back and forth for another twenty minutes.) McClurkin then asked, "So, it can't be forgotten?" I answered, "We of course would not object if a document withdrawing the permission was brought to us with Secretary Wilson's signature on it. Other than that, no attempts at 'canceling it' will lead to our 'canceling it.'" To this, McClurkin told me, "If that is the case, this is what I am going to do. I have received a request from the Department of Defense requesting that Wilson's statement be withdrawn. I am relaying this to you." I said flat out, "I will not accept it."

McClurkin was a smart and diligent diplomat. He came to Japan in April the following year. Over dinner, we reminisced about our argument that time. Just one year later, I learned in the newspaper that he suddenly died while on a business trip in London. He left behind a daughter of about fifteen or sixteen, and a modest but dignified wife, who at first glance looks a little bit older than her husband. I know this because I once met the family at the airport.

DEFENSE SECRETARY WILSON'S GAFFE

Secretary Wilson had something about him. He was a hard worker, having gone from a factory employee to president of General Motors. When he spoke to us, we felt this "something." As a result, he was also someone who would cause a commotion due to some of the words that came out of his mouth based on these experiences.

About two weeks before he met with us, Wilson went to Detroit to help in the campaigning for the elections. Detroit is a large industrial town and the leadership of the labor unions complained to Secretary of Defense Wilson "because the defense budget was too low, military procurements were decreasing and unemployment was rising." To which, Wilson responded:

I quite understand what you are saying. A long time ago, I was also a factory worker. At that time, wages were only 5 cents an hour and everyone worked hard. Sometimes, however, we were laid off and we had trouble surviving. Compared to then, today, the worker is quite lucky. People talk about unemployment. However, even if you wanted to work and couldn't find any employment, you still can collect unemployment insurance and live a life of ease. With dogs as well, there are different types. One is the type of dog that is well taken care of by their masters, being given meat and allowed to sleep all day in their dog house. The other is that which the master takes out for hunting and runs around. The former we call "kennel dogs" and the latter are "bird dogs." Comparing the two, it is much easier to be sympathetic to the "bird dogs."

This comment did not seem to cause a problem at the time, but a few hours later, the leadership of the labor union issued a statement criticizing "Secretary of Defense Wilson's likening of America's holy workers as dogs." Because America is the country of mass communications, the story became news from coast to coast within the day.

Because the Republican Party tended to be seen as the party of the rich, this comment by Wilson indeed infuriated the labor parties. After several days of commotion, President Eisenhower asked Wilson for an explanation. There were several Republican candidates who attributed blame to Wilson for their defeat in the midterm elections that November.

When Wilson met with us, he keenly asked us about the labor situation in Japan. Specifically, he asked if Japanese laborers had a strong desire to work. I responded "All are 'bird dogs.' However, the situation is difficult because the country is small, natural resources are scarce, and game is limited." Wilson, looking at his aide, laughed heartily.

YOSHIDA'S BUSINESS STYLE

There was one big difference between this year's meetings and the ones last year. That was that the U.S. side did not refer at all to Japan's domestic politics, namely "defense issues" and "economic problems." Since Prime Minister Yoshida's forced a spending limit of 100 million yen on the budget last year through a Cabinet decision, the Japanese economy no longer saw signs of inflation. Prices began to fall and trade increased. Compared to the year before, the economy was growing. As a result, the U.S. side probably had no complaints.

Regarding defense problems, the opening bold comment by Minister Aichi probably went a long way to answering American concerns. Moreover, following the truce on the Korean peninsula, the situation had relaxed somewhat so the pressing need to provide weapons and equipment to Japan had probably gone away. There were probably different circumstances, but on the U.S. side it seemed as if there was prior agreement that nothing would be said until the end on this issue. I think there may in fact had been some prior agreement.

Everyday spent in meetings meant that the day of Prime Minister Yoshida's arrival in New York was fast approaching. On the evening prior to his arrival, we flew from Washington up to New York. Early the next morning, we went to the pier to await the arrival of the *Queen Mary*. Yoshida gave a press conference aboard the sundeck of the *Queen Mary*. It was quite a scene—tall foreign reporters surrounded the short Yoshida, and what's more, a cameraman's bulb exploded when the flash went off.

Yoshida's motorcade of several black-colored cars, led by police motorcycles, made their way through the sleepy streets of New York before finding their way to the vacation home of [John D.] Rockefeller III. The whole trip took about an hour.

That morning a *New York Times* editorial entitled "Visitor from Japan" pointed out that:

> The Japanese Premier has been a lifelong champion of that democratic process and suffered in Japan for his championship. He has been labeled "pro-American." In addition to being an exponent of political liberty and the democratic process, Mr. Yoshida is an astute and accomplished politician. Mr. Yoshida has repeatedly paid high tribute to the quality of our occupation. It should be noted, however, that Mr. Yoshida made his own unique contribution to the success of our occupation through his wisdom, skill, and cooperation.

During the course of the evening, election results were gradually announced. Times Square did not stop moving until late that night. We returned to Washington the next morning, and continued our meetings there. However, since Yoshida's coming to New York, the number of events to participate in increased. On the 5th, we again went to New York for a Japan Society dinner party hosted by its chairman, Rockefeller III.

The dinner, attended by some 1200 people in the grand ballroom of the Waldorf-Astoria Hotel, was an unprecedented event for us Japanese. Yoshida, Alexander Wiley, Chairman of the Foreign Affairs Committee of the Senate, and Senator [William J.] Fulbright, of the famous Fulbright Bill, made speeches, along with some others. Wiley's speech stressed that the way to fight Communism in the region of Southeast Asia, including Japan, was the development of the economy and trade. The draft of this speech was probably written by the State Department, but the fact this view was impressed upon the chairman of the Foreign Affairs Committee, who held a high position, and that this was the subject of his speech was very meaningful for Japan in its current situation in the postwar. In addition, thanks to the presence of Rockefeller, the dinner was well attended. It was quite a blessing for us that he had become the chairman of the Japan Society.

Yoshida appears to have been busy in New York with these lunches and dinners. Nevertheless, being Yoshida, he brought us a present. He called us to the Embassy in Washington and told us, "When I was in New York, the presidents of National City and Chase National banks said that they wanted to be of assistance as Japan had a lot of savings. I responded that I have wanted to send some Japanese to South America to emigrate, and because we don't have any money, would like to borrow some. They all said that would not be a problem. I want one of you to go to New York and arrange this with them."

It was a vague request to be sure and we were troubled by it. In the end, Suzuki of the Finance Ministry went to New York and began negotiations. Just as Prime Minister Yoshida said, a loan became available. At the time it seemed like a joke, but today, thanks to Yoshida's style of business, a company devoted to assisting Japanese emigrate abroad has been created, sending Japanese to other countries, with dollars being loaned to that company.

PRIME MINISTER GOES TO WASHINGTON

Yoshida arrived in Washington in the evening of November 7. As he was received as an official state guest, which involves a lot of ceremony, we had quite a good feeling being whisked around in cars surrounded by police bikes. The handling by the Embassy's protocol officer was impressive, with the times and places of where we were expected next clearly laid out for us. Looking at a paper handed to the staff, on the morning after Yoshida's arrival, it stated, "present ourselves before Mrs. Yoshida."

During the three days Yoshida stayed in D.C., he met with the President, laid a wreath at the Tomb of the Unknown Soldier, conducted press interviews, met with the main cabinet members below Secretary of State Dulles, was invited to dinner with them and also reciprocated by inviting them, and gave us directions in our talks with the U.S. side. All of these things must have been a great strain for the elderly Yoshida. Despite this, he was in a good mood well into the evenings and would invite us in for some brandy. At these times, Yoshida talked about GARIOA: "Your education in the Finance Ministry was all about not repaying debt. This is unacceptable." On the plane ride home the next day, he described it as a national humiliation. (Incidentally, last year during negotiations the United States began talking about a willingness to possibly reduce the GARIOA.)

In the speech at the Press Club, Prime Minister Yoshida stated, "it appears that Communist China is accumulating a lot of capital right now. The development of Southeast Asia, on the other hand, is far behind. If these trends continue, the United States will lose its battle with Communism." He proposed a four billion yen investment plan. Within the U.S. government, there was uncertainty about the situation in China. Many people listened to what Yoshida had to say because most of the information relating to China came through Hong Kong and was unreliable. Moreover, in the Ikeda-Robertson talks of this year and last year, as well as the meetings in Mexico City the year before, the American side was already showing a strong interest in the development of Southeast Asia, and asked us if we had a concrete plan. This year, we were expecting this, and brought several memos with us. However, they were still too vague for the U.S. side and did not satisfy them. We also did not have any confidence. Unfortunately, this still seems to be the case today.

After Prime Minister Yoshida's speech, the assembled reporters asked several questions. One person asked, "As a result of the Bikini nuclear test, many Japanese died and were injured. According to Japanese newspapers, there is a great fear of 'atomic tuna.'" To this, Yoshida stood and answered: "I want to raise this issue more and more with the U.S. side." Everyone was surprised by his comment. Shimanouchi [Toshiro], who was acting as interpreter, hesitated and whispered something to Yoshida. Yoshida, smiling, got up again and said, "Excuse me. I heard the word 'tuna' used, so I assumed it had to do with the fact that the United States placed high duties on canned tuna." With this, everyone laughed.

PRESIDENT EISENHOWER'S LUNCHEON

Being invited to the White House by President Eisenhower for lunch was an interesting experience for me. On the U.S. side, surrounding President Eisenhower was Vice President [Richard M.] Nixon, Dulles (State), Wilson (Defense), [George M.] Humphrey (Treasury), Stassen (Foreign Operations), and other members of the Cabinet and staff, Allen [C.] Dulles, Director of the Central Intelligence Agency, Senator Alexander Smith, and others. On our side were the Prime Minister, the Ambassador, Minister Aichi, Sato Eisaku, and myself. When Nixon related during his visit to Japan the year before how the children in the countryside called out, "Nixon, Nixon" to welcome him, the President spoke about his time as Supreme Allied Commander in Europe and how the German children would call out "Hei Eich!," recognizing his German name.

During lunch, the Secretary of State raised a work-related matter with the President. This was the report of the U.S. B-29 being shot down over the island of Habomai by a Soviet MIG. Dulles told Ike, "Habomai is located in the waters off Hokkaido. Actually, Habomai is a part of Hokkaido. It is a small island." I think he wanted to show that he knew about Habomai as he had studied a lot about Japan in preparing the San Francisco Peace Treaty, but what I remember is his belief that Habomai is a part of Hokkaido.

The Prime Minister and the President met for about thirty minutes before the luncheon. As expected, the problem of Communism in East Asia was apparently the subject. I do not know the details of what was said, and probably should not write them here either.

PRIOR TO THE RELEASE OF THE
YOSHIDA-EISENHOWER STATEMENT

One of the other tasks given to the Aichi mission was to help prepare the draft joint statement that was to be released by Yoshida and Eisenhower at the time of the former's departure from Washington. As mentioned before, Minister Aichi raised this with Assistant Secretary Robertson at their first meeting. In fact, in a sense, it is probably more accurate to say that we had an idea of what the statement should look like in our heads from the beginning, with the discussions working backwards from there. When we departed Japan on October 17, we already had a draft statement prepared and were discussing it among ourselves.

The joint statement, released at 1:00 p.m. on November 10, was quite general. Because it was introduced in the newspapers, I will only list up the main topics here:

1. The Japanese and U.S. governments would continue to work toward world peace, and cooperate in promoting the prosperity of Asia.
2. The economic well-being of the Japanese people was a matter of importance to the free world. The achievement of improved economic conditions in Japan depends upon the ability to pursue sound internal policies and expansion of trade. The United States will continue to examine sympathetically means whereby it can assist.

3. Specific measures that the United States and Japan agreed to:
   a. United States would cooperate with Japan in its efforts to expand its foreign trade relations. (Author: This referred to entry into GATT and other matters.)
   b. The United States would sell to Japan agricultural commodities and that the proceeds of these sales would be used for Japan's domestic economic improvement.
   c. Japan would participate in economic development planning for Southeast Asia.
4. U.S. representatives expressed regret over the injuries to the Japanese at the time of the Bikini nuclear test, and emphasized their belief that peaceful uses of atomic energy would eventually become of great value to Japan and other friendly nations throughout the world.
5. Other issues, such as the disposition of Japanese assets in the United States, release of war criminals, the status of the Ryukyu and Bonin Islands, the return of the former inhabitants to the Bonin Islands.

Foreign commentators often say when reading this type of document, which on the surface seems vague but really is a well-thought-out statement, one must pay as much attention to the question "What is written here?" as to "What is not written here?" If this is true, then, in my opinion, compared to the statement issued at the end of the Ikeda-Robertson talks the year before, the biggest difference this time was the lack of any reference to "Defense Issues." I have already described above the reason or, at least, my guess for this omission. However, it is worth noting again as it shows a clear change compared to last year.

Next, the joint statement was rewritten at least six times after merging the two respective U.S. and Japanese drafts. In the beginning, the thing that we had most wanted to say was that Japan wanted to become a window or a bridge with Communist China. This may have been traitorous to Prime Minister Yoshida's own ideas. When we were in Japan, we raised the issue in memos for the Prime Minister, on which he would sometimes write in comments. According to them, Yoshida's views were:

China is a great country and the Chinese are a great people. However, I do not recognize the People's Republic or its Communist citizens. The Chinese people have a history of always assimilating things from the outside, and thus the communization of China and of its people is only a temporary thing. It would be a mistake to treat this phenomenon as something permanent. Next is the conservative viewpoint that because Japan is closing the window on China, Japan is becoming the "orphan of Asia." Japan should economically join forces with the countries of Southeast Asia to pull the Chinese mainland and its people away from the grips of Communism.

These were in general Prime Minister Yoshida's views on this issue. However, our feeling was that while China might assimilate Communism for a long time, politics was about everyday life, and thus we could not understand the closing of the window and being told to wait during that time. The fact that such a country and its people lived right next door was a reality which we could not close our eyes and avoid. We felt to do so was not intelligent politics.

Because of this, we brought the issue to Washington to take our chances there. In the initial draft of the statement, we proposed the following phrase: "Peace in Southeast Asia will come about more quickly if the intercourse between Japan and China are allowed to take place under a certain set of rules, rather than through large negotiations trying to clear huge hurdles."

If Prime Minister Yoshida had seen this, he would have likely been the first to object, but as it turns out, the State Department as well wasn't able to go along with it: "The fact of the matter is that U.S. policy toward China has come to an impossible juncture. Because the Congress is the way it is, there are different viewpoints. For the time being, just consider 'China' a taboo word." If this were the case, we responded, we could change the wording. We tried very hard to get this message, no matter how vague, into the final statement. Finally, on November 9, the following phrase was drafted: "The prosperity and security of Southeast Asia will not be had until expansion tendencies are ended and the people of Asia are free to come and go as they please." The State Department representatives approved this, and so, Minister Aichi and I went to see Prime Minister Yoshida.

The Prime Minister read it for a long time, and then finally said, "It appears to be good." We all breathed a sigh of relief. However, during the morning of November 10, hours before the two sides planned to release the joint statement in the afternoon, a representative from the State Department called. He told us, "Secretary Dulles will not support the wording on that passage. Not only that, but he received permission from Prime Minister Yoshida the evening before when they met to delete it from the statement."

The night before, Dulles had invited Prime Minister Yoshida and his delegation to his home for dinner. Dulles and Yoshida sat next to one another, and it was probably during their conversation that this point was raised. From the beginning, Prime Minister Yoshida was not overly interested in having a joint statement, so the above episode could very well have happened.

The statement was a joint one prepared by the State Department and the Japanese Embassy in Washington and, superficially, had nothing to do with the work of our mission. In fact, we had been involved unofficially until then, but now, with only three hours remaining to the release of the statement, we had to leave it to the Embassy. Despite this, Dulles, ever the lawyer, read over the statement carefully with a keen eye. For these reasons, these three or four lines were deleted at the last minute.

There was also one more thing that was deleted toward the end: "The contribution of Japan, through participation in the Colombo Plan or by other means, to the economic development of the free nations of Asia is to the mutual benefit of these countries." At the last minute, the name "Colombo Plan" was removed with the final phrase being, "Other steps were discussed, such as the establishment of a productivity program in Japan and the mutual benefits which might arise from Japan's participation with the other free nations of South and Southeast Asia in the economic development of that area." I missed the opportunity to hear why "Colombo Plan" was deleted from the final version. It may have been because there were some slight differences at the time between the British initiatives and the U.S. ones in the region. Within the limited scope of my imagination, it remains a big mystery.

THE *NEW YORK TIMES'* PREDICTION

Because the political situation in Japan was so complicated and a great deal of coordination was necessary on the way in which Yoshida should return to Japan, Secretary General Ikeda called from Tokyo to ask me to come home early.

Although there were some issues remaining with surplus agriculture negotiations, the joint statement was finished so Sato Eisaku and I departed Washington the next day, November 11, for Tokyo.

When I opened the *New York Times* on the airplane, there was a four-column story publishing the joint statement and an analysis of it. Ironically, however, just below that was a story with a Tokyo by-line. It read,

Tokyo, Thursday, Nov. 11 (AP)—Two Japanese leaders purged by the Allied occupation formally decided yesterday to form a new conservative party to oust the pro-United States Yoshida Government. Mamoru Shigemitsu, World War II Foreign Minister who signed Japan's surrender, and Ichiro Hatoyama, wartime Education Minister, agreed to form the new party Nov. 23. Messrs. Shigemitsu and Hatoyama have large followings in the Diet (lower house of Parliament), increasing the possibility that the Government will lose a vote of confidence planned by opposition conservatives and Socialists. Mr. Shigemitsu agreed to disband his Progressive party and urge its members to sign up with the new anti-Yoshida movement. Mr. Hatoyama, founder of Mr. Yoshida's Liberal party, is expected to lead into the new group thirty or forty disgruntled Liberals.

This report accurately predicted the situation at the time. However, what was incorrect was the fact that dissolution would not take place but instead the resignation of the Cabinet en masse.

PRIME MINISTER YOSHIDA'S DEPARTURE

Yoshida arrived at Haneda Airport on November 17, brimming with confidence. The number of people who turned out at the airport only added to this bright scene.

However, clouds were already beginning to form. It was a mere three weeks until Yoshida Shigeru, who led Japanese politics for almost 10 years and showed an indomitable spirit despite constant criticism, left the official residence in Meguro that he had come to get used to and move back to Oiso.

With this, a period of Japan-U.S. diplomatic history spanning a decade can be said to have come to an end.[2]

NOTES

1. The translator was unable to identify the full name of Moyer or the accuracy of the name, as such a name is not found in the State Department's *Foreign Service Lists* or the *Foreign Relations of the United States* for Japan for that time.

2. Yoshida would live until October 1967, primarily in Oiso, as an elder statesman, continuing to be consulted over the years by his "students." Ikeda would become Prime Minister in July 1960 following the resignation of Kishi Nobusuke after the passage of the revised U.S.-Japan Security Treaty. Ikeda served as Prime Minister through November 1964 when he resigned due to the discovery of throat cancer. He died in August 1965. Miyazawa, as mentioned in the translator's preface, became Prime Minister in November 1991.

Appendix

Letter from Joseph Dodge to Ikeda Hayato

Washington, D.C.
August 9, 1949

Dear Minister Ikeda,

As you can imagine, I have been following the reports on the situation in Japan with special interest. Since my return I have been on a regular schedule to Washington. At each visit I review the cables and reports received from Japan and meet with the authorities and representatives of each Government Department having a primary interest in following the Japanese problem. Also, I receive the *Nippon Times* and other Japanese publications, and follow articles appearing in the United States press.

We have observed the courage with which Prime Minister Yoshida, you, and others of your Administration have been meeting your problems. That these would occur was clearly seen by the authorities in Washington at the time the Stabilization Directive was considered and issued. None of the difficulties were unexpected. The situation in China was apparent and undoubtedly will affect Japanese trade until it is resolved. The heightened problems of the sterling bloc are an additional complicating factor.

In general it seems to be overlooked that the trend of world affairs makes it even more necessary to stabilize and correct the internal situation in Japan. What has been happening in other parts of the world emphasizes the need for the program already initiated in Japan. What was done in Japan actually has preceded a steadily increasing need for the type of action taken. The fact that a start has been made will prove to be both constructive and fortunate.

One of the fundamental problems of international trade arises from the creation of a domestic price level which seriously interferes with the expansion of foreign trade. This is becoming evident in several important areas of the world, as well as in Japan.

The preference of workers for the shadow of a high-money wage rate over the substance of real purchasing power, the prevalence in business and industry of uneconomic production, and extravagant non-productive government expenditures all combine to contribute to a progressively less competitive price-level in world markets.

During and after the war Japan could not supply its normal markets. In the meantime some of these markets have disappeared, have materially changed, or have shrunk. Many countries, which formerly depended on Japan for goods, have been busily engaged in learning to supply themselves. This leads to trade restrictions intended to protect their own developing production. Other countries are following the belief that their future welfare also depends on greatly increased production.

During the war and immediately thereafter the test of most economies was how much could be produced irrespective of cost. Now the principal task is to adjust an increasing volume of output more exactly to the demands of a growing foreign competition. An increased volume of production is not automatically followed by more exports and a better balance on foreign account. Therefore, production alone will not suffice to meet the problem. It must be combined with suitable economic and financial policies.

Currency and other trade restrictions have been multiplying rapidly, and foreign trade tends to become more and more rigid and compartmentalized. Some authorities already have reached the conclusion that many countries are in for a reduction in their standards of living, which will be forced by the further planned restrictions of trade. With this, there seems to be a total inability to comprehend the possibility of United States aid being reduced or ended and to adjust themselves to that idea.

Declining prices also suggest that we are entering a period of the most intense competition in international commerce. The problem of finding adequate foreign markets largely will depend upon more efficient, higher-quality production, and the assurance of competitive prices. Those with the lowest costs will acquire most of the business. And the high cost of government is included in the price of exports.

Japan's problem is to prepare itself now to engage in this intense world competition on an effective and self-sustaining basis. Japan can not provide for itself as a high-cost, low-quality producer. Fundamentally the Stabilization Program is aimed at ensuring Japan an opportunity to meet this world trade problem.

You will be interested to know that the problem of government subsidies has become a major one in countries other than Japan. Here are some pertinent reports.

Recently in Argentina the props under retain food prices, held at artificially low levels under a grotesque subsidy structure, were unceremoniously removed and overnight most of the basic food stuffs went up as much as one hundred percent.

With this year's Budget, the British have had to bring to an end the rise in government subsidies. Belgium has had to take similar action.

Other governments have had to take drastic measures of economy. In Italy one of the government agencies providing subsidies or relief funds to industry, the Fondo Industria Meccancia, is to be liquidated.

In France more than 200,000 posts in the Civil Service and the nationalized industries have been done away with, as a measure of economy, since the beginning of 1947. To cut losses, the French Cabinet decided certain government-owned aviation factories should be closed or returned to private management. The National Assembly has approved substantial economy cuts in expenditures, and authorized a wide reorganization of the railways.

The price of government in Great Britain today is 40 percent of the total of all private incomes. There certainly never has been any country which taxed itself to anything like this extent.

These are a few samples of the problems of other nations. They suggest that Japan is not alone with its problems, and that its problems do not differ a great deal from those of other nations. In actually meeting them with corrective action, Japan is on the way to obtaining sound long-term benefits and avoiding even more serious difficulties.

There are no needed anti-inflationary adjustments, or adjustments need to place Japan in a position to compete efficiently in world markets which can be made without creating problems. The change from a substantially uncontrolled high-cost economy, supported by handouts in the form of government subsidies and bank and government credit, to any more normal procedure is certain to bring some temporary embarrassments. The adjustments can be accepted and met as necessary and inherent to the situation, or avoided by a continued inflation with unquestionably disastrous results.

It is no surprise that exaggerations and alarms should arise from sources that in the past have advocated or encouraged the road of inflation for their own purposes. Any change from the flow of a progressive and extreme inflation inevitably encourages the internal enemies of the country to attempt to restore the progress of inflation or, failing that, plunge the country into a crisis. This is accomplished by spreading unwarranted seeds of fear.

One of the difficulties of correcting an inflation always arises from the fact that it has been extremely profitable for some, at the expense of most of the people; it has been a process that allowed many others to avoid making painful decisions; and it has minimized the consequences of financial mistakes. During an inflation people learn to act as though costs and money values did not matter, but it is becoming more certain every day that costs and prices are beginning to matter very much.

There has been and is an urgent necessity for the Stabilization Program. It is essential for the economic recovery of Japan. The objectives of stabilization and recovery are not in opposition, but are directly related and interdependent, and everyone in Japan has a personal stake in their achievement. It is an important and necessary step toward the eventual attainment of economic self-support and of optimum recovery under conditions of self-support.

While adjustments are taking place, in fact adverse effects are being minimized by substantial aid from the United States. Without this aid, the same problems of inflation or world trade conditions would have to be met with much greater penalties and difficulties, and with a much lower standard of living.

Alarmist reports and interpretations of currency and credit shortages appear to have little real foundation.

Reduction in the total of currency in circulation was intended and is to be expected. It is applied to an inflated price structure and an extensive higher-priced black market. It tends to increase the real value of the reduced monetary means, which is an anti-inflationary objective.

An inflation requires large amounts of currency both for legal use and for black market activities, conducted outside of banks. The continued ability of consumers to pay high black market prices for consumption goods under conditions where a substantial part of basic consumption requirements are supplied by the United States indicates a surplus of purchasing power. A decline in the volume of money can be almost as much of a deterrent to excessive consumption buying by those obtaining windfalls from inflation as ration coupons, and is much less complicated.

If an effective stabilization is carried through, it should encourage saving, reduce or eliminate the black market, increase production efficiency, and further lower prices, all of which permit an additional decline in the volume of currency in circulation. Inflation, black market activities, and a continual rise in prices destroy both monetary and moral values.

At a recent reported total of about 285 billion yen, the currency issue is still approximately 190 times what it was in the 1930–1934 period. It is approximately 70 times what it was at the end of the war. This is despite the substantial currency reduction brought about by the government action of 1946.

The level of production remains below that of the 1930–1934 period. It is ridiculous to attempt to pervert a 20 percent shrinkage in currency outstandings from an abnormal seasonal peak of approximately 350 billion yen to 285 billion yen, into a currency shortage or a forerunner of national disaster.

The alleged shortage of credit results from the demands for it created by high prices and high wages, and the general policy of over-lending to borrowers who have been permitted to become overloaded with unrepayable debt. This loose credit practice has contributed directly to the inflation spiral. It has been magnified by those who have borrowed freely and unwisely in the expectation of being able to repay the debt with a further inflated currency of less value. Anywhere these circumstances exist and loan credit standards are applied more carefully and realistically, credit is certain to become less available. But, the real fact is that there is a greater shortage of credit-worthy borrowers than of credit.

It is certainly true that more capital is needed in Japan for most forms of industry and commercial enterprise. Again this is a problem which is common to most of the rest of the world. But real capital either must be created or supplied from internal or external sources. Unfortunately, in Japan its internal production operations have tended to dissipate capital and not create it. The inflation process undermined both the incentives and capacities of Japan to create new capital, despite the abortive attempts of government to do so through excessive advances of public funds to industry and trade, obtained by the use of government credit and taxation. This only made the Stabilization Program more necessary. A sound foundation had to be laid for the creation and acquisition of real capital and its future constructive and economic use.

Apparently there is little realization in Japan that every dollar of the large amount of United States aid already provided Japan has supplied, to some degree, additional capital to Japan. This is true even if the assistance is represented by food, fertilizer, and medical or other supplies furnished under GARIOA appropriations. It does not necessarily solely apply to raw materials supplied by EROA appropriations. All forms of aid have allowed the Japanese an alternative use of their own resources which otherwise might have had to be used for the maintenance of mere existence.

If adequate tax revenues are maintained and government expenditures are reduced, there are mechanisms provided in both the Budget and the Counterpart Fund to meet any situation likely to develop which can be attributed to the financial changes that have recently taken place. Sound administration of the Counterpart Fund and Budget revenues and expenditures will do much to minimize the results of any additional factors of world disturbance.

Before we left Japan the mechanism for establishing and using the Counterpart Fund had been agreed. When the appropriate authorities agree upon and submit a program which conforms to the principles clearly established and publicized, governing the use of the Fund, this Fund can be activated.

Many of the proposals originally advocated appeared essentially political in their motives and inconsistent with the objectives and possibilities for the most productive use of the Fund. The delay in submitting a suitable program and the details of the proposed individual projects underlying the program only served to add to the difficulties of the United States authorities in analyzing and approving allocations and disbursements.

Nothing would be more inconsistent with international economic reality or more detrimental to the continued recovery of Japan and a continuation of United States aid than to accept the studied exaggerations of those who would attempt to reverse the Stabilization Program. The need for a rationalization of the domestic and export economy has only become more urgent. The return to any semblance of an inflationary program would serve to raise prices and further depreciate the Japanese international competitive position.

What Japan needs above everything else is to increase its productivity and its exports. Both are extremely low. Productivity is not the maximum quantity of production at any cost. It is the highest possible return on the use of all forms of productive resources. A world competitive ability only can be accomplished through increased efficiency of production, higher-quality products, and better distribution at reduced costs. None of these either can be or will be accomplished by a continued inflation, or by the continued use of the proceeds from the United States aid to cover the selling loses on production and exports.

There has been general astonishment here over the exaggerations of local conditions that appear to have little support from the underlying statistics of Japanese progress. The tendency of certain ostensible financial and economic authorities of Japan to over-estimate the adverse effects of the Stabilization Program and under-estimate or ignore any of its benefits causes more concern than any of the actual facts of the situation. Constructive attitudes are noticeably lacking. This suggests the possibility of a deliberate attempt to reverse the Stabilization Program and return to outright inflation.

The Stabilization Program has made possible definite steps of progress. One of many was the establishment of the single exchange rate. Mr. McDairmid put it very well when he pointed out that Japan has introduced a single rate without devices such as export subsidies, export taxes, and special import or export rates, that many countries, even some not violently disturbed by the war, have believed it necessary to employ. This is a real accomplishment.

For the first time prices and wages have shown signs of actual stabilization. Industrial activity has remained substantially stable. The actual rise in unemployment has been greatly exaggerated. Unemployment is reported at a small figure, when the tremendous postwar increase in the Japanese labor forces through overseas repatriation is taken into consideration.

The May decline in exports reflects the inflated forward-buying earlier in the year in anticipation of the exchange rate or of changes in local important controls elsewhere, as in India. Export trade prospects may have become more precarious and there may be added complications from any continued adverse turn in international trade conditions. But if so, that only highlights the need for rationalized production in export industries. Later reports show some recovery of exports in June and July.

The economic welfare of the Japanese people should be enhanced, not injured, by co-operative support of the stabilization program. The constant encroachment on the living standards of Japanese workers of spiralling [sic] consumer goods prices, and the parallel dissipation of productive resources into uses contributing little or nothing to the supply of essential goods, have been a direct result of inflation in Japan, as in several other countries. No development short of war itself could have been more damaging to the viability of the Japanese economy and, ultimately, to the real income of the Japanese consumer. To describe measures directed to the correction of this situation as an "austerity program" is surely a false interpretation of the facts. There is already ample evidence in Japan that the supply of food, clothing, and other essentials moving to the consumer through legitimate channels of trade is on the increase.

The termination of government deficit financing definitely strengthens government credit and should contribute to a more general and genuine market for government bonds. The fact that workers will be paid in a currency, the value of which does not continue to shrink, is an encouragement to thrift, saving, and investment.

It may be that the substntial [sic] isolation of Japanese public officials and the people of Japan from a general knowledge of what is occuring [sic] elsewhere in the world contributes to an unwarranted and distorted view of their own problems. Many other countries have comparable problems. This does not deny unfounded pessimistic and premature.

This is a test period for the Japanese people and the Japanese economy. The result of the test can not be determined in any sixty or ninety days. Certainly the honor and self-discipline of the people of Japan should be sufficient to meet the problems, particularly when this is being done with substantial assistance from the United States, which can not and will not be forthcoming from any other source.

Repeatedly the United States has accorded assistance to Japan on a large scale. The receipt of these resources has been of great value to Japan. Unfortunately, in too large a part, they have been put to uses which only served to postpone the internal adjustments that are necessary and inevitable.

It will be extremely difficult to convince the people and the Congress of the United States that a substantial part of this assistance should be continued without the clearest kind of evidence that the Japanese people have organized themselves to meet effectively their own problems.

There has been no change in the conviction here that the Stabilization Program was advisable and is absolutely necessary, in the interests of both Japan and the United States.

Very sincerely,

Joseph M. Dodge
United States Minister and Advisor

The Honorable Hayato Ikeda
Finance Minister
Ministry of Finance
Shinkuku [sic], Tokyo

Index

Acheson, Dean G., 48–49, 55, 57
Adenaur, Konrad, 61
Administrative Agreement, 58–60, 82
Aichi, Kiichi, 97, 105–6, 128–29,
  134–40, 144–45, 147
Akiyama, Konosuke, 94, 132n7, 96
Allison, John M., 39, 89, 98
Amami Oshima, 49, 65n6
Anderson, Samuel W., 99
Araki, Eikichi, 85, 88, 98, 107, 131
Asahi Shimbun, 20, 52, 81, 131, 132n5
Ashida, Hitoshi, 38, 45, 94
Aso, Kazuko, 42, 45

Bank of Japan, 10–12, 43, 70, 82–83
Bases (U.S.): offer of, 18–19, 21–25;
  problems associated with, 40, 52,
  58–61
Benson, Ezra T., 138
Bikini test, 136, 144, 146
Black, Eugene R., 70–72
Blair House, 103
Bonin Islands. *See* Ogasawara
Brown, Lloyd B., 115
Bungei Shunju, 60
Bunjito, 81, 83, 85
Burgess, W. Randolph, 107
Butterworth, W. Walton, 24

Central Liaison Office, xvi
Ceylon, 48, 51
Chase National Bank, 143
Chicago Sun Tribune, 123
China (Communist), 33
Chishima (see Kuriles)
Chitose (Hokkaido), 83
Clemenceau, Georges, 80, 134
COCOM, 101
Cold War, x
Colombo Plan, 148
Communist Party (of Japan), 9, 18, 83
Crown Prince, visit to U.S., 107
Counterpart Fund, 10

Democratic Liberal Party, 1, 3, 5–6,
  8–9, 29, 40–43, 65, 67, 76–77,
  79–81, 85–88, 94–95, 104, 133, 148
Democratic Party (Japan), 40–43, 45
Department of Agriculture, 138
Department of Army. *See* U.S. Army
Department of Commerce, 99, 105, 138
Department of Defense, 30, 40, 72, 103,
  111–12, 115, 127, 139–40
Department of State, 24, 26, 30, 39–40,
  70, 94, 98–99, 101, 103, 107, 118,
  124, 126, 128–30, 131n1, 137–38,
  143

Department of Treasury, 99
Diehl, William W., 98
Diet, 1, 22, 33, 34, 42, 45, 67–68, 76,
     79–81, 85–88, 92–94, 97, 105–6,
     129, 134, 145
Dirksen, Everett M., 88
Dodge, Joseph M., 1–13, 15, 17, 29–25,
     28, 32–35, 46, 47, 63–64, 70, 72–73,
     84, 98–104, 108, 114, 117–18, 127
Dodge Line, 5, 6, 15–18, 31
Draper, William H., 70
Dulles, Allen C., 44
Dulles, John Foster, 22, 25, 30, 38–40,
     48–49, 52–53, 55, 48, 58–60, 92–93,
     99, 100, 102, 107, 143–45, 147–48

Economic Cooperation Administration,
     115–16, 119, 121
Eichelberger, Robert L., 20
Eighth Army, 20
Eisenhower, Dwight D., 26, 80, 90, 108,
     117, 134, 141, 143, 145
Emperor: Article 7 of postwar
     Constitution, 78n3; radio address of,
     xii; meeting with Yoshida, 69
Erhard, Ludwig W., 72
Etorofu, 52, 56, 58, 61
Exchange rate, 10–12

FBI (Federal Bureau of Investigation),
     46
Fine, Sherwood, 7
Foreign Exchange Committee, 12
Foreign Ministers Conference, 21, 24
Foreign Operations Administration, 107,
     109, 128, 138
France, 52, 75
Francis, Clarence, 138
Franco, Francisco, 116
Fukunaga, Kenji, 67, 69, 78n1
Fukushima, Shintaro, 60
Fulbright, William J., 142

GARIOA (Government Appropriation
     for Relief In Occupied Areas), 3, 46,

91, 100, 102–3, 108, 117–18,
     122–23, 16–27, 129–30, 135, 144
GATT (General Agreement on Tariffs
     and Trade), 146
GHQ (General Headquarters, SCAP):
     1–3, 11–13, 15, 22, 24–25, 28–29,
     32–35; Economic and Science
     Section (GHQ), 2, 3, 13;
     Government Section, 34; Political
     Advisor Office, 39
Governors Association (*Chiji Kaigi*), 64
Gromyko, Andrei, 54
Gunma Prefecture, 83

Habomai Islands, 53, 57, 145
Hakone, 9, 43, 45
Hamamatsu (Shizuoka Prefecture): air
     school at, 71
Hashimoto, Kingoro, 9, 13n4
Hatoyama, Ichiro, 56, 62, 68, 75–76,
     80–81, 83, 85, 148
Hayashi, Hikosaburo, 94, 132n6, 96
Hemmendinger, Noel, 46–47
Hensley, M. Stewart, 22
Higashikuni, Naruhiko, xvi
Hirokawa, Kozen, 42–43, 77, 79–81
Hiroshima, xv
Hori, Shigeru, 44
Hozen Keizaikai, 77
Humphrey, George M., 108, 144

Ichimada, Hisato, 11, 47
Ikeda, Hayato, ix–xii, xvi, 3, 5–10,
     12–13, 15–29, 31–34, 38, 42–43,
     46–47, 59, 61, 63, 64, 70–71, 76–77,
     85, 89, 91–92, 95–106, 112–13, 115,
     117, 119, 122–23, 126–30, 131n1,
     134, 146, 148–49
Import-Export Bank, 18–20, 109, 117
Inagaki, Heitaro, 11
India, 67, 71, 105
Indochina, 23, 99. *See also* Southeast
     Asia
Indonesia, 39, 48, 51, 108
International Court of Justice, 117

International Monetary Fund, 70–71
Inukai, Takeru, 41
Iokibe, Makoto, xii
Ishibashi, Tanzan, 77–78, 80
Italy, 75, 92
Ito, Jufuku, 77
Izumiyama, Sanroku, 1

Japan Society, 142–43
Japan-U.S. Joint Committee, 82
Jayewardene, J. R., 51
Joint Chiefs of Staff, 21
Judd, Walter H., 114, 132n10

Kamakura, 87, 93, 96–97
Kato, Takeo, 94, 132n7
Keidanren (Federation of Economic
    Organizations), 84, 89
Kennedy, John F., xii–xiii
Keynes, John Maynard, 108
Khan, Chandri Mohammad Zafrulla, 51
Kimura, Tokutaro, 88–89
Kishi, Nobusuke, 87, 149
Kitamura, Tokutaro, 45
Kiuchi, Nobutane, 12
Kiyose, Ichiro, 86–87; Kiyose Theory,
    95
Kodama, Yoshio, 80
Kochikai (Ikeda Faction), xvi
Koizumi, Junichiro, xvii
Kokura City, 83, 132n2
Kono, Ichiro, 77–78, 80
Korean War, 23, 25, 30–31, 37, 45, 49,
    72, 81, 83–84, 90, 100–101, 108–9,
    126, 137, 139
Kowakudani, 43
Kunashiri, 52, 58, 61
Kuriles, 39–40, 42, 52–57, 65n3, 80,
    123
Kusunoki, Ayako, xii
Kyodo News Agency, 12
Kyoto, 25, 27, 33

Labor Party (UK), 51
Labor Standard Law, 33

Liberal Party of Japan. *See* Democratic
    Liberal Party
Liberal Democratic Party, xvi

Macapagal, Diosdado, 50
MacArthur, Douglas A., 15–17, 19, 22,
    24, 28–30, 34–35, 37, 50
Magnasum, Warren G., 88
Magruder, Carter B., 24
Manchukuo. *See* Miyazawa Kiichi, trip
    to
Maritime Police, 67
Marquat, William F, 1–3, 7, 17, 27–29,
    34, 37.
Martin, William McChesney, 73–74
Masuda, Kaneshichi, 38, 65n1, 41–43
McClurkin, Robert C., 122, 126, 130,
    131, 138–40
Meiji Constitution, xii
Miki, Bukichi, 79–80
Miki, Takeo, 41–43
Mills, John Stewart: *On Liberty*, xiv
Mindoha, 80, 131n1
Ministry of Agriculture, 32, 135
Ministry of Finance, x, 112
Ministry of Foreign Affairs (or Foreign
    Ministry), 60, 90
Ministry of International Trade and
    Industry, 11, 105
Miyazawa, Kiichi: as chairman of
    Liberal Democratic Party Executive
    Council, xvi; as a child and student,
    xiv–xv; as chief cabinet secretary,
    xvi; as director of Economic
    Planning Agency, xvi; as finance
    minister, xii, xvi–xvii; as Liberal
    Democratic Party treasurer, xvi; as
    minister for International Trade and
    Industry, xvi; as prime minister, ix,
    xvii; as secretary to finance minister,
    x, xvi, 3; election to Upper House,
    x–xi, xvi; Recruit scandal, xvi,
    xviiin21; retirement from politics,
    xvii; trip to Manchukuo, xv; trip to
    United States (1961), xii–xiii

Miyazawa, Koto, xiii
Miyazawa, Yoko, xv
Miyazawa, Yutaka, x, xiii–xiv
Mori, Yoshiro, xvii
Morrison, Herbert, 51
Moyer [first name unknown], 139
Mukai, Tadaharu, 79
Murakami, Kotaro, 97, 112
Murphy, Robert D., 114, 138
Musashi High School, xiv
Mutual Security Assistance, 83–93, 101,
    106, 109–10, 115–119, 121–22,
    124–131

Nagano Prefecture, 83
Nakamura, Shogo, 20
Nakasone, Yasuhiro, x, xvi, xvii
Nara City (Nara Prefecture), 82
Nash, Frank C., 109–10, 112
Nasu Imperial Villa, 69, 78n2
National Bank of Mexico (Banco de
    Mexico), 72–73
National City Bank, 143
National Personnel Authority, 28
National Police Reserves, 31, 63, 67,
    70–72, 81, 89
National Railways, 33
National Safety Agency, 67, 70, 89, 92,
    97, 111, 125, 139
National Safety Force, 31, 67, 70, 81,
    85, 88, 91–92, 94–96, 104,107, 111,
    114, 119–20, 124
New Dealers, 2–3, 5–7
New York Times, 21, 93, 122, 142, 148
Nishimura, Kumao, 50
Nishio, Suehiro, 38
Nixon, Richard M., 144–45
Nomizo, Masaru, 81
North Korea, 30, 33

Oasa, Tadao, 87, 13n4, 94, 96
Obuchi, Keizo, xii, xvii
Office of Budget Director, 98–99
Office of Economic Stabilization, 11
Office of Foreign Assistance, 99

Ogasawara Islands, 57–58, 101, 146
Ogata, Taketora, 79, 86, 87, 133
Ogawa, Heikichi, xiii
Ohori, Hiromu, 134
Oiso, 86, 132n3
Okazaki, Katsuo, 43, 45, 59–60, 90,
    102, 121
Okinawa, 49, 57–58, 101, 123, 146
Ono, Bamboku, 69
Overby, Andrew N, 138.
Oya, Shinzo, 1
Ozawa, Ichiro, x
Ozawa, Saeki, 42

Pakistan, 48, 51
Paul, Norman, 110
Peace Treaty. *See* Treaty of Peace with
    Japan
Peking. *See* People's Republic of China
Pentagon. *See* Department of Defense
People's Republic of China, 49, 50, 75,
    100–01, 122, 126, 144, 146–47
Perry, Matthew C., xviin5
Philippines, 39, 48, 50, 64, 108
Poland, 55
Potsdam, 53
Procurement Agency, 60
Progressive Party, 38, 71, 76, 79–81, 83,
    85–88, 93–96, 103–04, 133

Queen Mary, 142

Reconstruction Finance Corporation
    (Fukko Kinyu Kinko), 5
Reid, Ralph, 22, 24, 29, 64
Republic of China (Taiwan), 49, 67, 110
Republican Party, 17, 141
Reston, James, 21, 93
Rhee, Syngman, 93, 105, 111
Robertson, Walter S., 26, 47, 98–100,
    102, 104–05, 107, 111–13, 115,
    117–120, 129, 131, 134–36, 139,
    144–45
Rockefeller, John D. III, 129, 142
Romulo, Carlos P., 50

Royall, Kenneth C. 1
Russia: Russo-Japanese War, xviin5
Rusk, Dean, 59

Saiken Renmei (Japan Reconstruction League), 37
Sakai, Yoneo, 20
Sakhalin, 39, 40, 56–57, 65n3, 123
Sasebo, 82
Sastroamidjojo, Ali, 51
Sato, Eisaku, 79, 86–87, 145, 148
SCAP (Supreme Commander for Allied Powers). *See* GHQ
Schaffer, Fritz, 72
Self-Defense Force, 31, 104
Seiyukai, xiv
Shidehara, Kijuro, xvi
Shigemitsu, Mamoru, 26, 79–80, 85–87, 93–97, 103, 107, 133, 148
Shikotan, 53, 57, 123
Shimanouchi, Toshiro, 144
Shirasu, Jiro, 9, 36n3
Shoup, Carl S., 9, 17
Shoup Taxation Mission, 36n2
Shuto, Hideo, 11
Smith, H. Alexander, 49, 50, 144
Snyder, John W., 70, 72, 74, 84
Socialist Party of Japan, 18, 38, 71, 76, 80–83, 85, 87, 91, 148
Southeast Asia, 106, 121
South Korea, 23, 33, 92–93, 105, 109–10, 117, 120–22
Soviet Union, 18, 20–21, 23, 38–40, 45–49, 52–58, 65n3, 68, 75, 109–10. *See also* Russia
Stassen, Harold E., 107, 138, 144
Subardjo, Ahmad, 51
Sugamo Prison, 87
Sullivan, Charles A., 103–04, 111–12
Suzuki, Gengo, 97, 112, 116, 134, 143
Suzuki, Zenko, xvi

Tachikawa City, 82
Tadamigawa: power station, 70–71, 78n4

Taiwan. *See* Republic of China
Takasaki, Tatsunosuke, 71
Takeshita, Noboru, xvi
Takeuchi, Ryuji, 98, 134–35
Tohata, Shiro, 135
Tokyo Shimbun, 20
Tokyo University, xiv–xv
Tomabechi, Yoshizo, 41–43, 45
Toyoda, Teijiro, 44
Treaty of Peace with Japan: Diet support of, 40–45; drafts of, 38–40; negotiations/consultations over; reparations, 47–51; San Francisco Peace Conference, 45–57
Truman, Harry S., 1, 30, 37
Tsushima, Juichi, xvi
Tsutsumi, Yasujiro, 87

Uchinada (Ishikawa Prefecture), 82
Urruppu, 56
United Kingdom, 50–52, 56–58, 75, 108
United Press, 11
U.S. Air Force, 59
U.S. Army, 20–21, 26, 28
U.S. Embassy, Tokyo, 90, 92, 126. *See also* Allison, John M.
U.S. Federal Reserve, 73
U.S.-Japan Alliance, x
U.S.-Japan Student Conference, xv
Utsumi, Yasukichi, 9, 13n4

Valdes, Miguel Aleman, 73
Veronica, 74–75
Vorhees, Tracy S., 20

War Department, 22
Washington Post, 124
Watanabe, Takeshi, 27, 98
Watson, Thomas E., 71
West Germany, 46, 61, 75, 117, 127–28
Whitney, Courtney, 27–28, 34, 37–38
Wicks, Sinclair, 138
Wiley, Alexander, 142

Wilson, Charles E., 139–41, 144
Wilson, President Woodrow, 64
World Bank, 70–71, 101, 105, 109,
　117

Yalta Agreement, 40, 53, 57, 65n3, 80,
　114
Yamashita Steamship, xiii
Yamazaki, Takeshi, 38
Yokosuka City (Kanagawa Prefecture),
　83

Yoshida, Shigeru, ix–x, 1, 9, 15, 18–19,
　22–23, 25–26, 28–31, 38, 40–43,
　46–47, 49–52, 54, 56–58, 60–63,
　67–69, 71, 75–76, 79–80, 84–89,
　91–99, 101–07, 117, 130, 133–35,
　138, 141–47, 149; Yoshida Cabinet,
　1, 3, 5, 8–9, 23, 38, 40, 43, 45,
　51, 62–63, 67, 69, 75, 81, 84, 87–89,
　94, 105, 141; Yoshida Doctrine, x
Yoshitake, Eiichi, 42–43
Younger, Kenneth G., 58

About the Author and Translator

Miyazawa Kiichi was Japan's 78th prime minister, serving between November 1991 and August 1993. He was born in 1919 and as a member of the Japan-U.S. Student Association, traveled to the United States prior to the outbreak of war between Japan and the United States. As a junior official in the Finance Ministry, he served as an aide and interpreter to Minister Ikeda Hayato, who was Prime Minister Yoshida Shigeru's closest advisor. Miyazawa has served in top posts in the government and Liberal Democratic Party throughout his career. He retired from politics in 2003 and resides in Tokyo.

Robert D. Eldridge, Ph.D., is an associate professor of Japanese Political and Diplomatic History at the School of International Public Policy, Osaka University, Japan. He earned his doctorate at Kobe University and is the author of numerous works including *The Origins of the Bilateral Okinawa Problem* and *The Return of the Amami Islands*. He first interviewed Miyazawa in 1999 and has maintained a close relationship with him since.